Ireland Travel (

**Your Essential Companion to the Emerald Isle:
When to Go, What to See, Outdoor Adventures,
Local Cuisine, and Hidden Gems**

Logan Matthews

Logan Matthews Ireland Travel Guide 2025

Contents

Chapter 1: Introduction to Ireland

Welcome to Ireland

Ireland—a land of misty green hills, dramatic coastlines, lyrical storytellers, and timeless charm—awaits you with open arms and a soul-stirring embrace. This is a country where ancient myths whisper through moss-covered stones, music drifts from glowing pub doorways, and every turn down a country road feels like a step into a living postcard.

A Nation of Stories and Soul

To step foot in Ireland is to walk through layers of time. Its landscapes are etched with history: megalithic tombs older than the pyramids, medieval castles perched above wind-swept valleys, and quiet country lanes that once echoed with the footsteps of poets and revolutionaries. Yet Ireland is anything but stuck in the past. Its cities hum with creativity, innovation, and a warm hospitality that makes visitors feel like part of the family.

The Land Itself

Nicknamed the Emerald Isle for good reason, Ireland is a patchwork of lush pastures, rugged mountains, and glittering lakes. The Atlantic Ocean crashes against its western shores with cinematic drama, while the interior unfolds in tranquil beauty, dotted with stone walls, sheep-dotted hills, and villages that seem unchanged by time.

From the raw, windswept majesty of the Cliffs of Moher to the otherworldly basalt columns of the Giant's Causeway, from the mystical Ring of Kerry to the poetic beauty of Yeats Country, Ireland's natural wonders are nothing short of extraordinary.

Cities Full of Character

The capital, Dublin, pulses with youthful energy and literary prestige—home to James Joyce and Oscar Wilde, and host to some of the friendliest pubs in the world. Belfast, in Northern Ireland, tells its story through a powerful mix of art, history, and industrial pride, not least at the striking Titanic Belfast museum. Smaller cities like Galway, Kilkenny, Cork, and Derry/Londonderry each offer their flavors, from bohemian charm to medieval mystique.

People and Culture

Perhaps nothing endears Ireland to travelers more than its people. Renowned for their wit, warmth, and storytelling prowess, the Irish have a way of making strangers feel instantly welcome. Don't be surprised if a casual chat with a local turns into a treasured memory or an invitation to a music session that stretches into the wee hours.

The culture is rich with Gaelic traditions, foot-tapping folk music, and dancing that can ignite an entire village square. You'll find it in the cadence of a conversation, in the cozy ritual of a pub gathering, and in the solemn beauty of ancient ruins where silence speaks volumes.

Timeless and Transformative

Ireland is more than a destination—it's a feeling. Whether you're sipping whiskey by a turf fire, hiking through a glacial valley, or listening to waves crash against stone cliffs, there's a quiet magic here that lingers long after you've returned home. In 2025, Ireland continues to charm with a perfect blend of old and new, offering world-class cuisine, vibrant arts, and eco-conscious experiences without ever losing its essential soul.

So, whether you come in search of adventure, heritage, culinary delights, or simply the famous cead míle fáilte—"a hundred thousand welcomes"—you'll find it here in Ireland. Welcome to a land that feels like home, even if you've never been. Welcome to Ireland.

Why Visit Ireland in 2025: 10 Excellent Reasons to Go

Ireland is not simply a destination—it's an experience that stirs the soul. In 2025, this enchanting island offers even more reasons to discover its magic. Whether it's your first time or your tenth, Ireland promises something extraordinary at every turn. Here's why this is the year to go.

1. A Banner Year for Irish Heritage Celebrations ·

2025 marks a special calendar of national and regional anniversaries, showcasing everything from ancient Celtic rituals to more recent cultural milestones. Expect expanded festivals, pop-up exhibitions, reenactments, and live performances in castles, forests, and small-town squares across the island.

2. New Trails and Scenic Routes Unveiled

Nature lovers and hikers, rejoice: Ireland's renowned walking and cycling trails are expanding in 2025. The long-anticipated Trans-Ireland Greenway is opening new legs, linking riverside towns, rural heartlands, and dramatic coastlines, all while emphasizing eco-friendly travel and local storytelling.

3. A Culinary Scene in Full Bloom

Ireland's food scene has undergone a quiet revolution. In 2025, it shines brighter than ever with Michelin-starred restaurants, farm-to-table gastropubs, seafood shacks, and whiskey and gin distilleries offering immersive tastings. The island's culinary identity—once underrated—is now confidently world-class.

4. Reopened and Restored Historic Landmarks

This year brings the reopening of several iconic sites, including ancient abbeys, Celtic ringforts, and Victorian estates, many of which have been beautifully restored or enhanced with digital storytelling and immersive technology.

5. Smaller Crowds, Bigger Magic

Ireland remains less crowded than its mainland European neighbors, making it an ideal destination for travelers craving authenticity and breathing room. Even top attractions often allow for unhurried exploration, and it's still possible to stumble upon a cliffside ruin with no one else around.

6. Festivals, Music, and the Return of the Craic

Whether it's traditional fiddle music in a candlelit pub or open-air rock in Dublin, 2025's cultural calendar is bursting with festivals. Highlights include TradFest, Galway International Arts Festival, and Lisdoonvarna's famous matchmaking fest—each offering a unique way to tap into Ireland's boundless creativity and charm.

7. A Pilgrimage for Fans of TV, Film, and Literature

From "Game of Thrones" landscapes in Northern Ireland to the literary haunts of James Joyce and Seamus Heaney, Ireland is a wonderland for culture buffs. In 2025, new themed tours are launching, combining storytelling, history, and cinematic scenery.

8. Immersive Experiences for All Travel Styles

Whether you want to sleep in a castle, learn Gaelic in a coastal village, forage for wild herbs with a chef, or take a traditional Irish dancing class, 2025 is all about immersive, slow travel. The tourism sector is focused more than ever on meaningful connections over fast sightseeing.

9. Natural Beauty at Its Absolute Peak

From the wild drama of the Skellig Islands to the mirror-like stillness of Glendalough, Ireland's landscapes are a soul-nourishing balm. 2025 offers a fresh invitation to disconnect and rewild yourself, with growing support for eco-lodges, conservation tourism, and off-the-grid adventures.

10. A Warm Welcome That Feels Like Home

In a world that's fast, loud, and often impersonal, Ireland feels deeply human. The warmth of a local who gives directions with a story, the laughter over pints in a pub, the way strangers invite you into their world—it's hospitality that comes from the heart. In 2025, this spirit feels more important than ever.

Key Highlights of the Emerald Isle

Ireland is a land of captivating contrasts—wild, windswept cliffs and cozy, candlelit pubs; ancient ruins and dynamic cities; haunting myths and vibrant music. These key highlights bring together the most iconic and inspiring experiences the island has to offer—moments that define Ireland and linger in the soul long after the journey ends.

1. The Wild Atlantic Way

Stretching over 2,500 km along Ireland's rugged west coast, the Wild Atlantic Way is one of the world's most spectacular coastal drives. Winding past sheer cliffs, hidden coves, windswept beaches, and charming villages like Doolin and Clifden, it's a feast for the eyes—and the spirit. Don't miss the dramatic Cliffs of Moher, the remote Aran Islands, or the poetic beauty of Slea Head Drive on the Dingle Peninsula.

2. Dublin: A Capital of Literature and Life

Ireland's capital is a cosmopolitan blend of old and new, with Georgian architecture, buzzing cafes, riverside strolls, and a vibrant arts scene.

Tour the Trinity College Library to see the Book of Kells, walk in the footsteps of literary giants, sip Guinness at its source, or discover the city's rebellious history in its many museums and monuments.

3. The Ring of Kerry & Killarney National Park

A quintessential Irish journey, the Ring of Kerry encircles a landscape of lush valleys, shimmering lakes, rugged mountains, and seaside views. Stop at Muckross House, hike in Killarney National Park, cruise across Lough Leane, or watch the mist roll in over the Gap of Dunloe. It's nature in its most cinematic form.

4. Galway: The Bohemian Heart of the West

Colorful, artistic, and effortlessly cool, Galway is a city that lives to the rhythm of the street. It's known for its traditional music, seafood, street performers, and festivals—especially the Galway International Arts Festival. It's also your gateway to Connemara's wild beauty and the haunting serenity of Kylemore Abbey.

5. The Giant's Causeway

This geological marvel on Northern Ireland's north coast is steeped in myth and science. Over 40,000 interlocking basalt columns rise from the sea, forming a surreal and unforgettable landscape. Explore nearby Carrick-a-Rede Rope Bridge, Dunluce Castle, or follow the Causeway Coastal Route for breathtaking views.

6. Ancient East: Castles, Monasteries & Sacred Sites

Ireland's Ancient East is a treasure trove of heritage. Explore Newgrange, a Stone Age passage tomb older than the pyramids; the medieval city of Kilkenny; the spiritual solitude of Glendalough; or the towering ruins of the Rock of Cashel, once the seat of ancient kings and saints.

7. Belfast & Titanic Quarter

Belfast, Northern Ireland's dynamic capital, has transformed from a city of conflict to one of creativity and resilience. Visit the Titanic Belfast experience—voted the world's leading tourist attraction—or delve into political history through powerful street art and walking tours of the Falls and Shankill neighborhoods.

8. The Causeway Coast & Game of Thrones Territory

Fans of fantasy will delight in the real-world locations of the Game of Thrones series, scattered across the Antrim Coast. Discover the eerie beauty of Dark Hedges, the windswept Ballintoy Harbour, and Cushendun Caves, blending storytelling with stark natural beauty.

9. Castles, Clans & Country Estates

Ireland is a land of castles—some in ruins, others lovingly restored and open for overnights. Experience grandeur at Ashford Castle, explore the fairy-tale towers of Blarney Castle (and kiss the famous stone), or wander the haunting halls of Leap Castle, reputed to be Ireland's most haunted.

10. Music, Pubs & the Warmth of the People

Every journey in Ireland is enriched by the human touch—locals who share stories, laughter, and songs over a pint. Whether you're tapping your feet to a spontaneous trad session in a Galway pub, dancing at a festival in Dingle, or singing along with strangers in a Dublin snug, these moments become the heart of your adventure.

Essential Ireland Fast Facts

Before you set off on your adventure to the Emerald Isle, here are the key essentials to help you navigate Ireland with ease and confidence:

1. Location & Geography

- **Location:** Ireland is located in the North Atlantic Ocean, west of Great Britain.
- **Area:** 84,421 square kilometers (32,595 square miles), making it the 20th-largest island in the world.
- **Capital:** Dublin, situated on the east coast along the River Liffey.
- **Regions:** Ireland is divided into two distinct political entities: the Republic of Ireland (covering most of the island) and Northern Ireland (part of the United Kingdom).

2. Population

Population: Approximately 5 million people (Republic of Ireland); 1.9 million people (Northern Ireland).

Language: The official languages are Irish (Gaeilge) and English. English is the dominant language, but Irish is still spoken in certain regions, particularly in the Gaeltacht areas (Irish-speaking districts).

Time Zone: Ireland follows Greenwich Mean Time (GMT) during winter and Irish Standard Time (IST, GMT+1) during the summer months (Daylight Saving Time).

3. Currency & Money

Currency:

- The Republic of Ireland uses the Euro (€).
- Northern Ireland uses Pounds Sterling (£) as part of the UK.

ATMs & Credit Cards: Widely available, with most establishments accepting major credit cards. ATMs are accessible in cities, towns, and even smaller villages.

Tipping: Tipping is customary but not mandatory. In restaurants, 10-15% is typical if service is not included.

4. Weather & Climate

Climate: Ireland has a temperate maritime climate, with mild winters and cool summers. Rain is frequent throughout the year.

Average Temperatures:

- Summer (June to August): 15-20°C (59-68°F).
- Winter (December to February): 5-8°C (41-46°F).

Best Time to Visit: The summer months (May to September) offer the best weather and longest days, but the spring and autumn seasons can be just as rewarding, offering fewer crowds.

5. Electrical Information

- **Voltage:** 230V.
- **Plug Type:** Ireland uses Type G electrical outlets (three rectangular prongs). Travelers may need an adapter for devices with other plug types.

6. Health & Safety

- **Healthcare:** Ireland offers excellent healthcare services. Visitors from the EU can access healthcare with an EHIC card, while non-EU visitors should consider travel insurance.
- **Emergency Number:** Dial 112 or 999 for emergency services (ambulance, fire, or police).

7. Transportation

- **Public Transport:** Ireland has a well-developed public transport system, including buses, trains (Irish Rail), and ferries. Dublin's Luas tram and the DART suburban rail are popular for city travel.
- **Driving:** In Ireland, cars drive on the left-hand side of the road. Visitors from abroad should ensure they are comfortable with driving on the left before renting a car.
- **Domestic Flights:** Flights are available between major cities like Dublin, Cork, Galway, and Belfast, and can save time when traveling long distances.

8. Internet & Connectivity

- **Wi-Fi:** Wi-Fi is widely available in hotels, cafés, and public spaces. However, rural areas may have less reliable connectivity.
- **Mobile Roaming:** Ireland is part of the EU, so EU visitors can use their mobile phone plans without extra charges. For non-EU travelers, purchasing a local SIM card or opting for roaming is recommended.

9. Key Holidays & Festivals

- **St. Patrick's Day:** Celebrated on March 17th, this is Ireland's national holiday, with parades, parties, and festivals across the country.
- **Irish Independence Day:** Commemorates the signing of the Anglo-Irish Treaty on December 6, 1921.
- **Other Notable Festivals:** Galway International Arts Festival, Dublin Theatre Festival, Fleadh Cheoil (the largest traditional music festival in the world).

10. Important Laws & Customs

- **Drinking Age:** The legal drinking age in Ireland is 18.
- **Smoking:** Smoking is prohibited in enclosed public places, including restaurants, pubs, and public transport.

- **Punctuality:** The Irish are generally friendly and laid-back, but it's polite to arrive on time for appointments and reservations.

Understanding Irish Culture & Customs

Ireland is a country where tradition and modernity blend seamlessly, and its culture is a reflection of centuries of history, mythology, and evolution. As you explore the Emerald Isle, you'll encounter a rich tapestry of customs, values, and practices that define the Irish way of life. Whether you're sipping a pint in a local pub, enjoying a lively conversation, or admiring the country's art and literature, understanding the cultural nuances will make your experience even more enriching.

1. The Importance of Storytelling

Ireland's deep-rooted oral tradition is one of the pillars of its cultural identity. Storytelling, whether through literature, music, or casual conversation, is an integral part of Irish life. From ancient myths and legends like those of the Tuatha Dé Danann to modern works by authors such as James Joyce and Seamus Heaney, the Irish have long been masters of narrative. In Ireland, stories are often told with great flair, marked by humor, wit, and dramatic pauses. Even in everyday life, it's common to hear locals spinning tales, often with a humorous twist. In fact, "craic" (pronounced "crack") is a quintessential part of the Irish experience, referring not just to fun and entertainment but to the lively conversations and good company that accompany it.

2. Hospitality and the "Irish Welcome"

There's a saying in Ireland: "Céad Míle Fáilte," which means "A Hundred Thousand Welcomes." Irish hospitality is world-renowned, and visitors often remark on the warmth and friendliness of the locals. Whether you're in a bustling city or a small rural village, you're likely to find the Irish eager to share their time, stories, and sometimes even a pint. In many cases, you may be invited into someone's home, and it is customary to bring a small gift as a token of appreciation—flowers, chocolates, or something locally made. When entering a pub, it's common to offer a polite greeting to the bartender and fellow patrons. Don't be surprised if a conversation starts with "Where are you from?"—the Irish take genuine interest in getting to know newcomers.

3. Music, Dance, and the Arts

Music and dance are at the heart of Irish culture. The island is famous for its traditional music, with instruments like the fiddle, tin whistle, uilleann pipes, and bodhrán (a traditional drum) taking center stage in local performances. In pubs and cultural centers, you'll often hear live Irish folk music, where songs about love, life, and loss intertwine with the rhythms of the land. Irish dance, most famously represented by Riverdance, is another defining cultural aspect. It combines fast-paced footwork with fluid upper-body movements, often performed in competitive settings or as part of local festivals. Traditional Irish dance festivals (feiseanna) are held regularly, and they draw participants from around the world.

4. Respect for Tradition and Family

Irish culture places a high value on family and community. The close-knit nature of families, particularly in rural areas, fosters strong bonds. Sunday gatherings and family meals are sacred traditions, and it's common for multiple generations to live under the same roof or nearby. The older generation in Ireland is respected for its wisdom, and their stories often form the foundation of familial connections. Religion, especially Catholicism, has historically played a significant role in shaping Irish identity. While modern Ireland has become more secular in recent decades, religious traditions like attending Mass on Sunday or celebrating saints' feast days still influence many Irish customs. Many of the island's most beautiful landmarks—churches, abbeys, and shrines—are steeped in this spiritual heritage.

5. Humor and Wit

The Irish are renowned for their dry, self-deprecating humor. It's not uncommon to hear quick-witted remarks that reflect a mix of charm, irony, and sometimes even sarcasm. Humor is often used to navigate life's challenges, and the Irish have a knack for turning even the most difficult situations into something to laugh about. If you find yourself the subject of good-natured teasing, don't take it personally; it's a sign of affection, not offense.

6. The Pub Culture

The Irish pub is an institution that transcends just a place to drink. It's a space for socializing, storytelling, and community bonding.

The pub is often the heart of a town or village, where people gather to relax, enjoy music, discuss politics, or simply pass the time with friends. In larger cities like Dublin, Galway, and Cork, pubs are an integral part of the nightlife scene, each with its unique atmosphere. A traditional pub may have live folk music in the evenings, while others offer a more contemporary vibe. It's customary to buy a round of drinks for your group, and if you're new to the pub, expect some conversation to come your way, along with a pint of Guinness or a glass of Irish whiskey.

7. Irish Festivals and Traditions

Festivals are a significant part of Irish culture, celebrating everything from music to food to literature. The most famous of all is St. Patrick's Day, celebrated on March 17th. What began as a religious feast day for Ireland's patron saint has evolved into a global celebration of all things Irish, marked by parades, festivals, and the ubiquitous wearing of green. Other key festivals include the Dublin Theatre Festival, the Galway International Arts Festival, and Fleadh Cheoil, the world's largest celebration of traditional Irish music. Throughout the year, towns and villages host local festivals celebrating everything from food to folklore, making every visit to Ireland an opportunity to experience something uniquely Irish.

8. The Role of the Irish Language (Gaeilge)

Although English is the predominant language, Irish (Gaeilge) is an integral part of the cultural fabric. Spoken predominantly in the Gaeltacht (Irish-speaking regions) located along the western seaboard, Irish is taught in schools across the country, and efforts are being made to revive its use in daily life. Visitors will often encounter Irish road signs, place names, and traditional songs in Irish. Understanding even a few basic phrases like "Dia dhuit" (hello) or "Slán" (goodbye) can go a long way in connecting with the locals.

9. Attitudes Toward Nature and the Land

The Irish have a deep respect for nature, and this is reflected in their relationship with the land, especially in rural communities. The rolling hills, rugged coastlines, and ancient forests are not merely places of beauty—they are part of Ireland's collective identity. Hiking, walking, and outdoor activities are central to life, and preserving the environment is increasingly important in Irish society.

It's common to hear locals speak with reverence about the land, and many will gladly share their knowledge about the flora and fauna in their area.

10. A Rich Literary Tradition

Ireland has a remarkable literary tradition, producing some of the world's greatest writers, including W.B. Yeats, Oscar Wilde, Samuel Beckett, and James Joyce. Dublin was designated a UNESCO City of Literature in 2010, and literary tours through the capital and beyond showcase the legacy of these literary giants. The Irish also take great pride in their tradition of poetry and oral storytelling, where even the most casual conversation can feel like a well-crafted tale.

Chapter 2: Planning Your Irish Trip

Best Time to Visit by Season & Region

Ireland's climate is unique, characterized by mild temperatures, frequent rain, and ever-changing weather. The best time to visit depends on your priorities — whether you're seeking ideal weather, fewer crowds, or a taste of specific regional experiences. Understanding the nuances of each season and how they vary across Ireland's regions will allow you to make the most of your time in the Emerald Isle.

Spring (March to May)

Why Visit: Spring is one of the most magical times to visit Ireland. With the landscape bursting into vibrant greenery and the first signs of flowers blooming, this season offers mild weather, fewer tourists, and plenty of festivals.

Weather: Temperatures range from 8°C to 14°C (46°F to 57°F). Expect some rain, but you'll enjoy more sunshine as the days get longer.

Highlights:

- **St. Patrick's Day (March 17th):** Celebrated across Ireland, especially in Dublin, with parades, festivals, and a chance to experience the country's cultural heritage.
- **Wildflower Blooms:** The Irish countryside comes alive with colorful wildflowers, particularly in the Kerry and Wicklow mountains.
- **Festivals:** Alongside St. Patrick's Day, the Dublin Dance Festival and Galway Arts Festival (late spring) kick off the cultural calendar.

Best Regions:

- **Dublin:** Perfect for experiencing St. Patrick's Day and the city's vibrant cultural scene.
- **Kerry and Clare:** The landscapes are stunning, and the weather is mild, ideal for hiking in the Killarney National Park or along the Cliffs of Moher.

Summer (June to August)

Why Visit: Summer is peak tourist season in Ireland, marked by long daylight hours, lively festivals, and perfect weather for outdoor activities.

It's the ideal time for those who want to enjoy Ireland's stunning landscapes and rich cultural events.

Weather: Average temperatures range from 14°C to 19°C (57°F to 66°F), with the possibility of occasional showers. It's the warmest time of the year, but rain is still frequent.

Highlights:

- **Festivals:** Ireland's summer calendar is packed with events, such as the Galway International Arts Festival, the Kilkenny Arts Festival, and Feis Ceoil (the largest traditional music competition).
- **Outdoor Activities:** Perfect weather for exploring the Ring of Kerry, Connemara, or cycling through the Great Western Greenway.
- **Beaches:** With mild temperatures, the beaches of Cork and Wexford become popular, though still relatively uncrowded compared to other European beaches.

Best Regions:

- **Dublin:** A vibrant mix of festivals, theater, and bustling cafés. You can also enjoy evening strolls along the River Liffey with long daylight hours.
- **Kerry:** Known for its coastal scenery, the Ring of Kerry and Dingle Peninsula are breathtaking in the summer months.
- **West Coast (Clare, Galway, and Mayo):** Ideal for exploring the Aran Islands or hiking the rugged coastline.

Autumn (September to November)

Why Visit: Autumn in Ireland is a wonderfully tranquil time to visit. The crowds thin out, the landscape shifts to autumn hues, and the weather remains relatively mild. It's perfect for those who want to enjoy Ireland's natural beauty without the peak-season hustle.

Weather: Average temperatures range from 10°C to 15°C (50°F to 59°F). The weather is still mild in September, but rainfall increases in October and November.

Highlights:

Autumn Foliage: The landscape turns golden with fall colors, making it the ideal time for scenic drives through regions like Wicklow, Kerry, and Donegal.

Harvest Festivals: Ballymaloe Harvest Festival in County Cork celebrates the autumn harvest with local food, music, and crafts.

Less Crowded: Popular tourist sites like the Cliffs of Moher or Blarney Castle are much quieter in autumn, offering a more relaxed experience.

Best Regions:

- **Wicklow:** Known for its stunning autumn colors, Glendalough and Wicklow Mountains National Park are especially beautiful in fall.
- **Cork and Kilkenny:** These regions host harvest festivals and are perfect for indulging in local cuisine and culture.
- **Donegal:** The northwest offers a rugged, windswept beauty with fewer tourists during this time of year.

Winter (December to February)

Why Visit: Winter is the quietest season in Ireland, and while the weather can be cold and unpredictable, it also offers unique experiences, from cozy pubs with roaring fires to fewer crowds at popular tourist attractions.

Weather: Temperatures range from 4°C to 9°C (39°F to 48°F). Ireland rarely experiences snow, but it can be damp and chilly, especially in coastal areas.

Highlights:

- **Festive Atmosphere:** The Christmas period in Ireland is enchanting, with festive markets in Dublin, Galway, and Belfast. Traditional Irish holiday foods and mulled wine add to the experience.
- **Cultural Experiences:** Visit Ireland's world-class museums and galleries, like the National Gallery of Ireland or the Chester Beatty Library in Dublin, for indoor cultural exploration.
- **Off-season Tranquility:** Popular tourist sites are quiet, and you can enjoy Ireland's dramatic landscapes almost entirely to yourself.

Best Regions:

- **Dublin:** Ideal for exploring museums, theaters, and cozy pubs during the festive season.
- **Belfast:** Explore the vibrant city with fewer tourists. The Titanic Museum and St. George's Market are especially atmospheric during winter.

- **Cork and Kerry:** Experience Ireland's natural beauty at a slower pace, without the crowds of the high season.

Regional Considerations

While Ireland is a relatively small island, the weather and experiences can vary greatly from one region to another:

East Coast (Dublin, Wicklow, Wexford): This area tends to have milder winters and drier conditions, though rain is frequent. Dublin is a lively city year-round, with cultural events taking place throughout all seasons.

West Coast (Galway, Clare, Mayo): The west coast is often more exposed to Atlantic weather, which means more frequent rain and wind. However, it also has some of the country's most stunning natural landscapes, including the Cliffs of Moher, Connemara, and the Aran Islands.

North (Donegal, Antrim, Derry): Donegal and Northern Ireland experience colder, windier conditions, particularly in winter. However, the natural beauty, including the Giant's Causeway, makes it worth a visit year-round.

Month-by-Month Guide to Visiting Ireland in 2025

January

January in Ireland is the coldest month of the year, with temperatures averaging around 4°C to 7°C (39°F to 45°F). It's a quiet time to visit, with fewer tourists and the winter landscapes offering a serene atmosphere. Rain is frequent, and daylight hours are limited, so it's ideal for those who want to experience the peaceful side of Ireland. While some attractions may have reduced hours, it's a great time for indoor cultural experiences, such as visiting museums or cozying up in a traditional pub by a roaring fire. If you visit in January, expect chilly weather, but also enjoy the tranquility of the off-season.

February

February remains cold, with average temperatures similar to January. The early part of the month sees quieter crowds, with fewer tourists around the popular sites. However, late February brings the first signs of spring, and the landscape starts to look greener. Rainfall is still high, and while snow is rare, it can occasionally blanket the higher altitudes of places like Wicklow or the Mourne Mountains.

Ireland's cultural scene remains lively in cities like Dublin, with concerts, art exhibitions, and theater productions offering indoor entertainment. It's a good month for those looking to avoid crowds while still enjoying a variety of activities.

March

March signals the beginning of spring, and the temperature begins to rise slightly, reaching around 5°C to 9°C (41°F to 48°F). While the weather can still be unpredictable, Ireland's cultural calendar comes to life, particularly with St. Patrick's Day on March 17th. This is the best time to experience Ireland's festivities, as parades, music, and dancing fill the streets of Dublin, Cork, Galway, and beyond. The landscape starts to bloom with early wildflowers, making it a great month for nature lovers. Although there is still a chance of rain, the celebrations and cultural experiences make it a vibrant time to visit.

April

April is a wonderful time to experience Ireland, as the country is coming into full spring. Average temperatures range from 8°C to 12°C (46°F to 54°F), and rainfall is still frequent but more manageable than in the winter months. The countryside is vibrant with blooming flowers, and the weather is generally mild, although the occasional cold snap is still possible. The Easter holiday brings several festivals and events, and it's also a time when many attractions begin to open for the season. If you're visiting in April, you'll enjoy fewer crowds than in summer while still having access to many outdoor and cultural activities.

May

By May, the days are noticeably longer, and the weather starts to warm up, with temperatures averaging between 9°C and 14°C (48°F to 57°F). This is one of the best months to visit Ireland, as the crowds haven't yet reached their summer peak, but the weather is ideal for outdoor activities. The countryside is in full bloom, with lush greenery and colorful wildflowers, especially in places like the Kerry and Wicklow mountains. It's a great time for hiking, cycling, and exploring Ireland's scenic beauty. Various cultural festivals, such as the Dublin Dance Festival, kick off, adding to the lively atmosphere.

June

June marks the start of summer in Ireland, and the weather improves significantly with temperatures ranging from 12°C to 17°C (54°F to 63°F).

This is the beginning of the high tourist season, especially in popular destinations like Dublin, Galway, and the Ring of Kerry. The days are long, with up to 17 hours of daylight in some parts of the country. This makes it an excellent time for outdoor activities, whether you're hiking, exploring the beaches, or cycling along the scenic routes. While there may still be occasional showers, June offers some of the best weather for exploring Ireland's natural beauty and vibrant towns.

July

July is one of the warmest months in Ireland, with temperatures averaging between 14°C and 19°C (57°F to 66°F). The weather is mild, making it perfect for outdoor exploration and enjoying the country's coastal regions. The tourist season is in full swing, so popular destinations will be busier, but this also means more events, festivals, and activities. Ireland hosts a range of summer festivals, including the Galway International Arts Festival and Kilkenny Arts Festival. The longer daylight hours also mean more time to explore, whether you're wandering through cities or hiking in the mountains.

August

August is another peak month for tourism in Ireland, with temperatures remaining warm at around 15°C to 19°C (59°F to 66°F). The country is in full summer mode, with festivals, outdoor concerts, and sporting events taking place across the country. It's an excellent time to visit if you enjoy the lively atmosphere and want to experience Ireland's cultural scene at its best. While some areas can get crowded, particularly in cities like Dublin and Galway, the pleasant weather and long days make it ideal for exploring the countryside, from the Cliffs of Moher to the beaches of Wexford and Cork.

September

September is one of the best times to visit Ireland, as the summer crowds start to dissipate, but the weather remains relatively mild, with temperatures ranging from 12°C to 16°C (54°F to 61°F). This is harvest time, and the Irish countryside is a beautiful mix of autumn colors. It's the perfect month for outdoor activities such as hiking, cycling, or exploring the scenic routes, such as the Ring of Kerry. The days are still long, and while there may be a bit more rain, September offers the perfect balance of mild weather and fewer tourists. This is also the month when Ireland's cultural festivals, like the Ballymaloe Harvest Festival, take place.

October

October sees a noticeable drop in temperatures, averaging between 9°C and 14°C (48°F to 57°F). The autumn colors begin to peak, especially in places like Wicklow and Kerry, making it an excellent month for scenic drives or hiking. While rain is frequent, the fall foliage creates a striking contrast against the rugged landscapes, providing excellent photography opportunities. The crowds are much thinner than in summer, so you can enjoy the sights at a more relaxed pace. Festivals such as the Dublin Theatre Festival and Cork Film Festival add a cultural touch to the month, making it a fantastic time for a more intimate Irish experience.

November

November brings colder weather, with temperatures ranging from 5°C to 9°C (41°F to 48°F). The days are shorter, and rain becomes more frequent, but the autumn landscapes are still beautiful, especially as the last of the fall foliage lingers. This is a quiet time to visit, with fewer tourists around, allowing you to experience Ireland's natural beauty and historical sites in peace. Many attractions may begin to close for the winter, but indoor activities such as visiting museums, galleries, and enjoying Ireland's legendary pub culture remain great options. It's a peaceful month to experience the real Ireland without the hustle and bustle of peak season.

December

December is cold, with temperatures ranging from 4°C to 8°C (39°F to 46°F), and the weather is often damp, but the holiday spirit fills the air. Cities like Dublin, Cork, and Galway are beautifully decorated for Christmas, and festive markets spring up in major cities. It's an excellent month for those who enjoy cozy winter activities, like visiting Christmas markets, enjoying traditional Irish food, and sipping on mulled wine by the fire. While the weather can be unpredictable, the Christmas atmosphere, combined with fewer tourists, makes it a charming time to visit if you don't mind the cold.

Best Time to Visit Ireland by Interest

Ireland offers something for everyone, regardless of your interests. Whether you're a nature lover, history enthusiast, or foodie, the best time to visit depends on what you're looking to experience.

For Outdoor Adventures & Nature Exploration

Best Time: May to September

Why: During these months, Ireland's weather is mild, making it perfect for hiking, biking, and outdoor exploration. You can hike the Wicklow Mountains, enjoy the scenic Ring of Kerry, or explore the Wild Atlantic Way with pleasant weather and longer daylight hours. The landscapes come alive with vibrant green fields and blooming flowers in spring and early summer, while autumn offers stunning foliage in parks like Killarney National Park.

For Festivals & Cultural Experiences

Best Time: March to August

Why: Ireland's rich cultural scene is showcased in numerous festivals throughout the year. March, particularly around St. Patrick's Day (March 17), offers vibrant celebrations in Dublin and other cities. For art lovers, the Galway International Arts Festival in July and the Kilkenny Arts Festival in August are key highlights. The Dublin Theatre Festival in October also provides an excellent mix of contemporary performances.

For History & Heritage Exploration

Best Time: April to October

Why: The milder weather during these months allows for easier exploration of Ireland's many historical landmarks, castles, and museums. Spend time at Kilmainham Gaol in Dublin, the Rock of Cashel in Tipperary, or the Cliffs of Moher for a combination of natural beauty and historical significance. With fewer tourists in the off-season, you can enjoy historical sites without the crowds, especially in September and October.

For Food Lovers & Culinary Delights

Best Time: June to September

Why: Summer months bring the harvest season, providing fresh, local produce and plenty of opportunities to sample Irish specialties. Dublin, Cork, and Galway are renowned for their vibrant food scenes, with farmers' markets offering fresh local cheeses, meats, and vegetables.

Festivals like Taste of Dublin in June showcase the best of Irish food, while seafood lovers can enjoy freshly caught fish along the coast in Galway and Kinsale.

For Peaceful Escapes & Relaxation

Best Time: November to February

Why: If you're looking for a peaceful retreat away from the crowds, winter months are perfect. Dublin and Cork offer cozy pubs, while the West of Ireland and Connemara provide serene landscapes ideal for reflection and quiet walks. The cooler temperatures and festive atmosphere make it a great time for relaxation. If you enjoy low-season prices and fewer tourists, this period is ideal for unwinding.

For Photography & Scenic Landscapes

Best Time: May to October

Why: Ireland's landscapes are breathtaking year-round, but the summer months offer the best conditions for photographers. Early summer sees lush green fields, vibrant wildflowers, and the clearest skies, while autumn provides stunning golden and red hues across the countryside. Popular spots like the Cliffs of Moher, Connemara, and The Burren are even more dramatic with the changing light.

For Family Vacations & Kid-Friendly Activities

Best Time: June to August

Why: Ireland's family-friendly atmosphere shines during the summer months when schools are out and the weather is warm enough for outdoor activities. Explore places like Dublin Zoo, Killarney's Muckross House (perfect for family tours), or enjoy a family day out in Belfast's Titanic Quarter. Summer also offers many festivals with family-friendly performances, making it a great time for all ages to enjoy Ireland together.

For Golf Enthusiasts

Best Time: May to September

Why: Ireland is renowned for its stunning golf courses, many of which are set against dramatic coastal backdrops.

Ballybunion, Royal County Down, and Lahinch offer world-class golfing experiences. The summer months provide the best weather conditions for a day on the green, with long daylight hours and mild temperatures.

Entry Requirements & Visas

Ireland is part of the Common Travel Area (CTA), which includes the United Kingdom, the Republic of Ireland, the Isle of Man, and the Channel Islands. This arrangement impacts visa requirements for travelers, and the specific entry conditions depend on your nationality and travel purpose. It's essential to check updated information before traveling to ensure a smooth entry into the country.

General Entry Requirements for Ireland

Passport: All travelers must present a valid passport when entering Ireland. Ensure your passport is valid for at least three months beyond the date you intend to leave Ireland.

Visa Requirement: Whether or not you need a visa to enter Ireland depends on your nationality and the length of your stay.

Who Needs a Visa?

Ireland has a visa policy that varies by country. Citizens of some countries require a visa to enter Ireland, while others are visa-exempt for short stays (usually up to 90 days). Generally, the visa policy applies to non-EU/EEA nationals.

1. EU/EEA and Swiss Citizens: Citizens from EU member states, the European Economic Area (EEA), and Switzerland do not require a visa to enter Ireland. They are free to travel and stay within Ireland for up to 90 days without restrictions.

2. Visa-Exempt Countries: Citizens of certain countries do not need a visa for short stays (tourism, business, etc.) of up to 90 days. These countries include:

- United States
- Canada
- Australia
- New Zealand
- Japan
- South Korea
- Israel

- And several others

If you are from one of these countries, you can travel to Ireland for up to 90 days without a visa. However, immigration officials at the port of entry may ask to see evidence of your return flight or sufficient funds for your stay.

3. Countries That Require a Visa: Nationals of countries not on the visa-exempt list will need to apply for a visa to enter Ireland. Examples of countries that require a visa include:

- China
- India
- Russia
- Nigeria
- South Africa

If you're from one of these countries or any other visa-required nation, you must apply for an Irish visa before traveling.

Types of Visas for Ireland

Depending on your purpose of visit, you may need to apply for one of the following types of visas:

1. Short Stay Visa: This is the most common visa for tourists, business travelers, and those visiting friends or family for short periods (usually up to 90 days).

2. Long Stay Visa: If you intend to stay in Ireland for longer than 90 days, for example for study, work, or family reunification, you will need to apply for a long-stay visa. These visas allow stays for up to one year or longer, depending on the type of visa.

3. Transit Visa: If you are traveling through Ireland to another country (for example, on a layover), you may require a transit visa. This is applicable if you plan to stay in Ireland for less than 24 hours.

4. Study Visa: If you're planning to study in Ireland for more than 90 days, you will need to apply for a student visa. You will need to provide evidence of admission to a recognized educational institution and proof of sufficient financial resources.

Visa Application Process

The process of applying for an Irish visa generally involves the following steps:

1. Check if You Need a Visa: Determine whether you need a visa based on your nationality and the purpose of your visit.

2. Complete the Visa Application Form: You must complete the visa application form online at the Irish Naturalisation and Immigration Service (INIS) website. This can be done at least three months before your planned travel.

3. Gather Required Documents: The documents typically required for an Irish visa application include:

- A valid passport
- Completed visa application form
- Passport-sized photos
- Proof of travel (such as a flight itinerary or travel bookings)
- Evidence of accommodation (hotel bookings, invitation letters from family/friends)
- Financial evidence (bank statements or pay slips showing that you can support yourself during your stay)
- Visa fee payment (visa fees vary depending on the type of visa and your nationality)

4. Submit Your Application: Submit the completed application form and required documents at the nearest Irish Embassy or Consulate. In some cases, you may be required to attend an interview.

5. Wait for a Decision: Visa processing times can vary depending on the embassy or consulate. Typically, short-stay visa applications take around 6 to 8 weeks to process. Be sure to apply well in advance to avoid delays.

Customs & Immigration

When you arrive in Ireland, you will go through passport control and immigration checks. At this stage, you'll need to:

- Present your passport (and visa, if required).
- Answer questions about the purpose and duration of your stay.

- Provide proof of return travel, accommodation, or sufficient funds, if requested.

If you're arriving from outside the Common Travel Area (CTA) (which includes the UK, the Channel Islands, and the Isle of Man), you will be subject to immigration controls.

Special Note: The Common Travel Area (CTA)

While Ireland is not part of the Schengen Area, it has an agreement with the UK, the Channel Islands, and the Isle of Man, known as the Common Travel Area. This means that:

- UK and Irish citizens can travel freely between Ireland and the UK without passport controls.
- People traveling from the UK to Ireland may not need to go through additional immigration checks, depending on their travel route.
- However, travelers from outside the CTA, such as from the United States, Canada, or India, must still go through Irish immigration controls when entering Ireland.

Important Tips for Travelers

Check for Updates: Visa and entry requirements can change, so always check the Irish government's official website for the most current information before planning your trip.

Be Aware of Visa Duration: Make sure your visa allows you to stay for the appropriate length of time and is valid for the entire duration of your visit.

Proof of Financial Means: Be prepared to show evidence that you can financially support yourself during your stay (such as bank statements or sponsor letters) when applying for a visa or entering Ireland.

Vaccinations & Health Guidelines

Traveling to Ireland in 2025 is a generally safe and straightforward experience in terms of health and hygiene. The country boasts a modern healthcare system, a clean water supply, and excellent medical services. Still, it's important to prepare for your trip by following updated health recommendations and ensuring necessary vaccinations and travel insurance are in place.

Routine Vaccinations

All travelers should be up to date on routine vaccinations before entering Ireland. These include:

- MMR (Measles, Mumps, Rubella)
- DTP (Diphtheria, Tetanus, Pertussis)
- Polio
- Varicella (Chickenpox)
- Annual Influenza Vaccine
- COVID-19 (Latest Booster, if recommended in your country)

These are typically covered in most national immunization programs and are particularly important for travelers who plan on spending time in crowded areas, using public transport, or attending festivals and public gatherings.

Recommended Vaccines for Travelers

While no vaccinations are legally required for entry into Ireland, the following are recommended depending on your personal health, travel style, and length of stay:

- **Hepatitis A:** Transmitted through contaminated food or water, though rare in Ireland, it's advisable if you're traveling from a region where Hep A is more common.
- **Hepatitis B:** Recommended for longer stays or for those who might require medical treatment during their time in Ireland.
- **Rabies:** Only advised for travelers planning outdoor activities in rural areas, such as hiking or caving, where they might encounter bats or stray animals.

COVID-19 Protocols (2025 Update)

Ireland has relaxed most pandemic-era travel restrictions, but a few protocols remain in place as part of general public health policy:

- No mandatory testing or quarantine is currently required for travelers from most countries.
- Travelers should carry proof of vaccination or recent recovery from COVID-19, especially if planning to attend large public events or visit healthcare facilities.

- Mask-wearing remains optional but is encouraged in medical settings and on public transport during flu season or when experiencing symptoms.

Always check your airline and the connecting country's rules, as some may maintain their COVID-related entry requirements.

Healthcare System & Access

Ireland provides high-quality healthcare through both public and private systems.

- **EU/EEA Travelers:** Should carry a European Health Insurance Card (EHIC) for access to public healthcare services at reduced or no cost.
- **Non-EU Visitors:** Strongly advised to purchase comprehensive travel insurance that includes coverage for medical expenses, evacuation, and emergencies.

Pharmacies are widespread, well-stocked, and usually open Monday to Saturday. In major cities, 24-hour or late-night pharmacies are available.

Emergency Medical Services

- **Emergency Number:** Dial 112 or 999 for ambulance services in Ireland.
- Hospitals and clinics are located throughout the country, with top-quality medical centers in cities like Dublin, Cork, Galway, and Limerick.

Water & Food Safety

- Tap water in Ireland is safe to drink throughout the country.
- Food safety standards are high; restaurants, pubs, and markets follow strict health regulations.
- Street food, where available, is generally clean and safe.

Weather-Related Health Tips

Ireland's weather can change quickly, often presenting four seasons in a single day. Be prepared for:

- Sudden rain showers – carry a lightweight rain jacket.
- Mild but damp winters – dress in layers to stay warm.
- UV exposure – In summer, even cloudy days can bring UV rays; sunscreen is advisable.

Allergies & Special Health Needs

Those with food allergies, asthma, or chronic health conditions should travel with a doctor's note and a sufficient supply of prescribed medication. English is spoken throughout Ireland, making communication with medical professionals straightforward. Many restaurants are allergy-aware and clearly label their menus with allergens, including gluten, dairy, and nuts.

Final Tip: A visit to Ireland rarely presents major health concerns, but taking a proactive approach with vaccinations, insurance, and a travel health kit ensures peace of mind and a worry-free journey.

Budgeting Your Trip: Cost Breakdown

Ireland offers a wide range of travel experiences suited to nearly every budget—from cozy countryside getaways and road trips to high-end city breaks with Michelin-starred meals. Understanding how to budget your trip effectively helps maximize your experience while keeping finances in check. This breakdown covers average costs across accommodation, transport, meals, attractions, and incidentals, with tips for saving and splurging wisely.

Accommodation Costs

Ireland caters to all types of travelers with accommodations ranging from countryside hostels to luxury manor houses.

- **Budget travelers** can expect to pay around €30–€60 ($33–$66) per night for a bed in a hostel or a basic guesthouse. Many budget options offer breakfast and free Wi-Fi.
- **Mid-range accommodations**, including comfortable hotels, B&Bs, and boutique stays, usually range from €90–€150 ($99–$165) per night. These often include breakfast and better amenities like parking and en suite bathrooms.
- **Luxury stays**, whether in five-star hotels or castle retreats, generally start at €250 ($275) and can rise to €500 ($550) or more per night, especially in peak season or premium locations like Dublin, Galway, or the Ring of Kerry.

Tip: Booking in advance during peak travel months (May–September) can help lock in better rates.

Food and Dining

The cost of food varies depending on where and how you eat, with hearty Irish portions often delivering good value.

- A **casual café breakfast** or lunch runs between €8–€15 ($9–$17). Coffee and a pastry will cost about €5 ($5.50).
- **Pub meals**, a classic way to enjoy Irish hospitality, range from €14–€25 ($15–$28) for mains such as Irish stew, fish and chips, or a burger with sides.
- **Dinner in a mid-range restaurant** will typically cost €25–€45 ($28–$50) per person, excluding drinks. A three-course meal with wine or craft beer might push the total closer to €60–€80 ($66–$88).
- **Fine dining experiences**, including Michelin-starred restaurants, begin at €90–€120 ($100–$132) per person, with tasting menus and wine pairings increasing the final bill considerably.

Tip: Many pubs serve hearty and affordable lunches with generous portions.

Transportation

Getting around Ireland offers both flexibility and scenic pleasure, whether you're taking a train or cruising down a coastal road.

- **Car rental** is the most popular option for travelers who want freedom. Expect to pay €35–€60 ($39–$66) per day for a compact vehicle, excluding fuel, insurance, and any added driver fees. Fuel prices average around €1.80 ($2.00) per liter (about €6.80 / $7.50 per gallon).
- **Public transportation** is affordable and reliable between cities. A train ticket from Dublin to Galway costs approximately €20–€35 ($22–$39) one way, depending on booking time and class. Intercity buses are slightly cheaper, at €10–€25 ($11–$28).
- **Local transit** within cities (bus, tram) typically costs €2.00–€3.50 ($2.20–$3.85) per ride, with day passes available for around €8–€10 ($9–$11).

Tip: For rural exploration, especially in counties like Clare or Donegal, renting a car gives the most flexibility.

Attractions and Activities

Ireland's best offerings often lie in its landscapes, which are free to enjoy, but many cultural sites and guided experiences have entrance fees.

- **National parks and natural sites** are often free, though parking may cost around €5 ($5.50) per visit.
- **Admission to castles, museums, and cathedrals** typically ranges from €8–€15 ($9–$17). Popular attractions like the Guinness Storehouse in Dublin or Blarney Castle in Cork may cost €20–€30 ($22–$33).
- **Guided tours**, such as a full-day tour to the Cliffs of Moher or a Game of Thrones filming location tour, are priced from €45–€85 ($50–$94).
- **Outdoor activities** like kayaking, cycling tours, or horseback riding range from €40–€70 ($44–$77) depending on the location and duration.

Tip: The Heritage Card (€40) grants access to many state-run attractions and can pay for itself in 3–4 visits.

Entertainment and Nightlife

Ireland's social scene is part of its charm, from live traditional music in a pub to plays in historic theaters.

- A **pint of Guinness** or craft beer usually costs €5.50–€7.00 ($6–$7.70), with slightly higher prices in Dublin.
- **Live music venues and pubs** may charge a small cover fee of €5–€10 ($5.50–$11), but many traditional sessions are free with drink purchases.
- **Theater tickets**, such as a performance at Dublin's Abbey Theatre, typically range from €25–€60 ($28–$66) depending on seat and production.

Incidentals & Souvenirs

- **Budget:** €5–€10/day for snacks, public restrooms, postcards, or minor tips.
- **Mid-range:** €20–€50/day for crafts, local gifts, books, or artisanal food.
- **Luxury:** Designer shopping, fine woolens, or crystalware can exceed €100+ per item.

Money-Saving Strategies

- Travel in the shoulder seasons (April, October) to save on accommodation and flights.
- Choose self-catering accommodation or shop at local supermarkets for breakfast and snacks.
- Use Leap Cards for public transport savings in cities like Dublin.

- Opt for combo passes for attractions or take advantage of free-entry days at national museums.

Splurge-Worthy Experiences

- A night in a historic castle hotel
- Dinner at a Michelin-starred restaurant in Dublin, Cork, or Galway
- A private chauffeur tour of the Wild Atlantic Way
- Tickets to a traditional Irish music session or theatre performance

Daily Budget Estimates (Per Person)

Budget travelers: €60–€90 ($66–$99) — includes hostel stay, casual meals, public transport, and a few low-cost attractions.

Mid-range travelers: €150–€250 ($165–$275) — includes mid-range accommodation, dining in pubs or casual restaurants, car rental or rail travel, and entrance to top attractions.

Luxury travelers: €350–€600+ ($385–$660+) — includes upscale lodging, fine dining, private tours, car hire with full insurance, and high-end cultural or adventure experiences.

Currency, Credit Cards & ATMs

Understanding how money works in Ireland can make your journey smoother and more enjoyable. Ireland is largely cashless-friendly, yet carrying a small amount of cash is still wise, especially when visiting rural areas, traditional markets, or independent shops.

Currency in Ireland

The official currency of the Republic of Ireland is the euro (€). Banknotes come in denominations of €5, €10, €20, €50, €100, €200, and €500, although €200 and €500 notes are rarely used. Coins include €1 and €2, along with smaller cent coins (1c to 50c).

Northern Ireland, part of the United Kingdom, uses the British pound sterling (£). If your travels take you north of the border, plan accordingly or exchange euros for pounds. Many card payment systems in Northern Ireland, however, accept both currencies electronically.

Credit & Debit Card Use

Credit and debit cards are widely accepted throughout Ireland, especially Visa and Mastercard. American Express is less commonly accepted but can still be used in hotels, higher-end restaurants, and some larger retailers.

- Tap-and-go (contactless) payments are the norm across Ireland, and mobile wallets like Apple Pay and Google Pay work almost everywhere.
- Smaller pubs, rural shops, or market stalls may prefer cash, especially in remote areas, so it's wise to carry some euros for emergencies or small purchases.

Tip: Inform your bank of your travel dates in advance to avoid fraud alerts or service disruptions.

ATMs (Bank Machines)

ATMs, locally called cashpoints, are easy to find in cities, airports, shopping areas, and even most small towns. Most machines accept international debit and credit cards and operate 24/7.

- Use ATMs attached to banks whenever possible for better exchange rates and lower fees.
- Some ATMs may offer "dynamic currency conversion," giving you the option to be charged in your home currency. Decline this and opt to be charged in euros for a more favorable rate.

Withdrawal Tips:

- Check with your home bank to know international withdrawal fees and daily limits.
- Consider using travel-friendly cards with no foreign transaction fees, such as Wise, Revolut, or travel-focused credit cards.

Exchanging Currency

Currency exchange services are available at major airports, train stations, and in tourist-heavy cities like Dublin, Cork, and Galway. However, exchange rates at airports tend to be less favorable than in banks or post offices.

If you prefer to carry cash into the country, consider exchanging a small amount beforehand and withdrawing more as needed from ATMs once you arrive.

Banking Hours and Currency Exchange

Banks in Ireland usually open from 9:30 AM to 4:30 PM, Monday to Friday, with some city branches offering limited Saturday hours. Currency exchange services are available at banks, exchange bureaus, airports, and post offices. However, exchange rates at airports and hotels tend to be less favorable. For better rates and lower commissions, consider using bank-affiliated exchange services in town centers or withdrawing directly from an ATM.

Tipping in Ireland

Tipping is appreciated but not obligatory. In restaurants, leaving 10%–15% for good service is standard, unless a service charge has already been added. For taxis, rounding up to the nearest euro is common. Porters and hotel staff may be given a few euros for assistance.

Packing Guide for Irish Weather

Ireland's weather is famously unpredictable—think sunshine one moment and a soft drizzle the next. No matter the season, packing smartly ensures you're comfortable, dry, and ready to enjoy everything from lush green hills to lively city streets. Layering is your best friend, and versatility is key.

General Essentials – Year-Round Must-Haves

- **Waterproof jacket with hood** – A lightweight, breathable rain jacket is non-negotiable. Showers can pop up anytime.
- **Comfortable walking shoes** – Choose sturdy, waterproof footwear suitable for cobblestone streets and rural paths.
- **Umbrella (small, wind-resistant)** – Handy for city walks, though less practical on blustery coastal days.
- **Warm layers** – Bring sweaters, fleece tops, or insulated vests—even in summer evenings, temperatures can dip.
- **Daypack or crossbody bag** – Weather-resistant with space for snacks, a water bottle, and layers you'll shed or add.
- **Adapters & converters** – Ireland uses the Type G plug (UK-style, 230V voltage), so bring a universal adapter if needed.
- **Reusable water bottle** – Tap water is safe and clean, and many spots offer refill stations.

Spring (March – May)

Expect cool temperatures (40s–60s °F / 5–16°C) and frequent showers.

- Light waterproof coat or parka
- Long-sleeve shirts and base layers
- Warm scarf and gloves (especially in March)
- Jeans or quick-drying pants
- Lightweight beanie or hat for wind protection

Summer (June – August)

Temperatures are mild (50s–70s °F / 10–21°C), with longer daylight hours—but showers still come and go.

- Breathable shirts and light sweaters
- A couple of warmer layers for evenings
- Convertible pants or capris
- Sunglasses and sunblock (yes, even in Ireland!)
- Swimsuit and towel for wild swimming or coastal dips
- Bug spray if visiting lakes or boggy regions

Autumn (September – November)

Crisp air, changing leaves, and misty mornings mark the season. Temps hover between 40s–60s °F (5–15°C).

- Waterproof hiking boots
- Thermal socks
- Insulated vest or light down jacket
- Earth-tone clothing that blends well for photography
- Gloves and a hat by late October

Winter (December – February)

While not extreme, Irish winters are damp and chilly (30s–50s °F / 0–10°C) with short daylight hours.

- Heavy coat or wool-blend outerwear
- Thermal base layers
- Wool sweaters or fleece-lined tops

- Gloves, scarf, and beanie
- Waterproof boots with a good grip for icy walks
- Indoor shoes or slippers if staying in traditional B&Bs

For the Countryside & Outdoor Adventures

- Quick-dry hiking trousers or leggings
- Moisture-wicking socks
- Rain pants for hikes or bike rides
- Binoculars for birdwatching or coastal spotting
- Portable charger for long days out

City Explorers & Culture Seekers

- Smart-casual outfit for dining out or theatre nights
- Foldable tote for markets or souvenirs
- Lightweight accessories to switch up outfits
- Power bank and local SIM (or eSIM) for navigation

Bonus Tips

- **Pack in layers**, not bulk. The weather may swing across seasons in a single day.
- **Choose neutral colors** that mix and match easily and hide mud or rain spots.
- **Don't overpack**—most towns have shops with outdoor gear if needed, especially in hiking hubs like Killarney or Dingle.

Travel Insurance & Safety Tips

Ireland is widely regarded as one of the safest and most welcoming destinations in Europe. But like any international journey, preparation is essential. Travel insurance adds a layer of protection, while understanding local safety norms ensures peace of mind throughout your trip.

Why Travel Insurance Matters

Even in a low-risk country like Ireland, unexpected events can disrupt your journey. Comprehensive travel insurance covers a range of potential issues:

- Trip cancellations or delays due to weather, illness, or emergencies
- Medical expenses not covered by your home health provider

- Lost or delayed baggage
- Theft or loss of valuables
- Adventure sports or rental car coverage, if applicable

A typical travel insurance policy for a 10-day trip might cost between $50–$150, depending on your age, trip cost, and coverage level. Look for providers that offer 24/7 assistance and flexible cancellation options.

Tip: Always review the policy details and exclusions. Some providers may not cover pre-existing conditions or high-risk activities unless specified.

Personal Safety in Ireland

Ireland consistently ranks as one of the safest destinations for travelers. Violent crime is rare, and locals are generally friendly and helpful. Still, it's wise to take basic precautions:

- **Keep your valuables secure** – Use a money belt or crossbody bag in busy areas.
- **Avoid leaving bags unattended** in restaurants or public transit.
- **Stay alert at night** – Irish cities are lively, but stick to well-lit streets and avoid parks after dark.
- **Watch for pickpockets** in tourist-heavy areas like Temple Bar (Dublin), Galway's Latin Quarter, or Cliffs of Moher parking areas.

Driving Safety

If renting a car:

- Drive on the left-hand side of the road.
- Roads in rural areas can be narrow and winding—drive cautiously, especially in bad weather.
- Roundabouts are common; yield to traffic from the right.
- Always carry a valid driver's license, and consider getting an International Driving Permit if your license is not in English.
- Most cars in Ireland have manual transmissions; request an automatic in advance if needed.

Weather Awareness Ireland's weather is changeable, and storms occasionally cause delays in ferry crossings, flights, or driving conditions.

Monitor Met Éireann (Ireland's national weather service) for up-to-date forecasts, especially during autumn and winter.

Emergency Services

Ireland has a well-developed emergency infrastructure. The emergency number for police, ambulance, and fire is 112 or 999 (either works from any phone). Response times in urban areas are quick, and most staff speak English.

Pharmacies (often marked "chemist") are widespread and a good first stop for minor medical issues. Many offer basic consultations.

Health Tips

- Tap water is safe to drink.
- No special vaccinations are required for travel to Ireland.
- If you take prescription medication, carry it in its original packaging along with a doctor's note.
- For EU travelers, a European Health Insurance Card (EHIC) provides access to public healthcare.

Useful Safety Apps

- Google Maps or Citymapper for real-time navigation and transit info
- SmartTraveler (for U.S. citizens) or equivalent for your country's embassy alerts
- WhatsApp for free calls and messaging over Wi-Fi
- Emergency App by IFRC for disaster alerts and tips

Chapter 3: Getting There & Around Ireland

Major Airports and Arrival Tips

Ireland is well-connected to the rest of the world through several international and regional airports. Whether arriving from North America, continental Europe, or the UK, you'll find modern facilities, efficient immigration processes, and convenient onward travel options. Knowing what to expect when you land makes your arrival smooth and stress-free.

Major Airports in Ireland

Dublin Airport (DUB) – Eastern Ireland

As the country's primary international gateway, Dublin Airport is located about 10 km (6 miles) north of the city center. It handles the majority of international flights, including direct services from North America, the Middle East, and across Europe.

- **Terminals:** Two (T1 for short-haul and T2 for long-haul)
- **Transport:** Taxis, Aircoach, Dublin Bus, and rental cars are easily accessible. Expect a 25–40 minute ride into central Dublin.
- **Facilities:** Currency exchange, car rental desks, SIM card kiosks, tourist information centers, and free Wi-Fi are all available.

Cork Airport (ORK) – Southern Ireland

Ireland's second-largest airport lies approximately 8 km (5 miles) south of Cork city. It primarily serves regional European routes with some seasonal international flights.

- **Transport:** Buses, taxis, and car hire are on-site. Travel time to Cork city center is about 15–20 minutes.
- **Best For:** Travelers heading to the south coast, including Kinsale, the Ring of Kerry, and West Cork.

Shannon Airport (SNN) – Western Ireland

Located in County Clare, Shannon is ideal for exploring the Wild Atlantic Way, the Cliffs of Moher, and the Burren. It offers transatlantic service and connections to several European hubs.

- **Transport:** Rental cars are highly recommended due to rural surroundings, though bus services to Limerick and Galway are available.
- **U.S. Preclearance:** Shannon has full U.S. customs and immigration preclearance, allowing travelers to arrive in the U.S. as domestic passengers.

Knock (Ireland West Airport – NOC) – Northwest Ireland

This regional airport serves the west and northwest, including counties Mayo and Sligo. Flights mostly come from the UK and select European destinations.

Transport: Car rental is the most practical option; public transport is limited.

Belfast Airports – Northern Ireland (UK Jurisdiction)

Belfast International Airport (BFS) and George Best Belfast City Airport (BHD) serve Northern Ireland.

If arriving in Belfast and traveling to the Republic of Ireland, be aware of currency differences and passport checks, even though there are no physical border controls.

Arrival Tips for First-Time Visitors

- **Passport Control:** EU/EEA and Swiss nationals use the EU lanes, while others, including U.S., Canadian, and Australian passport holders, go through the non-EU lanes. Ensure your passport is valid for at least six months beyond your arrival date.
- **Customs:** Ireland has separate customs rules from the UK. If traveling from outside the EU, be mindful of limits on alcohol, tobacco, and luxury goods.
- **Pre-book Transfers:** If arriving at night or on a holiday, it's wise to pre-book taxis or airport shuttles, especially outside of Dublin.
- **SIM Cards & Connectivity:** SIM cards and eSIM options are available at kiosks or convenience stores inside major airports. Vodafone, Three, and Eir are the main providers.
- **Car Rental:** For countryside exploration, consider renting a car. Most rental desks are located in or adjacent to airport terminals. Drivers must be at least 21 (age varies by company), and driving is on the left.
- **Tourist Information Desks:** Staff can assist with maps, bookings, and local tips—especially helpful if your itinerary isn't finalized.

Ferries & Cross-Channel Travel

Traveling to Ireland by sea offers a scenic, flexible, and often underrated alternative to flying. Ferries are particularly popular among travelers from the UK and mainland Europe who wish to bring their vehicles, avoid luggage restrictions, or enjoy a more leisurely journey across the waters of the Irish Sea or the English Channel.

Main Ferry Routes to Ireland

From Great Britain to the Republic of Ireland

Holyhead (Wales) to Dublin (Port of Dublin). This is the busiest and most direct route, with crossings operated by Irish Ferries and Stena Line. The journey typically takes around 2 hours for a fast ferry or 3 hours and 15 minutes for a conventional ferry. Departures run multiple times daily.

Fishguard (Wales) to Rosslare (County Wexford) Operated by Stena Line, this route connects southern Wales to Ireland's southeast coast. It takes about 3 hours and 30 minutes and is ideal for those heading to Waterford, Kilkenny, or the scenic Copper Coast.

Pembroke (Wales) to Rosslare Irish Ferries offers this route with crossings of approximately 4 hours. It's a favorite for travelers with caravans or those touring the southeast countryside.

Liverpool (England) to Dublin P&O Ferries provides overnight and daytime crossings, with journey times of around 8 hours. This route is particularly useful for freight, vehicles, and travelers based in northern England.

Cairnryan (Scotland) to Belfast or Larne (Northern Ireland), Stena Line and P&O Ferries operate frequent sailings, taking 2 to 2.5 hours. From Belfast or Larne, it's an easy drive to explore the Causeway Coast or cross into the Republic via Donegal.

From France to Ireland

Cherbourg to Dublin or Rosslare, Brittany Ferries and Irish Ferries offer overnight services (17–19 hours), particularly popular in the summer months. These are great options for travelers from Western or Southern Europe, especially those planning to drive in Ireland.

Roscoff to Cork, Brittany Ferries runs a seasonal service connecting northwest France to southern Ireland, ideal for exploring Cork, Kerry, and the Wild Atlantic Way.

Cherbourg to Cork (newer seasonal route) This extended option offers an overnight crossing directly to Ireland's southwest, reducing driving time for travelers focused on the Atlantic coast.

What to Expect Onboard

Modern ferries are equipped with comfortable lounges, restaurants, Wi-Fi, duty-free shopping, children's play areas, and private cabins (especially useful for overnight routes). Vehicle decks accommodate cars, campervans, and motorbikes. Passengers can also travel as foot passengers on most services. Cabin upgrades are often available, especially on longer crossings. Booking in advance is recommended, particularly during the summer holidays or around major Irish festivals.

Ferry Travel with Vehicles

If you're planning to bring a vehicle, it's advisable to book in advance. Vehicle bookings often require longer lead times, especially during peak seasons (spring to autumn). Ferries are equipped with space for cars, motorhomes, motorcycles, and bicycles, making it easy to explore Ireland at your own pace.

Travel Tip: Remember to check that your car insurance covers driving in Ireland. If you're planning to rent a vehicle in Ireland, make sure to select a car that suits your needs for both city driving and rural exploration.

Traveling Without a Vehicle

For those traveling without a car, ferries are equally convenient. Many ferry routes offer comfortable seating areas, restaurants, shops, and lounges, making the journey relaxing. You can also bring bikes, allowing you to explore Ireland's towns and cities at a leisurely pace.

Travel Tip: If you're traveling on foot, be sure to check if you need to make reservations in advance. Some ferries have limited space for pedestrians, especially during busy periods.

Booking Your Ferry Tickets

Booking ferry tickets is simple and can be done online through the ferry operator's website. It's advisable to book early during the peak summer season (June–August) to secure the best prices and availability.

Popular Ferry Operators:

- Stena Line
- Irish Ferries
- P&O Ferries
- Brittany Ferries

Booking Tips:

- Consider return tickets if you plan to leave and return via the same port, as round-trip tickets can sometimes offer discounts.
- Look for special offers on websites or third-party booking platforms to get the best rates.

Ferry Schedules & Timings

Ferry schedules vary depending on the route and time of year. Most ferry operators offer flexible schedules, with more frequent sailings in the summer months. Always check the timetable close to your departure date, as weather conditions or operational issues might cause delays or cancellations.

Tips for a Smooth Ferry Journey

- **Booking:** Reserve well ahead for the best prices, especially if bringing a vehicle. Many ferry operators offer flexible tickets and bundled deals with accommodation.
- **Check-In:** Arrive at least 45–60 minutes before departure if traveling with a vehicle. Foot passengers may check in 30 minutes prior.
- **Travel Insurance:** Ensure your policy covers ferry travel, including delays or cancellations due to rough seas.
- **Driving in Ireland:** Vehicles arrive ready to drive on the left-hand side. Ensure your insurance is valid for use in Ireland and Northern Ireland if crossing the border.
- **Food and Refreshments:** Meals are typically not included in ticket prices, but onboard restaurants serve full meals, snacks, and drinks.

Rail & Sail Packages

For those without a car, several operators offer combined train and ferry tickets from cities like London, Manchester, and Glasgow to Dublin or Rosslare. These packages include rail travel to the departure port and ferry transfer, often at discounted rates—an ideal choice for budget-conscious or environmentally-minded travelers.

Trains, Buses & Coaches: Public Transport Guide

Ireland's public transport network offers a fantastic way to explore the island, from its bustling cities to its rural towns and coastal villages. Whether you're traveling across the vibrant streets of Dublin, discovering the scenic beauty of the West Coast, or venturing into the heart of the Irish countryside, public transport provides an affordable and convenient means of travel. This section explores Ireland's train, bus, and coach services, offering insights into the networks, routes, tips, and the best ways to get around.

Trains in Ireland: Exploring the Rail Network

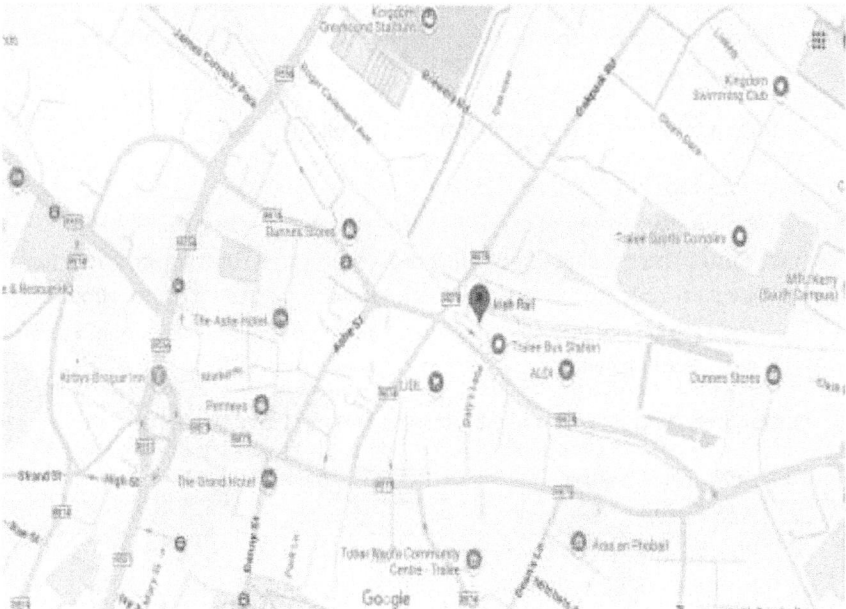

Ireland's rail network is extensive, connecting major cities, towns, and rural areas. The Irish rail system is operated primarily by Irish Rail (Iarnród Éireann), and while it's not as extensive as some larger European networks, it still provides a convenient and scenic way to travel.

Main Train Lines in Ireland

1. Dublin to Cork (Heuston Station to Kent Station)

- **Duration:** Approximately 2.5 hours
- **Frequency:** Frequent daily departures, every 1–2 hours during peak times
- **Route:** The train journey between Dublin and Cork is one of the most popular and scenic in Ireland, passing through rolling green hills and picturesque towns. The route offers comfortable seats, free Wi-Fi, and a cafe car for refreshments.

2. Dublin to Galway (Heuston Station to Ceannt Station)

- **Duration:** Around 2.5 to 3 hours
- **Frequency:** Multiple daily services, every 2–3 hours
- **Route:** The journey from Dublin to Galway takes you across Ireland's midlands, offering views of lakes, rivers, and farmland. This is one of the best ways to explore the west of Ireland, with Galway's vibrant cultural scene awaiting you.

3. Dublin to Limerick (Heuston Station to Colbert Station)

- **Duration:** 2–2.5 hours
- **Frequency:** Frequent services, with departures every 1–2 hours
- **Route:** The Dublin-Limerick line crosses through rural countryside, making it ideal for tourists looking to experience Irish nature en route. Limerick, a city known for its medieval history and the mighty River Shannon, is a rewarding destination to explore.

4. Dublin to Belfast (Connolly Station to Lanyon Place Station)

- **Duration:** 2 hours
- **Frequency:** Hourly service
- **Route:** This cross-border route connects the Republic of Ireland with Northern Ireland, offering scenic views of the countryside. The journey to Belfast is an excellent option for travelers exploring both parts of the island.

5. Dublin to Waterford (Heuston Station to Plunkett Station)

- **Duration:** 2 hours
- **Frequency:** Multiple daily services
- **Route:** A shorter, pleasant train ride from Dublin to Waterford takes you through the scenic landscapes of Ireland's southeast. Waterford is famous for its crystal, medieval architecture, and maritime history.

Train Tickets & Travel Passes

Ticket Options: Tickets for train travel in Ireland are available online, via mobile apps, or at ticket booths and machines at stations. You can choose from single, return, or multi-ride tickets, depending on your travel plans.

Discounts & Travel Passes:

- **Leap Card:** A contactless smart card offering discounted fares for frequent travel in Dublin and surrounding areas. It's not valid for intercity trains but offers savings on local travel.
- **Irish Rail's Family Ticket:** Offers discounts for families traveling together (2 adults + 2 children).
- **Saver Tickets:** Discounted tickets are available if booked in advance, ideal for those who plan their journeys ahead of time.

Booking Tips:

- **Advance Booking:** Booking tickets in advance can often save money, especially for intercity journeys.
- **Railcards for Tourists:** Irish Rail offers various discount cards for tourists, such as the Discover Ireland Rail Pass, which provides unlimited travel for a set number of days.

Train Travel Tips

Punctuality: Irish trains are generally punctual, but delays can occur, particularly on busy routes. Always check the real-time timetable via the Irish Rail website or app before your departure.

Comfort: Trains are typically comfortable with generous seating and onboard amenities like Wi-Fi and power outlets. First-class carriages provide extra space and comfort for a slightly higher fare.

Accessibility: Most major stations and trains are wheelchair accessible. Some stations offer assistance for passengers with reduced mobility, but it's advisable to inform the operator in advance.

Buses in Ireland: A Versatile & Affordable Option

Buses are the backbone of Ireland's public transport system, connecting cities, towns, villages, and remote areas. With an extensive network, buses offer one of the most convenient and cost-effective ways to travel in Ireland.

Key Bus Operators

1. Bus Éireann

Bus Éireann is the main national bus service provider in Ireland, operating services to and from all major cities and rural areas. They offer services to Dublin, Cork, Galway, Limerick, and beyond, as well as rural and regional routes.

Popular Routes:

- Dublin to Cork
- Dublin to Galway
- Dublin to Kilkenny
- Galway to Limerick

Bus Éireann Services:

- **Expressway Routes:** Faster services connecting major cities.
- **Local Services:** Serving smaller towns and villages.
- **School Services:** School buses run during term time and are open to the public during off-peak hours.

2. Dublin Bus

Dublin Bus provides an extensive urban bus network within Dublin, offering routes to suburbs, landmarks, and tourist destinations. It's ideal for getting around Dublin and reaching nearby areas.

Route Highlights:

- **Airport Route (747 & 757):** Direct service to Dublin Airport from various parts of the city.
- **City Tour Routes:** Dublin Bus also runs city tours, providing a guided experience for tourists.

3. Citylink & GoBus

These companies specialize in intercity routes, particularly for travelers who wish to travel between Dublin and other major destinations in the west or south, such as Galway, Limerick, and Cork.

Popular Routes:

- Dublin to Galway
- Dublin to Limerick
- Galway to Cork

Bus Fares and Tickets

- **Leap Card:** Valid for Dublin Bus services and offers discounted fares. You can top up the card online or at retail locations.
- **Single Tickets:** Available on most buses. If you're traveling outside Dublin, you can purchase tickets directly from the driver, though exact change is required.
- **Bus Éireann Tickets:** Bus Éireann tickets can be purchased online, at stations, or on the bus. For intercity services, booking is recommended.

- **Discounted Tickets:** Students, seniors, and groups can often avail themselves of discounted bus fares.

Bus Travel Tips

Route Planning: Check schedules and timetables before your journey, especially for rural routes, as they may not run as frequently.

Luggage: Buses are generally comfortable for luggage, but if you're traveling with large bags or suitcases, ensure there's enough room in the luggage compartment.

Real-Time Tracking: Many bus operators provide real-time tracking via mobile apps, so you can see when your bus is due to arrive.

Accessibility: Dublin Bus is largely accessible, and most buses feature low floors for ease of access. Other operators may offer limited services for disabled passengers, so it's best to check in advance.

Coaches: Long-Distance Travel Across Ireland

Coaches are a fantastic way to travel longer distances and explore more remote areas. Operators like Bus Éireann, Citylink, and GoBus provide comfortable long-distance travel, making it ideal for those seeking scenic routes or budget-friendly options for cross-country exploration.

Popular Coach Routes:

- **Dublin to Galway:** Coaches operate regularly on this route, taking about 2.5 hours to reach Galway, with departures throughout the day.
- **Dublin to Limerick:** Coaches take approximately 2.5 hours and are ideal for travelers looking for a direct, no-frills option.
- **Dublin to Cork:** The coach journey to Cork lasts around 3.5 hours, with both daytime and evening services available.
- **Dublin to Killarney:** Coaches to Killarney take about 4.5 hours, and it's a great choice for those traveling from the capital to County Kerry.

Tourist Coaches: Coaches also provide scenic tours of Ireland's major attractions, including the Ring of Kerry, Cliffs of Moher, Giant's Causeway, and Blarney Castle. These tours are guided and provide insightful commentary on Ireland's history and landscapes. Many tours depart from Dublin, with packages including transportation, hotel accommodations, and guided visits to key sights.

Comfort and Amenities: Coaches tend to be equipped with larger seats, air conditioning, Wi-Fi, and power outlets. Some premium coaches also feature onboard catering, making them an ideal choice for longer journeys.

Booking Coach Services: Booking tickets for coaches can be done through individual company websites, mobile apps, or at stations. Most services offer flexible and refundable options, especially in the low season.

Getting Around Cities: Urban Public Transport

Dublin

Dublin has a comprehensive public transport system, including Dublin Bus, LUAS (the light rail tram), and DART (the Dublin Area Rapid Transit train). The Leap Card is valid on all these services, providing an easy way to move around the city with contactless payment.

- **Dublin Bus:** Serving both central and suburban areas, Dublin Bus has an extensive network of routes.
- **LUAS:** The two LUAS lines, Red and Green, are fast and efficient, connecting areas like Tallaght, Rathmines, and Sandyford to the city center.
- **DART:** The DART connects Dublin to coastal towns such as Dún Laoghaire, Howth, and Malahide. It's an excellent way to enjoy the coast while traveling to scenic areas outside the city.

Other Cities

Cork: Cork City Bus is the primary public transport provider, with a well-connected network covering all major districts and surrounding areas. Cork is also one of the few cities in Ireland with a fully integrated bike-share scheme.

Galway: Galway's City Bus service operates routes around the city, providing easy access to sights like Eyre Square, Salthill, and the Latin Quarter.

Limerick: Limerick's Bus Éireann services provide connections to key neighborhoods and outlying areas, including scenic routes along the Shannon River.

Best Practices for Public Transport in Ireland

- **Plan:** Always check timetables and plan your journey to avoid unnecessary stress, especially if you're traveling long distances or using rural services.

- **Time Management:** Allow extra time for delays, particularly in busy cities or on routes serving rural areas.
- **Travel Passes:** Consider purchasing travel passes or discount cards for frequent use. These passes can significantly lower the cost of traveling by train, bus, or coach.

Renting a Car in Ireland: What You Need to Know

Renting a car in Ireland opens the door to unparalleled freedom and exploration. While public transportation is effective for traveling between cities and popular tourist areas, many of Ireland's most breathtaking sights—rugged coastlines, remote villages, ancient ruins, and hidden beaches—lie off the beaten path. A rental car enables travelers to craft their itinerary, follow scenic byways, and discover the country on their terms. However, there are several important aspects to understand before hitting the Irish roads.

1. Eligibility and Requirements

Driver's License

Travelers from the EU/EEA, the UK, the US, Canada, Australia, and most other countries can legally drive in Ireland with their full, valid domestic license. The license must be in English or accompanied by an International Driving Permit (IDP) if it is not. Drivers must have held their license for at least 2 years to rent with most agencies.

Age Restrictions

The minimum age to rent a car in Ireland is generally 25, although some rental companies allow drivers aged 21–24 with a young driver surcharge and more limited vehicle options. Most agencies impose an upper age limit (often 75) and may require a medical certificate or driving history documentation for older drivers.

Credit Card and Identification

Renters must present a major credit card in their driver's name. Some agencies accept debit cards but often require a larger deposit. A passport or national ID card is also required for identification at pickup.

2. Choosing the Right Vehicle

Manual vs. Automatic

The majority of vehicles in Ireland have manual transmissions. Automatics are available but limited in supply and generally more expensive. It's best to book automatic cars well in advance, especially during peak travel months (May–September).

Size Matters

Ireland's roads, particularly in rural areas and the west (like the Ring of Kerry or Connemara), can be extremely narrow. Opting for a smaller car will make navigating tight country lanes easier and reduce stress. SUVs and larger vehicles are best reserved for those with extensive experience driving in Europe.

Fuel Type

Cars typically run on either petrol (gasoline) or diesel. Diesel vehicles often offer better mileage, which is helpful for long trips, though they may cost slightly more to rent.

3. Insurance: What's Required and What's Not

Insurance is one of the most complex parts of renting in Ireland. Most quotes include the legally required Collision Damage Waiver (CDW), but the excess (deductible) can be as high as €2,500. To reduce this excess, consider purchasing:

- **Super CDW (SCDW):** Reduces or eliminates the excess liability. Available directly from the rental agency.
- **Third-Party Insurance:** Some credit cards (especially premium ones like Visa Infinite or Mastercard World Elite) include rental car coverage in Ireland, but Ireland is often excluded in their terms. Confirm with your card provider before relying on this.
- **Personal Liability Coverage:** Damage to third parties is usually included, but check for confirmation.
- **Tire and Windshield Coverage:** These are commonly excluded in standard packages but can be added.

Be prepared for hard sales tactics at the counter. Understanding your needs in advance can save money and stress.

4. Driving in Ireland: What to Expect

Left-Side Driving

Ireland drives on the left side of the road. This takes some adjustment for drivers from countries with right-hand traffic. Roundabouts, turning lanes, and narrow roads are the most challenging aspects for first-timers.

Road Conditions

- **Motorways (M-roads):** High-quality, fast, and tolled in places (e.g., M50 in Dublin).
- **National Routes (N-roads):** Well-maintained, linking major towns and regions.
- **Regional and Local Roads (R and L-roads):** These range from decent to very narrow and winding, especially in the west and on the Wild Atlantic Way.

Speed Limits

- Motorways: 120 km/h (74 mph)
- National roads: 100 km/h (62 mph)
- Regional roads: 80 km/h (50 mph)
- Urban areas: 50 km/h (31 mph)

Signage Ireland uses kilometers, not miles. Signage is mostly in English, though in Gaeltacht (Irish-speaking) areas, such as parts of Galway and Donegal, signs are in Irish only.

Roundabouts: used frequently instead of traffic lights. Yield to traffic already in the roundabout, and remember to go clockwise (left entry).

Parking Pay: Attention to signs indicating permit-only areas or metered parking. Most towns and cities have paid parking zones, and fines are enforced. Many villages and attractions offer free or low-cost parking. Consider downloading local apps like ParkMagic or ParkingTag for cashless payments.

Tolls: apply mainly to motorways. Most tolls can be paid at booths, but the M50 in Dublin uses an automated system (eFlow). If using the M50, ensure your rental company handles the toll, or pay online by 8 p.m. the next day to avoid penalties.

5. Navigation and Fuel

Navigation Google Maps and Waze works well in Ireland. GPS units are available for rent, but using your phone with a local SIM or roaming plan is often more effective. Be aware that the mobile signal may drop in remote regions, so offline maps are a good backup.

Fueling Up, Petrol stations are widely available, especially along national roads and in cities. Rural areas have fewer stations, so plan accordingly. Stations are usually full-service or self-service, with diesel often cheaper than petrol. Always double-check the fuel type of your rental before filling up.

Prices fluctuate, but in 2025, expect to pay:

- Around €1.80–€2.00 per liter for petrol (approx. $7.30–$8.10 per gallon)
- Around €1.70–€1.90 per liter for diesel (approx. $6.90–$7.70 per gallon)

6. Picking Up and Dropping Off

Airports. The most popular rental pickup points are:

- **Dublin Airport (DUB)** – extensive choice, 24/7 service
- **Shannon Airport (SNN)** – convenient for the west of Ireland
- **Cork Airport (ORK)** – ideal for southern adventures
- **Knock and Kerry airports** – smaller but useful for regional travel

City Center Locations Dublin, Galway, Limerick, and Cork have downtown offices. Note that city pickups may be slightly more expensive due to congestion fees or parking charges.

One-Way Rentals One-way rentals within Ireland are possible, though often incur a fee. Dropping off in Northern Ireland may not be allowed or may come with an additional cross-border fee.

7. Driving to Northern Ireland

Crossing the border between the Republic of Ireland and Northern Ireland (UK) is completely open, with no passport checks or customs. However:

- Inform the rental company and ensure cross-border travel is permitted.
- Insurance must explicitly cover driving in the UK.
- Speed limits in Northern Ireland are in miles, not kilometers.

8. Travel Tips for a Smooth Ride

- Practice caution on rural roads, where livestock, tractors, and cyclists are common.
- In remote areas, mobile coverage may be limited. Always carry a paper map or download offline maps.
- Avoid driving in central Dublin, where traffic is heavy, parking is limited, and public transport is more efficient.
- If unfamiliar with roundabouts or left-side driving, consider starting your journey outside major cities for an easier adjustment.
- Book your rental car well in advance, especially during festivals or peak summer months.

Scenic Drives & Road Trip Routes

Ireland's spellbinding landscape is best experienced behind the wheel, where winding coastal roads, lush countryside, dramatic cliffs, ancient ruins, and charming villages unfold around every turn. Whether you're seeking windswept ocean views or tranquil green valleys, the Emerald Isle offers some of Europe's most unforgettable scenic drives.

The Wild Atlantic Way (West Coast, 2,500 km / 1,553 mi)

The Wild Atlantic Way is one of the longest defined coastal routes in the world, stretching from Kinsale in County Cork to Malin Head in County Donegal. This journey hugs Ireland's rugged western edge, where crashing waves meet towering cliffs and timeless villages.

Highlights Include:

- **Mizen Head:** Ireland's most southwesterly point, with a dramatic cliff-top footbridge.
- **The Ring of Kerry:** A circular route in County Kerry with panoramic mountain and ocean views.
- **Cliffs of Moher:** Towering over the Atlantic, one of Ireland's most iconic sights.
- **Connemara:** A tapestry of bogland, lakes, and stone walls in Galway, with a deep-rooted Irish culture.
- **Slieve League:** Some of the highest accessible sea cliffs in Europe in County Donegal.

This route is ideal for travelers with at least two weeks and a sense of adventure. While you could technically drive it in a week, its full magic reveals itself slowly, in the unplanned detours and seaside towns along the way.

The Ring of Kerry (County Kerry, 179 km / 111 mi)

The Ring of Kerry offers one of the most picturesque circular drives in Europe. Starting in Killarney, it winds through a dramatic landscape of mountains, lakes, coastal cliffs, and colorful villages.

Key Stops:

- **Ladies View and Moll's Gap:** Stunning views over Killarney National Park.
- **Skellig Ring:** A detour worth every minute, offering views of Skellig Michael, a 6th-century monastic site and a UNESCO World Heritage Site.
- **Waterville and Sneem:** Quaint villages known for their charm and scenery.
- **Kenmare:** A vibrant town known for artisanal crafts and gourmet food.

Early starts are recommended, especially in summer, as the narrow roads can become congested with tour buses. Driving counterclockwise is often advised to avoid the larger traffic flow and get better access to scenic pull-outs.

The Causeway Coastal Route (Northern Ireland, 212 km / 132 mi)

Running between Belfast and Derry/Londonderry, the Causeway Coastal Route showcases the dramatic northern coastline of the island and weaves past legendary landmarks and Game of Thrones filming locations.

Must-Sees:

- **Giant's Causeway:** An extraordinary volcanic formation with hexagonal basalt columns.
- **Carrick-a-Rede Rope Bridge:** Suspended high above the Atlantic, connecting the mainland to a tiny island.

- **Dark Hedges:** An enchanting tree-lined road made famous by Game of Thrones.
- **Dunluce Castle:** A medieval ruin perched on the cliff's edge.

This route combines natural beauty with myth and legend. It can be driven in two days, but three to four days allow time for hiking, photography, and savoring the region's renowned whiskey and seafood.

The Dingle Peninsula (County Kerry, 47 km / 29 mi - Slea Head Drive)

Though much shorter than its neighbor, the Ring of Kerry, the Dingle Peninsula packs in immense beauty. The Slea Head Drive, starting and ending in the colorful harbor town of Dingle, circles the western tip of the peninsula.

Highlights:

- **Slea Head:** Dramatic ocean cliffs with views across to the Blasket Islands.
- **Gallarus Oratory:** A dry-stone chapel dating back over 1,000 years.
- **Inch Beach:** A long strand perfect for walking or surfing.
- **Dunquin Pier:** A wildly photogenic spot where boats once ferried islanders to and from the mainland.

This drive can be done in an afternoon, but Dingle's thriving music scene, artisan shops, and sea safaris make it well worth an overnight or two.

The Copper Coast (County Waterford, 166 km / 103 mi)

This lesser-known stretch of Ireland's southeast coast offers dramatic cliffs, peaceful coves, and a glimpse into the island's ancient geological past. The route runs from Tramore to Dungarvan through the Copper Coast UNESCO Global Geopark.

What to Look For:

- **Annestown and Bunmahon Beaches:** Remote and peaceful stops for a picnic or a stroll.
- **Copper Coast Drive:** A short but spectacular route through coastal cliffs and sea stacks.
- **Waterford Greenway:** Rent a bike and ride along Ireland's longest off-road trail.

Perfect for those seeking serenity and avoiding the crowds, the Copper Coast is often overlooked by international tourists, making it all the more special.

The Boyne Valley Drive (Ancient East, approx. 100 km / 62 mi)

This route through Ireland's Ancient East is a pilgrimage into the island's mythological and historical heart. Centered in County Meath, it's home to some of the oldest man-made structures in Europe.

Top Sights:

- **Brú na Bóinne:** Home to Newgrange, Knowth, and Dowth, megalithic passage tombs that predate the Pyramids.
- **Hill of Tara:** Ancient seat of Ireland's high kings.
- **Trim Castle:** The largest Anglo-Norman castle in Ireland.
- **Loughcrew Cairns:** Neolithic burial mounds with carved stone art.

The Boyne Valley is ideal for a one- or two-day road trip from Dublin and offers fascinating insights into Ireland's ancient soul.

The Wicklow Mountains Scenic Loop (County Wicklow, 130 km / 80 mi)

Just a short drive from Dublin, this loop through the Garden of Ireland delivers forested hills, shimmering lakes, and remote mountain passes.

Key Stops Include:

- **Glendalough:** A serene valley with a 6th-century monastic settlement and hiking trails.
- **Sally Gap and Wicklow Gap:** Two of Ireland's most scenic driving routes, especially atmospheric in fog or snow.
- **Powerscourt Estate:** A magnificent house and gardens with views of the Sugarloaf Mountain.

- **Lough Tay:** Also known as the Guinness Lake for its dark water and pale beach "foam."

Best enjoyed on a clear day, this drive offers solitude and spectacle, and is easily completed in a day trip from Dublin.

Tips for Scenic Driving in Ireland

- **Allow extra time** for unexpected photo stops, traffic delays, and winding roads that demand slow speeds.
- **Start early** in the day to avoid traffic and maximize daylight, especially important during winter months.
- **Fill up with fuel** before venturing into rural or coastal areas, where petrol stations may be few and far between.
- **Respect speed limits**, especially on narrow regional roads, and be cautious when encountering sheep, cyclists, or slow-moving tractors.
- **Plan for weather:** Irish weather can be unpredictable. Roads may be slick in rain or foggy in the hills, but the mist often adds to the enchantment.

Local Transport: Taxis, Biking & Walking

Getting around Ireland is relatively easy, whether you're exploring vibrant cities or venturing into the countryside. Ireland's local transport options cater to all types of travelers, from urban explorers to nature enthusiasts seeking quiet walks or scenic bike rides.

Taxis in Ireland

Taxis are a reliable and convenient way to travel, particularly in cities and towns. They are widely available and provide door-to-door service, but they can be a bit pricey, especially for long journeys or trips outside urban areas.

How to Find a Taxi:

- **City Centers:** In major cities like Dublin, Cork, Galway, and Belfast, taxis are readily available at taxi ranks, usually near train stations, major intersections, and popular areas.
- **Hail on the Street:** Taxis can be hailed directly on the street, though this is more common in urban areas. If you're in a rural location, it's better to pre-book.

- **Pre-booking:** For convenience and sometimes better rates, you can call a taxi company or use apps like MyTaxi (now Free Now), Uber, or local taxi service apps available in various cities.

Taxi Fares:

- **Dublin:** The base fare is around €4.00, with an additional €1.00 per km.
- **Outside Major Cities:** Fares may be higher in rural areas due to longer distances. Rural taxis might also charge a fixed rate for trips to nearby towns or attractions.
- **Airport Transfers:** Taxis from Dublin Airport to the city center typically cost between €25-€35, depending on traffic.

Travel Tip: Always confirm the fare before starting your journey, as some taxi services may charge an extra fee for airport pick-ups, late-night journeys, or heavy luggage.

Biking in Ireland

Ireland is one of the best places in Europe for cycling, offering diverse landscapes, from flat coastal paths to rolling hills and rugged mountains. Whether you're looking for an adventure or just a scenic, leisurely ride, biking is a wonderful way to explore the country at your own pace.

Cycling Routes:

The Great Western Greenway (Mayo): This 42 km off-road cycling trail follows the route of an old railway line from Westport to Achill Island, offering stunning views of the countryside and the Atlantic Ocean.

The Waterford Greenway: A 46 km path that runs from Waterford to Dungarvan, perfect for cyclists who enjoy coastal views, tunnels, and viaducts.

Ring of Kerry: A popular route for serious cyclists, this challenging circuit through County Kerry offers panoramic views of mountains, lakes, and beaches.

Belfast's Lagan Towpath: This scenic route offers a 16 km bike ride along the River Lagan, ideal for those looking for an easy ride in a city setting.

Bike Rentals:

City Rentals: In cities like Dublin, Cork, and Galway, bike rental services are available for daily or weekly hires. Dublin has a bike-sharing system called Dublinbikes, which allows you to pick up and drop off bikes at various locations across the city. Prices typically start around €2 for 30 minutes.

Touring Bikes: Many areas with cycling routes also offer touring bike rentals. These bikes are suited for long-distance rides, and most rental shops provide equipment like helmets and panniers.

Travel Tip: Always wear a helmet when cycling in Ireland, especially on more challenging routes. Make sure to check the condition of the bike before setting off, and use bike locks for safety when leaving it unattended.

Walking in Ireland

With its picturesque landscapes and charming towns, Ireland is a paradise for walkers. Whether you're strolling through the streets of Dublin, hiking up mountains in the west, or rambling along tranquil coastal paths, walking offers a wonderful way to immerse yourself in Irish culture and nature.

Popular Walking Routes:

Kerry Way: A 214 km long-distance trail through County Kerry, this walk offers some of the most spectacular views of Ireland's rugged coastline, valleys, and mountains. The route can be tackled over several days or completed in sections.

Dublin's City Walks: Dublin offers numerous walking tours of its historical landmarks, including visits to Trinity College, St. Stephen's Green, Dublin Castle, and Temple Bar. You can enjoy the city's literary history with walking tours focusing on famous writers like Joyce, Yeats, and Beckett.

Cliffs of Moher Coastal Walk: The 19 km walk along the cliffs provides breathtaking views of the Atlantic Ocean and surrounding countryside, with the iconic cliffs towering over 200 meters above the sea.

Wicklow Way: This 131 km trail takes you through the Wicklow Mountains, with scenic views of lakes, valleys, and forests. It can be tackled over several days or enjoyed in sections.

Walking Tours:

Guided Tours: In cities like Dublin, Cork, Galway, and Belfast, you'll find a variety of guided walking tours. These can range from historical and cultural tours to food or pub tours, giving you a deeper understanding of local life and history.

Self-Guided Tours: Many cities have free or inexpensive self-guided walking tours available via apps or downloadable PDFs. These can be a great way to explore at your own pace without a guide.

Travel Tip: Wear comfortable shoes for walking, especially in rural areas where paths can be uneven or muddy. Always bring a jacket or layers, as Irish weather can change rapidly, even in summer.

Practical Tips for Local Transport

- **Taxis:** If you need a taxi at peak times (like Friday or Saturday nights), book in advance or allow for longer waiting times.
- **Biking:** Many rural areas in Ireland may have narrow roads without bike lanes, so always stay alert, especially when cycling on busy roads or near traffic.
- **Walking:** When walking in urban areas, always use designated pedestrian crossings and be cautious around busy roads. Ireland's rural walking paths may be unmarked, so it's best to carry a map or use a GPS app.

Chapter 4: Where to Stay

Accommodation Types in Ireland

Ireland offers a wide variety of accommodation types to suit different tastes, budgets, and travel preferences. From luxury stays in historic castles to charming countryside B&Bs, each option provides its own unique experience, allowing visitors to immerse themselves in the rich culture and scenic beauty of the Emerald Isle.

Hotels

Ireland's hotel scene ranges from luxurious five-star establishments to more affordable mid-range options, providing comfortable stays in both cities and rural areas. Hotels are particularly popular in major cities like Dublin, Cork, Galway, and Limerick, where they are often centrally located for easy access to attractions, dining, and nightlife.

Luxury Hotels: In urban centers, luxury hotels like The Merrion in Dublin or The Westbury provide upscale amenities such as fine dining, spas, and concierge services. These hotels cater to both business and leisure travelers, offering impeccable service and prime locations.

Mid-Range Hotels: These offer a balance of comfort and affordability, with well-appointed rooms and essential amenities like Wi-Fi, restaurants, and fitness centers. Chains such as Clayton Hotels and Jurys Inn are common mid-range options, often located near major tourist spots.

Budget Hotels: For those on a tighter budget, affordable hotels provide basic accommodations, usually in convenient locations near public transport or key attractions. These are ideal for short stays where comfort and convenience are the primary considerations.

Bed & Breakfasts (B&Bs)

B&Bs are one of the most popular types of accommodation in Ireland, known for their welcoming atmosphere and personalized service. They offer an intimate, homely experience, making them perfect for those who want to connect with local hosts and experience traditional Irish hospitality.

Traditional B&Bs: Found across the country, these family-run establishments typically offer private rooms with en-suite bathrooms and serve hearty breakfasts, including Irish favorites like bacon, eggs, and soda bread.

Guesthouses: Similar to B&Bs, guesthouses are often larger and more formal but still maintain a homely feel. They may offer additional services such as laundry, packed lunches, or evening meals. Guesthouses are commonly located in both urban and rural settings.

Farm Stays: For an authentic rural experience, farm stays provide a chance to stay on working farms. Guests can enjoy home-cooked breakfasts made from locally sourced produce, and sometimes participate in farm activities, making this a great choice for those seeking a connection to the Irish countryside.

Hostels

Hostels are a budget-friendly accommodation option, especially popular among backpackers, students, and solo travelers. They provide affordable rates, with both shared dormitories and private rooms available. Hostels are ideal for those looking to meet other travelers and enjoy a social atmosphere.

Youth Hostels: Offering dormitory-style rooms, these hostels are designed for young travelers who don't mind sharing space with others. Most hostels include communal kitchens, free Wi-Fi, and often organize social events or city tours.

Private Rooms: Many hostels also offer private rooms, which can be a good compromise between affordability and privacy. These rooms are usually simple but comfortable, with the advantage of sharing common facilities like kitchens and lounges with other guests.

Boutique Hostels: In larger cities like Dublin, boutique hostels are becoming more popular. These hostels offer stylish decor, enhanced amenities, and a more upscale experience while still keeping rates affordable. These are great options for those seeking a unique, trendy vibe.

Self-Catering Accommodation

Self-catering options offer visitors the freedom to cook their own meals and enjoy more space and privacy during their stay. This type of accommodation is ideal for families, groups, or long-term travelers who prefer more control over their food and living arrangements.

Holiday Cottages: These standalone properties, often located in picturesque countryside locations, offer guests the chance to experience a home-away-from-home. Fully equipped with kitchens, living rooms, and outdoor spaces, holiday cottages are perfect for those looking for a quiet retreat or a base for outdoor activities.

Apartments: Available in most urban and tourist areas, apartments provide a more independent living situation, often with easy access to local attractions. Many apartments offer full kitchens, living areas, and sometimes even balconies or terraces for enjoying the surrounding views.

Glamping: For a more luxurious camping experience, glamping options are becoming increasingly popular across Ireland. These are often upscale tents or yurts that come with comfortable beds, electricity, and other modern conveniences, allowing guests to enjoy nature without sacrificing comfort.

Guesthouses & Inns

Guesthouses and inns offer a more intimate and personal experience than larger hotels while still providing comfort and privacy. These types of accommodations are often family-run businesses, offering local knowledge and personalized service.

Inns: Typically located in smaller towns and rural areas, inns provide both accommodation and meals. Many Irish inns are situated along scenic routes or close to major landmarks, offering a great place to relax after a day of sightseeing.

Boutique Guesthouses: These accommodations combine the charm of a traditional guesthouse with stylish, modern interiors. Boutique guesthouses often offer gourmet breakfasts, locally sourced ingredients, and personalized attention to each guest. These are a great choice for those looking for a more refined yet intimate experience.

Luxury & Boutique Stays

For travelers seeking a more extravagant experience, Ireland offers a range of luxury accommodations that blend historic charm with world-class service and amenities.

Castle Hotels: Ireland is famous for its many castles, some of which have been transformed into luxury hotels.

Staying in a castle like Dromoland Castle or Ashford Castle is a once-in-a-lifetime experience, offering grandeur, beautiful grounds, fine dining, and even activities such as falconry or archery.

Boutique Hotels: These small, stylish hotels are often located in prime city locations or scenic, off-the-beaten-path areas. With unique interior design, attention to detail, and top-notch service, boutique hotels in Ireland offer a more personalized, intimate alternative to larger hotel chains.

Spa Hotels: Ireland's luxury hotels often feature exceptional spa facilities, offering treatments that range from massages to facials, in tranquil, scenic settings. These properties are ideal for those seeking relaxation and rejuvenation during their stay.

Camping & Caravan Parks

Camping offers an affordable and adventurous way to experience Ireland's natural beauty. Whether you're pitching a tent in the countryside or staying in a fully-equipped caravan, camping is a great option for nature lovers.

Traditional Campgrounds: For those seeking a rustic experience, Ireland has numerous campgrounds that cater to tents and campervans. These parks often provide essential facilities like bathrooms, showers, and shared kitchens.

Caravan Parks: Caravan parks offer more comfort, with mobile homes or static caravans available for rent. These parks are often located in scenic areas and may offer additional amenities such as playgrounds, restaurants, or swimming pools.

Farm Stays

For a truly authentic experience, farm stays allow travelers to immerse themselves in Ireland's rural lifestyle. Staying on a working farm provides an opportunity to learn about Irish farming practices, sample local produce, and enjoy a peaceful, countryside escape.

Agricultural Tourism: These stays typically involve living in traditional farmhouses or newer accommodations on the farm. Guests may be invited to help with chores, such as milking cows or collecting eggs, offering a hands-on, educational experience.

Working Farms: Some farms operate tours or offer activities that allow guests to interact with animals and explore the farm's landscape, making this a great choice for families or animal lovers.

Best Areas to Stay in Major Cities & Regions

Ireland's towns, cities, and rural regions each offer distinct personalities, landscapes, and atmospheres. Whether the trip revolves around vibrant urban culture, serene countryside escapes, or coastal beauty, the choice of where to stay plays a major role in shaping the experience. From the Georgian charm of Dublin's neighborhoods to the dramatic coastline of the Wild Atlantic Way, selecting the right area can enhance both convenience and enjoyment.

Dublin: Ireland's Capital and Cultural Hub

Ireland's dynamic capital is a patchwork of diverse neighborhoods, each catering to different travel styles. Whether it's nightlife, history, or a quiet, elegant base for exploration, Dublin's districts provide plenty of variety.

Temple Bar: Known for its buzzing nightlife, cobbled streets, and vibrant arts scene, Temple Bar suits travelers who want to stay in the heart of the action. Expect live music, street performers, and easy access to major attractions like Dublin Castle and Trinity College.

St. Stephen's Green & Grafton Street: Offering a balance of elegance and accessibility, this area appeals to those who enjoy luxury shopping, Georgian architecture, and proximity to leafy park spaces. Upscale hotels and boutique stays are plentiful.

Ballsbridge & Donnybrook: Located just south of the city center, these upscale residential neighborhoods provide a quieter, more refined experience with beautiful homes, embassies, and excellent restaurants. Ideal for families or couples seeking tranquility.

Smithfield & Stoneybatter: North of the River Liffey, this increasingly trendy area features indie cafés, contemporary apartments, and access to the Jameson Distillery and Phoenix Park. Perfect for creatives and younger travelers.

Cork: The Rebel City's Creative Corners

Ireland's second-largest city offers a rich blend of cultural, culinary, and historical highlights, with areas suited to both lively urban exploration and peaceful riverside walks.

City Centre (Grand Parade, Oliver Plunkett Street): Ideal for those seeking quick access to restaurants, galleries, and pubs. Many of Cork's top museums, markets, and venues are within walking distance.

Shandon & Sunday's Well: Overlooking the River Lee, this neighborhood offers a more authentic and residential feel, paired with lovely views and proximity to the Cork Butter Museum and St. Anne's Church.

Douglas & Blackrock: Suburban but still convenient, these neighborhoods provide access to coastal walks and peaceful parks. Families and longer-term travelers find comfort in these scenic, quieter districts.

Galway: Bohemian Vibes on the Atlantic Coast

A bohemian gem on Ireland's west coast, Galway blends artistic flair, medieval history, and coastal charm. It serves as both a destination and a gateway to Connemara and the Aran Islands.

Latin Quarter & Eyre Square: Staying near Eyre Square or within the Latin Quarter places visitors at the center of Galway's energy, with traditional pubs, live music, shops, and cafes all just steps away.

Salthill: For travelers drawn to the sea, this charming coastal suburb offers sandy beaches, a long promenade, and beautiful views of Galway Bay. It's especially appealing in the summer months and great for families.

Claddagh & The West End: These historic districts blend residential serenity with quirky charm. Popular with locals, this area provides access to small art galleries, traditional bakeries, and lesser-known eateries.

Limerick: Ireland's Rising Cultural City

Limerick's vibrant arts scene, historical landmarks, and position along the River Shannon make it an appealing stop, especially for those venturing into western or southwestern Ireland.

City Centre (O'Connell Street & King's Island): Close to King John's Castle and the Hunt Museum, this part of the city is ideal for those interested in history and riverside walks. Accommodations include stylish hotels, guesthouses, and urban apartments.

Castletroy: Home to the University of Limerick, this leafy suburb is relaxed and modern, ideal for travelers who prefer quieter surroundings and access to the scenic River Shannon Walkway.

Kilkenny: Medieval Magic in the Southeast

Steeped in medieval history and rich in festivals, Kilkenny charms with its narrow lanes, castle views, and vibrant crafts scene.

Kilkenny City Centre: For a truly immersive experience, staying near Kilkenny Castle or along the Medieval Mile places visitors within easy reach of key sites, from Rothe House to traditional pubs and craft workshops.

John's Quay & Canal Walk: This riverside area is quieter but still central, offering lovely walks, tranquil settings, and quick access to cafes, shops, and galleries.

Killarney: Gateway to the Ring of Kerry

As a major stop along the Ring of Kerry and a gateway to Killarney National Park, this town is ideal for nature lovers and heritage seekers.

Killarney Town Centre: With its lively atmosphere, charming streets, and proximity to jaunting car rides and scenic lakes, the town center suits visitors eager to explore without needing a car.

Muckross & Fossa: For a more peaceful, scenic base, the areas surrounding Muckross House or closer to the lakes provide stunning views, forest trails, and easy access to the park. These are excellent for couples or travelers focused on outdoor adventure.

Dingle Peninsula: Atlantic Beauty & Gaelic Spirit

Small yet packed with character, the Dingle Peninsula provides coastal charm, Gaeltacht (Irish-speaking) culture, and dramatic views of the Atlantic.

Dingle Town: The harborfront town offers lively music, exceptional seafood, and easy access to scenic drives like Slea Head. Ideal for visitors who enjoy walkable villages and authentic Irish culture.

Ventry & Ballyferriter: These smaller villages offer tranquility and proximity to some of the region's best beaches. Perfect for those seeking peaceful stays and immersive cultural experiences.

The Burren & Cliffs of Moher Region

This rugged region of County Clare is famed for its stark beauty, ancient sites, and dramatic coastal scenery.

Doolin: A beloved base for exploring the Cliffs of Moher and The Burren, Doolin combines traditional music, welcoming pubs, and ferry access to the Aran Islands.

Ballyvaughan & Kilfenora: Located further north, these villages offer a slower pace, rich archaeological history, and beautiful walking routes through the Burren National Park.

Belfast (Northern Ireland): Urban Renaissance in Northern Ireland

Northern Ireland's capital offers a blend of Victorian architecture, Titanic heritage, and modern cultural resurgence.

Cathedral Quarter: This artistic and historic area is known for its creative spirit, buzzing nightlife, and cobbled alleys filled with bars and murals.

Queen's Quarter: Centered around Queen's University and the Botanic Gardens, this neighborhood is green, youthful, and filled with museums, cafés, and bookstores.

Titanic Quarter: For travelers intrigued by maritime history, this modern riverside area offers sleek accommodation near the Titanic Belfast museum and historic shipyards.

Derry / Londonderry: Walled City Wonder

Known for its preserved city walls and vibrant political history, Derry blends deep storytelling with a thriving arts scene.

City Centre (Within the Walls): Staying within the 17th-century city walls puts visitors steps away from museums, murals, and cozy pubs.

Waterside: Across the River Foyle, this area offers a quieter atmosphere and great views of the historic cityscape, especially from the Peace Bridge.

Remote, rugged, and mystical, Connemara is ideal for solitude seekers, road-trippers, and lovers of raw natural beauty.

Clifden: The informal capital of Connemara, Clifden provides a small-town feel with vibrant dining and shopping options and is well-positioned for exploring Sky Road and the surrounding countryside.

Roundstone & Leenane: Sleepier coastal villages like Roundstone offer dramatic ocean views and artist studios, while Leenane sits by Killary Fjord with hiking trails and serene waters.

Unique Stays: Farmhouses, Thatched Cottages & Manor Houses

Ireland's charm isn't just found in its castles, cliffs, or cobbled cities—it's also woven into the character of its accommodations. For travelers who seek a more authentic and memorable experience, staying in a traditional farmhouse, a centuries-old thatched cottage, or a stately manor house offers a glimpse into the soul of Irish heritage. These types of lodgings are not only rich in atmosphere but also serve as living stories—each telling its tale of time, tradition, and local pride.

Farmhouses: A Taste of Rural Irish Life

Far removed from the hum of the city, Irish farmhouses deliver peace, pastoral beauty, and genuine hospitality. Often family-run, these homes sit on working farms where guests can enjoy everything from homemade bread and fresh eggs to views of roaming sheep and green hills that stretch to the horizon.

Atmosphere & Amenities

Farmhouse stays offer a warm, homey feel with rustic charm. Stone walls, wood-burning stoves, and handmade quilts are common features, and hosts typically provide home-cooked breakfasts made from locally sourced ingredients. Visitors can expect a slower pace of life, perfect for unplugging and reconnecting with nature.

Location & Experience

Found across Ireland's countryside—from the dairy farms of County Kerry to the sheep-dotted fields of Connemara—these accommodations often provide access to hiking trails, fishing spots, and quiet village life. Some hosts offer guided farm walks, demonstrations of traditional farming techniques, or hands-on experiences like milking cows or baking soda bread.

Who It's For

Travelers craving authenticity, families looking to introduce children to rural life, or couples on a romantic countryside escape will find farmhouse stays a wholesome and heartwarming option.

Thatched Cottages: Stepping Into an Irish Fairytale

The iconic image of a whitewashed cottage with a thatched roof set against rolling hills or coastal cliffs is not a postcard fantasy—it's a real and deeply rooted part of Ireland's rural architecture. Staying in a thatched cottage means immersing oneself in a tradition that has endured for centuries.

Architecture & Ambiance

Built with thick stone or mud walls and featuring roofs made from straw, reed, or rushes, these cottages offer insulation, character, and deep historical charm. Interiors vary from simple, cozy furnishings with open hearths and exposed beams to thoughtfully renovated spaces blending modern comforts with old-world aesthetics.

Where to Find Them

County Clare and the Dingle Peninsula are dotted with traditional thatched cottages, many located in protected heritage areas. The cottages in Adare, County Limerick—one of Ireland's prettiest villages—are particularly renowned, while the remote Inisheer (Inis Oírr) island offers unforgettable stays in stone-and-thatch dwellings set against the Atlantic.

Why It's Special

Staying in a thatched cottage transports travelers to a different time. It evokes the simplicity and serenity of a bygone age, where peat fires crackle and the modern world fades into the background.

These cottages often provide stunning views, secluded locations, and a romantic, storybook atmosphere that's ideal for artists, couples, and solo travelers alike.

Manor Houses: Elegance in the Irish Countryside

Grand without being imposing, Ireland's manor houses embody grace, history, and impeccable hospitality. Many of these estates date back to the 18th or 19th century and were once the private homes of the Irish gentry. Today, they welcome guests into a world of refined comfort and pastoral beauty.

Heritage & Hospitality

Manor house accommodations typically feature elegant interiors with antique furnishings, drawing rooms with fireplaces, and expansive gardens. Some retain elements like grand staircases, walled gardens, and old libraries, while others have been modernized to offer spa treatments, gourmet dining, and concierge service.

Diverse Settings

Manor houses can be found near lakes, in woodland estates, or on coastal bluffs. Ballyvolane House in County Cork combines Georgian grandeur with a relaxed, family-run ethos—plus it's the birthplace of the award-winning Bertha's Revenge Gin. In County Mayo, Enniscoe House offers lakeside tranquility and a working organic farm, while Gregans Castle Hotel in the Burren blends historic architecture with gourmet experiences.

Experiences Offered

Many manor houses curate experiences for guests: falconry displays, foraging walks, guided history tours, and even horseback riding. Some operate under the "Blue Book" collection—a prestigious group of Irish country homes and boutique hotels celebrated for exceptional service and culinary excellence.

Ideal For

Lovers of history, culture, and high-end travel will feel at home in a manor house. These stays are perfect for special occasions, honeymoons, or anyone looking to explore Ireland in style while enjoying personalized attention and timeless surroundings.

Planning a Unique Stay

While hotels and B&Bs are plentiful, it's the unique stays that make an Irish journey unforgettable. Many of these options are family-run or operated by locals deeply rooted in their community and heritage. Booking early is advisable, particularly in the spring and summer months, when demand is highest. In some remote areas, these types of stays are not unique but also the most authentic and enriching way to connect with the land and its people.

Travel Tip: Consider pairing different styles of stay—perhaps two nights in a manor house followed by a few nights in a thatched cottage by the sea. This not only enhances the experience but also offers a broader view of Ireland's cultural landscape.

Family-Friendly Accommodation Options

Ireland is a wonderful destination for family travel, with its rich storytelling tradition, castles that inspire imaginations, and nature that invites adventure. When it comes to where to stay, the country offers a wide variety of family-friendly accommodations suited to different travel styles, budgets, and needs. From hotels with kids' clubs to self-catering cottages and countryside farm stays, families are warmly welcomed across the Emerald Isle.

1. Hotels with Family Perks

Urban comfort, countryside charm, and full-service amenities.

Many Irish hotels understand the unique needs of families. Expect spacious family rooms, adjoining suites, complimentary cots or rollaway beds, child-proofing features, and often even small perks like coloring books or children's toiletries. Many larger hotels also offer indoor pools, playgrounds, and kids' clubs during peak seasons.

Recommended:

- **Fota Island Resort, County Cork** – Luxury suites, child-friendly dining, kids' clubs, and proximity to Fota Wildlife Park.
- **Clayton Hotel Limerick** – Spacious family rooms with river views and pool access.
- **Castleknock Hotel, Dublin** – Near the Phoenix Park Zoo, this hotel features a spa for parents and games for kids.

Hotels like these typically offer breakfast-included packages and high flexibility for families needing early check-ins or late checkouts.

2. Self-Catering Holiday Homes and Cottages

Space, privacy, and the comforts of home.

For families who appreciate room to spread out or prefer cooking their own meals, self-catering stays are ideal. These can range from coastal cottages to modern apartments in towns and cities. Many come with secure outdoor space, laundry facilities, and cozy lounges where the family can unwind after a long day of exploring.

Why do they work well?

- A kitchen for managing picky eaters or allergies.
- Multiple bedrooms for privacy and naps.
- Gardens or patios where children can play safely.
- Often located near beaches, lakes, or countryside walking trails.

Popular providers include Trident Holiday Homes, Dream Ireland, and Airbnb listings across family-friendly counties like Kerry, Donegal, and Wexford.

3. Farm Stays and Rural B&Bs

Hands-on experiences, fresh air, and warm Irish hospitality.

A farm stay gives children an unforgettable taste of rural life—collecting eggs, petting goats, or watching sheepdog demonstrations. Parents benefit from the slower pace and home-cooked meals. These accommodations often have only a few rooms, making them ideal for families wanting a quiet, personal experience.

Standout stays:

- **Abbeyfield Farm, County Kildare** – Working farm with horseback riding and archery.
- **Coolanowle Country House, County Carlow** – Organic farm stay with family rooms and lakeside walks.
- **Ballybur Castle, County Kilkenny** – A self-catering stay in a renovated 16th-century tower with modern comforts and a sense of adventure.

4. Glamping and Eco-Friendly Lodges

Outdoor excitement with cozy comforts.

Glamping is an increasingly popular option for families seeking adventure without sacrificing comfort. Safari tents, yurts, and treehouses are available across Ireland. Many are set within safe, enclosed environments where children can roam, and some offer on-site activities like ziplining, kayaking, or treasure hunts.

Favorites for families:

- **Emerald Glamping, Offaly** – Family tents with bunk beds and wood stoves, plus a giant trampoline and board games.
- **Rock Farm Slane, County Meath** – Located on an organic farm with a riverside setting, ideal for cycling, paddling, and picnicking.
- **Podumna Village, County Galway** – Quirky wooden pods with shared kitchens and a play area in a central town setting.

5. Family Suites in Castle Hotels

A touch of magic with room to spare.

Staying in a castle can feel like stepping into a storybook—and many Irish castles have been transformed into luxurious, family-friendly hotels. These properties often provide expansive suites, lush gardens, and plenty of safe outdoor space for young explorers.

Top picks:

- **Ashford Castle, County Mayo** – One of Ireland's finest, offering falconry lessons, horseback riding, and family-size suites.
- **Dromoland Castle, County Clare** – Babysitting services, interconnecting rooms, and child-friendly fine dining make it a regal yet accessible choice.
- **Ballyseede Castle, County Kerry** – Family rooms with antique furnishings, and resident Irish wolfhounds to delight younger guests.

6. Budget-Friendly Hostels and Family Inns

Affordable, social, and often surprisingly stylish.

For families on a budget, modern hostels and family inns across Ireland offer practical lodging with shared or private family rooms, kitchens, and sometimes communal games rooms. Hostels are often centrally located near public transport and offer convenience with minimal fuss.

Examples:

- **Sleepzone Hostel, Galway** – Clean family rooms, close to Eyre Square and museums.
- **An Óige Dublin International Hostel** – Central and budget-friendly, with family dorm options.
- **The Hideout Hostel, Dingle** – Within walking distance to the aquarium, beaches, and ice cream parlors.

7. Coastal and Lakeside Retreats

Serene settings and plenty of splash time.

Lodgings near Ireland's coastlines or lake districts are ideal for families who love outdoor activities. Properties often include kayaking or fishing gear rentals, while children can enjoy safe beaches or countryside bike trails right at their doorstep.

Locations worth considering:

- **Lough Derg** – Self-catering lodges near the water, ideal for paddle boarding and cycling.
- **West Cork coastline** – Clusters of cottages near Blue Flag beaches like Inchydoney or Barleycove.
- **Achill Island** – Remote, quiet stays with beach access and dramatic scenery.

What Makes a Stay Truly Family-Friendly?

When choosing family accommodations in Ireland, it's not only about the facilities, but about the experience. Look for places that offer:

- **Safety:** Enclosed gardens, stair gates, child-proofing.
- **Convenience:** Laundry access, high chairs, easy parking.
- **Entertainment:** Books, board games, playrooms, or on-site animals.
- **Hospitality:** Hosts who genuinely enjoy welcoming children make all the difference.

Whether you're chasing rainbows in the hills of Wicklow or searching for seals in Sligo, the right family-friendly base transforms your journey into something comfortable, safe, and filled with joy.

Budget vs. Luxury: Insider Booking Tips

Ireland's charm lies not only in its windswept cliffs and cozy pubs but in the diversity of its accommodations. From five-star castles to wallet-friendly hostels, there's a place to suit every traveler's style and budget. Understanding the landscape of Irish lodging can help stretch a euro or make a splurge truly unforgettable. Whether traveling on a shoestring or indulging in premium comfort, choosing the right accommodation is as much about strategy as it is about preference.

Understanding the Accommodation Spectrum

Budget travelers often seek value, location, and basic comforts. Options typically include hostels, B&Bs, guesthouses, holiday parks, and self-catering apartments.

Luxury travelers look for elegance, bespoke service, memorable settings, and exceptional dining. This includes five-star hotels, boutique inns, manor houses, castle estates, and designer lodges.

Tips for Booking on a Budget Without Sacrificing Quality

1. Embrace Midweek Travel

Room rates in Ireland tend to spike over weekends and during school holidays. Traveling midweek—especially Tuesday through Thursday—can unlock significantly lower prices in both cities and rural destinations.

2. Choose Guesthouses or Family-Run B&Bs

Ireland's traditional bed-and-breakfast culture offers warm hospitality, home-cooked meals, and insights from locals. They often cost less than hotels while offering far more character. Look for those with high ratings on Booking.com or B&B Ireland.

3. Stay Just Outside the Hotspots

In Dublin, for example, staying in Dún Laoghaire or Malahide provides access to the city via rail or bus, often at half the price of central hotels.

Near the Cliffs of Moher, choosing a B&B in Lahinch instead of Doolin can reduce costs without sacrificing location.

4. Leverage Hostel Privates and Hybrid Lodgings

Hostels have evolved. Many now offer private family rooms with en-suite bathrooms, free Wi-Fi, and breakfast. Properties like Generator Dublin or Sleepzone Galway blend affordability with sleek design.

5. Book Direct When Possible

Many small lodgings offer a lower rate if booked directly through their websites or via email. Some even include perks like free breakfast or late check-out for doing so.

6. Look for Self-Catering Options

A cottage or apartment with a kitchen lets travelers save on meals while experiencing Ireland like a local. Weekly rentals are common, especially along the Wild Atlantic Way and in the countryside.

Tips for Booking a Luxury Experience Without Overspending

1. Travel in Shoulder Seasons

Late April to early June and September to mid-October offer prime weather with fewer crowds and better rates. Luxury hotels often run seasonal offers that include spa treatments or gourmet dinners.

2. Use Upgrade-Friendly Booking Channels

Sites like Virtuoso, The Leading Hotels of the World, and Mr & Mrs Smith often include room upgrades, early check-in, or €100 resort credits with booking. Loyalty programs like American Express Fine Hotels & Resorts or Visa Luxury Hotels offer similar perks.

3. Go Boutique, Not Just Big-Name

Some of Ireland's finest luxury stays are independently run. Gregans Castle Hotel in County Clare, The Twelve Hotel in Galway, or Ballynahinch Castle in Connemara offer award-winning comfort and charm without the markup of corporate chains.

4. Consider Packages and Experiences

Many luxury properties offer packages that combine accommodation with fine dining, falconry, golf, or spa experiences. While seemingly pricier, these packages often deliver higher value than paying à la carte.

5. Use Local Travel Advisors or Destination Experts

Smaller travel agencies based in Ireland often have relationships with high-end hotels and can secure unpublished rates or exclusive experiences. This is especially valuable for castle stays or private estate rentals.

General Booking Strategies That Benefit All Budgets

1. Book Early for Peak Season

From mid-June to August and around major holidays like St. Patrick's Day, accommodations across Ireland fill quickly. Booking 6–9 months in advance ensures better choices, especially in small towns with limited options.

2. Use Meta-Search Tools Wisely

Platforms like Trivago, Google Hotels, and HotelsCombined show price comparisons across booking platforms. These tools help spot deals and identify which sites offer the best perks for the price.

3. Read the Fine Print

Cancellation policies vary widely. Flexible bookings may cost a bit more upfront, but provide peace of mind. Always check if breakfast, parking, or Wi-Fi is included, especially in city-center hotels.

4. Stay Loyal—Literally

Signing up for programs like Marriott Bonvoy, IHG One Rewards, or Small Luxury Hotels INVITED can build status that leads to room upgrades, late check-outs, and discounted stays, even after just a few bookings.

Matching Accommodation to Experience

- **For road-tripping families:** Look for holiday parks, farm stays, or self-catering cottages with laundry facilities and parking.

- **For couples on a romantic escape:** Boutique hotels or countryside manor houses offer intimacy and atmosphere.
- **For solo explorers or students:** Hostels and pod hotels provide affordable, sociable environments in central locations.
- **For heritage lovers:** Castle hotels, Georgian townhouses, and converted abbeys offer immersive, historic experiences—often at reasonable rates when booked off-season.
- **For outdoor enthusiasts:** Lodges near national parks or coastal trails often offer gear rentals, guides, and local tips.

When to Splurge vs. When to Save

Splurge on:

- A final-night stay in a castle or historic estate
- A hotel with breathtaking views (e.g., Cliffs of Moher, Ring of Kerry, or the lakes of Killarney)
- A location central to a bucket-list event or activity (e.g., Galway Arts Festival, Dublin's New Year Festival)

Save on:

- Overnights during long drives when proximity matters more than luxury
- Chain hotels or airport stays where comfort trumps character
- Multi-night city stays where you'll spend most of your time exploring, not relaxing indoors

Chapter 5: Top Experiences & Must-See Attractions

Bucket List: Unforgettable Experiences in Ireland

Ireland is a land of natural wonders, rich history, and vibrant culture, where every corner seems to offer something truly memorable. From the rugged coastlines of the Wild Atlantic Way to the ancient ruins and charming villages, the Emerald Isle has a plethora of must-see destinations and experiences that should be on every traveler's bucket list. Whether you're an adventurer, history buff, or culture seeker, Ireland offers unique moments that will leave you awestruck.

1. The Cliffs of Moher: Majestic Sea Views

The Cliffs of Moher, one of Ireland's most iconic natural landmarks, stand tall at over 700 feet above the Atlantic Ocean. This awe-inspiring stretch of cliffs, located on the western edge of the country in County Clare, provides panoramic views of the Aran Islands, Galway Bay, and the wild Atlantic Ocean. The cliffs are home to a variety of seabirds, including puffins, making it a popular spot for birdwatching. Walk along the cliffside pathways and feel the wind as you take in one of the most breathtaking landscapes in Ireland.

Location: County Clare, Ireland, part of the Wild Atlantic Way.

Insider Tips:

- Visit early or late in the day to avoid crowds and experience the cliffs in quieter, softer light.
- Dress warmly, as the weather can be unpredictable and winds can be strong.
- For the best photo opportunities, walk along the upper paths near O'Brien's Tower.

2. The Ring of Kerry: A Scenic Drive Through Paradise

The Ring of Kerry is a 111-mile circular route that showcases the best of County Kerry's natural beauty. This drive takes you through lush green valleys, along dramatic coastlines, past pristine beaches, and quaint villages. Highlights include Killarney National Park, Torc Waterfall, and Muckross House, a Victorian mansion surrounded by gardens and lakes. This scenic route offers numerous opportunities for hiking, cycling, and exploring traditional Irish culture in small towns like Killorglin and Kenmare.

Location: County Kerry, southwest Ireland

Starting Point: Typically begins and ends in Killarney

Insider Tips:

- Drive counter-clockwise to avoid getting stuck behind tour buses.
- Start early to enjoy quieter roads and sunrise views.
- Take the Skellig Ring detour for fewer crowds and dramatic coastal cliffs.

3. Dublin: The Heartbeat of Irish Culture

Dublin, Ireland's vibrant capital, is a city teeming with history, culture, and charm. It's home to some of the country's most renowned attractions, including Trinity College and the Book of Kells, Dublin Castle, and St. Patrick's Cathedral. The city also boasts a dynamic nightlife scene, particularly in the Temple Bar district, where traditional Irish pubs and live music fill the air. Don't forget to visit the Guinness Storehouse to learn about the history of Ireland's most famous beer and enjoy a pint in the Gravity Bar with panoramic views of the city.

Location: East coast of Ireland, at the mouth of the River Liffey

Province: Leinster | County: Dublin

Insider Tips:

- Visit Trinity College Library early to avoid queues and enjoy a quieter viewing of the Book of Kells.

- Skip Temple Bar prices—find better-value pubs with live music in Camden Street or Capel Street.
- Use the DART train for quick seaside escapes to Howth or Dalkey.

4. The Giant's Causeway: Nature's Geological Wonder

Located in Northern Ireland, the Giant's Causeway is a UNESCO World Heritage site famous for its unique geological formations. The site consists of around 40,000 interlocking basalt columns created by volcanic activity millions of years ago. Steeped in myth and legend, the Giant's Causeway is a must-see for anyone traveling to Ireland, offering both a fascinating natural spectacle and an enchanting atmosphere.

Location: Bushmills, County Antrim, Northern Ireland BT57 8SU

Info Line: +44 28 2073 1855

Insider Tips:

- Visit at sunrise or sunset for magical lighting and fewer crowds.
- Wear sturdy shoes—the rocks can be slippery, especially when wet.
- Stop by the Visitor Centre for interactive exhibits and local folklore.

5. Killarney National Park: Ireland's Scenic Jewel

Killarney National Park, located in County Kerry, is a breathtaking expanse of lakes, forests, and mountains covering over 25,000 acres. It is home to Ireland's only native red deer herd and encompasses landmarks like Muckross House, the Lakes of Killarney, and the Gap of Dunloe. The park's beauty lies in its diversity— tranquil waterways, ancient oak woodlands, and towering peaks like Torc Mountain. It's ideal for hikers, photographers, and nature lovers. The blend of cultural heritage and pristine wilderness makes it a highlight of any Irish itinerary.

Location: County Kerry, Southwest Ireland – Adjacent to the town of Killarney

Info Line: +353 64 663 0085

Insider Tips:

- Visit early morning to avoid crowds and catch the mist over the lakes.
- Rent a bike in Killarney town to explore scenic trails easily.
- Don't miss the short hike to Torc Waterfall for incredible photo ops.

6. The Aran Islands: A Step Back in Time

The Aran Islands—Inishmore, Inishmaan, and Inisheer—lie off the coast of County Galway, accessible by ferry or small plane. These windswept islands preserve a way of life that feels untouched by modernity.

Ancient stone forts, like the cliffside Dún Aonghasa, overlook the wild Atlantic, while Gaelic remains the spoken language in many homes. Cyclists and walkers will find tranquility among dry-stone walls, open fields, and timeless landscapes. Traditions thrive in the form of hand-knitted Aran sweaters, currach fishing boats, and folk tales shared in cozy village pubs. A visit to the Aran Islands is a quiet immersion in heritage, community, and Ireland's raw, coastal beauty.

Location: Off the coast of County Galway, reachable by ferry from Rossaveal or Doolin, or by air from Connemara Airport.

Insider Tips:

- Rent a bike to explore at your own pace—cars are limited.
- Visit early or late in the day to avoid peak ferry crowds.
- Bring cash; ATMs are limited and card acceptance is spotty.

7. Connemara: Wild Beauty and Untamed Landscapes

Connemara, located in the west of County Galway, is a region of wild beauty, rugged mountains, tranquil lakes, and endless expanses of unspoiled wilderness. The area is perfect for hiking, cycling, and photography. Visit Kylemore Abbey, a stunning Benedictine monastery nestled beside a lake and surrounded by mountains. Connemara is also known for its unique Gaelic culture, vibrant music scene, and picturesque villages like Clifden and Roundstone.

Location: West of County Galway, stretching from Oughterard to Clifden and down to Roundstone.

Insider Tips:

- Visit during golden hour for breathtaking light on the landscape.
- Rent a bike in Clifden and cycle the Sky Road for epic views.
- Try Connemara lamb or local mussels in a traditional pub.

8. Blarney Castle: Kiss the Blarney Stone

Blarney Castle, nestled in the lush countryside of County Cork, is one of Ireland's most beloved attractions. Built nearly 600 years ago by the powerful MacCarthy clan, the castle is famed for the legendary Blarney Stone set high in its battlements. Kissing the stone, said to bestow the "gift of eloquence," involves leaning backward over a drop (safely guided, of course), making it one of Ireland's most memorable travel experiences. The castle grounds are equally enchanting, with magical gardens, mystical rock formations, and a Poison Garden filled with fascinating (and dangerous) plants. Beyond the myth, Blarney offers a beautiful blend of history, legend, and landscape.

Location: Blarney, County Cork, Ireland

Opening Hours: Daily, 9:00 AM – 5:00 PM (varies by season)

Phone: +353 21 438 5252

Insider Tips:

- Arrive early to avoid long queues for the stone.
- Wear comfortable shoes for climbing steep, narrow stairs.
- Don't miss the Rock Close – a hidden garden full of druidic lore.

9. The Dingle Peninsula: A Seaside Escape

The Dingle Peninsula, located in County Kerry, offers some of Ireland's most scenic drives, beaches, and historical sites. The Slea Head Drive takes you along the coastline, past ancient forts, beehive huts, and dramatic cliffs. The town of Dingle is famous for its friendly atmosphere, seafood restaurants, and the beloved dolphin Fungie, who has been a resident of the harbor for years. The peninsula is a great base for hiking, cycling, or just relaxing by the sea.

Location: County Kerry, Southwest Ireland

Insider Tips:

- Visit early morning or late afternoon to avoid tourist bus crowds.
- Hike to Eask Tower for panoramic views over Dingle Bay.
- Try Murphy's Ice Cream—handmade with local milk and sea salt.

10. The Rock of Cashel: A Majestic Hilltop Fortress

Perched atop a limestone outcrop in County Tipperary, the Rock of Cashel commands sweeping views of Ireland's lush Golden Vale. Once the seat of Munster kings and later a powerful ecclesiastical site, its impressive complex includes a 12th-century round tower, Cormac's Chapel with rare Romanesque frescoes, and a majestic Gothic cathedral. Legend links the site to Saint Patrick, who is said to have converted King Aengus here in the 5th century. As one of Ireland's most iconic historic landmarks, it offers a stunning blend of myth, architecture, and medieval power, all set against a timeless landscape.

Location: Cashel, County Tipperary, Ireland

Insider Tips:

- Visit early in the morning or late afternoon for fewer crowds and golden light for photos.
- Don't miss the 360-degree views from the outer walls—perfect for panoramic shots.
- Combine your visit with nearby Hore Abbey, a peaceful and often overlooked ruin visible from the Rock.

11. The Burren: A Unique Limestone Landscape

The Burren in County Clare is a geological wonder, famous for its vast limestone landscape, unusual plant life, and rich archaeological history. The region is home to ancient tombs, stone forts, and hidden caves. It's also a hotspot for botanists, as it hosts plants from both Mediterranean and Arctic climates. The Burren National Park offers scenic walking trails where visitors can explore the unique beauty of this karst landscape.

Location: The Burren, County Clare, Ireland (Nearest town: Ballyvaughan)

Insider Tips:

- Visit in late spring or early summer for peak wildflower blooms.
- Explore on foot—The Burren Way walking trail offers access to hidden gems.
- Stop by the Burren Perfumery for botanical scents inspired by local flora.

12. Galway: The City of Tribes

Galway, often called the "City of Tribes," is a lively and colorful city on Ireland's west coast. Known for its arts, music, and festivals, Galway offers a blend of medieval streets and modern flair. The city is also a gateway to the Aran Islands and the Cliffs of Moher.

Visit the Galway Cathedral, stroll along the Spanish Arch, and enjoy the lively atmosphere of Shop Street. Galway is also famous for its traditional pubs where you can enjoy live Irish music.

Insider Tips:

- Visit Eyre Square for a taste of local culture and Galway's lively atmosphere.
- Don't miss the Galway Market, open on weekends, for artisanal foods and crafts.
- Take a boat trip to the Aran Islands for a quiet retreat and stunning views.

13. Take a Whiskey Tour: Discover Ireland's Liquid Gold

Ireland is world-renowned for its whiskey, and a guided tour through its distilleries offers an unforgettable experience. Start your journey in Dublin, home to iconic distilleries like the Jameson Distillery Bow St. and the Teeling Distillery, where you can witness the meticulous process of crafting the smooth, rich whiskey that Ireland is famous for. For a more scenic experience, head to Kilbeggan Distillery in County Westmeath, the oldest licensed distillery in Ireland, or explore the Midleton Distillery in County Cork, where the renowned Jameson is produced. The tours take you through the history of whiskey, from its ancient origins to modern-day innovation. Taste various expressions, learn the art of blending, and appreciate the nuances of each sip.

Insider Tips

- **Book in advance:** Popular distilleries like Jameson can fill up fast, especially in peak seasons.
- **Wear comfortable shoes:** Distillery tours often involve walking or climbing stairs.
- **Don't skip the tasting session:** It's the highlight of every tour and a great opportunity to compare different whiskey styles.

14. Skellig Michael: A Remote Monastic Island

Skellig Michael, a UNESCO World Heritage site, is a stunning island off the coast of County Kerry, Ireland. It is famous for its well-preserved monastic settlement dating back to the 6th century, perched atop dramatic cliffs. The island is home to beehive huts, stone paths, and a breathtaking panoramic view of the Atlantic Ocean. Accessible only by boat, the climb to the monastic site involves navigating over 600 steep steps, offering a challenging yet rewarding experience. Skellig Michael gained international fame as a filming location for Star Wars: The Last Jedi. This remote and rugged location is a must-visit for history enthusiasts, nature lovers, and adventure seekers.

Location: Skellig Michael is situated approximately 8 miles off the coast of Portmagee, County Kerry.

Insider Tips:

- **Book early:** Boat trips to Skellig Michael are limited, especially during peak season. Secure your spot in advance.
- **Dress appropriately:** Prepare for wind and rain, as conditions can change rapidly on the island.
- **Take the tour:** Knowledgeable guides will enhance your experience with stories about the island's history and wildlife.

15. Wicklow Mountains: Ireland's Garden County

County Wicklow, known as the "Garden of Ireland," offers some of the most beautiful natural landscapes in the country. The Wicklow Mountains National Park features rugged mountains, glacial lakes, and sweeping valleys. Highlights include the stunning Glendalough Valley, with its early Christian monastic site, and Powerscourt Estate, which boasts beautiful gardens and views of the Sugarloaf Mountain. Wicklow is ideal for hiking, photography, and discovering Ireland's ancient history.

Insider Tips:

- **Early Start:** Beat the crowds by visiting early in the morning, especially in popular spots like Glendalough.

- **Hiking Gear:** Wear sturdy footwear for hiking, as trails can be muddy, especially after rain.
- **Local Pubs:** Stop by a cozy local pub, such as The Wicklow Heather in Laragh, for hearty Irish food and a warm drink.

16. Brú na Bóinne – Newgrange and Knowth

Brú na Bóinne is one of the most significant Neolithic landscapes in the world, home to the passage tombs of Newgrange, Knowth, and Dowth. These monumental burial chambers predate Stonehenge and the Egyptian pyramids by centuries. Newgrange, the most famous, is renowned for its alignment with the winter solstice, when the rising sun illuminates the inner chamber. Intricately carved stone art, ceremonial passageways, and cosmological significance make the site an awe-inspiring testament to prehistoric engineering, spiritual practice, and astronomical knowledge. A visit offers insight into the lives and beliefs of Ireland's ancient peoples, set in a rolling countryside filled with myth and meaning.

Location: County Meath, about 40 minutes north of Dublin

Insider Tips:

- **Book Ahead** – Entry to Newgrange and Knowth is only via guided tours from the Brú na Bóinne Visitor Centre; pre-booking is essential in high season.
- **Visit in Winter** – December's winter solstice lottery offers a chance to experience the rare alignment of sunlight through the tomb.
- **Don't Skip Knowth** – Often overshadowed by Newgrange, Knowth has the most decorated stones and provides fascinating context to the complex.

Chapter 6: Nature & Outdoor Adventures

Wild Atlantic Way: Road Trip Itinerary & Highlights

The Wild Atlantic Way is one of the world's longest defined coastal routes, stretching over 2,500 km from the windswept Inishowen Peninsula in County Donegal to the picturesque town of Kinsale in County Cork. Traversing nine counties and three provinces, this unforgettable road trip captures the raw beauty of Ireland's Atlantic coast—cliff-lined seascapes, hidden coves, traditional fishing villages, and ancient landmarks. It's a journey that weaves nature, culture, and history into every bend of the road.

Itinerary Overview: North to South

1. County Donegal (Inishowen Peninsula to Slieve League Cliffs)

Highlights:

- Malin Head, Ireland's northernmost point, with dramatic views and historic signal towers.
- Fanad Head Lighthouse, perched above crashing waves and sea arches.

- Glenveagh National Park, home to red deer and a fairytale castle.
- Slieve League Cliffs, nearly three times higher than the Cliffs of Moher but far less crowded.

Tip: Donegal is best enjoyed slowly—detour off the main route for isolated beaches and quiet valleys like Glencolmcille.

2. County Sligo & Mayo

Highlights:

- Benbulben, a tabletop mountain steeped in mythology.
- Strandhill, known for surfing and seaweed baths.
- Downpatrick Head, with its blowhole and sea stack, Dun Briste.
- Achill Island, a windswept paradise with Blue Flag beaches and mountain drives.

Tip: Try the Great Western Greenway for a cycling adventure through Mayo's wild countryside.

3. County Galway (Connemara & The Aran Islands)

Highlights:

- Sky Road in Clifden, a looped drive with panoramic ocean views.
- Kylemore Abbey, nestled in the shadow of the Twelve Bens.
- Connemara National Park, ideal for hiking, pony trekking, and wildlife spotting.
- Inishmore (Aran Islands), where Irish is still spoken, and Iron Age forts like Dún Aonghasa tower above sheer cliffs.

Tip: Catch the ferry from Rossaveal and rent a bike to explore Inishmore at your own pace.

4. County Clare

Highlights:

- The Burren, a vast limestone landscape dotted with ancient tombs and wildflowers.
- Cliffs of Moher, Ireland's most iconic coastal vista, is best viewed at sunrise or sunset.

- Doolin, the traditional music capital of Ireland.
- Loop Head Peninsula, a hidden gem with dramatic cliffs and dolphin spotting.

Tip: Skip the Cliffs' main car park and hike from Doolin for a quieter and more scenic approach.

5. County Kerry (Dingle Peninsula & Ring of Kerry)

Highlights:

- Dingle Town, a charming harbor with colorful buildings and lively pubs.
- Slea Head Drive, a circular route along cliffs, beaches, and ancient stone forts.
- Skellig Michael, a UNESCO site accessible by boat (seasonal).
- Killarney National Park, offers lakes, castles, and forested trails.

Tip: The Ring of Kerry can get congested—consider the lesser-known Ring of Beara for a peaceful, equally stunning alternative.

6. County Cork (West Cork & Kinsale)

Highlights:

- Mizen Head, the southernmost point of mainland Ireland, with a dramatic footbridge over the ocean.
- Barleycove Beach, a golden sandy stretch perfect for a picnic.
- Sheep's Head Peninsula, great for walkers seeking solitude and sea views.
- Kinsale, the culinary capital of the Wild Atlantic Way, with cobbled lanes, galleries, and gourmet restaurants.

Tip: Stay overnight in Kinsale to savor its restaurants and walk the Scilly Walk at golden hour for breathtaking harbor views.

Wild Atlantic Way Road Trip Tips

- **Car Hire:** Essential for freedom to explore smaller villages and off-the-beaten-path locations. Opt for a compact car on narrow rural roads.
- **Driving Direction:** Most travelers go southbound from Donegal to Cork, but the reverse is equally rewarding, depending on the season and flight routes.
- **Time Needed:** For a relaxed journey, allow 2–3 weeks. For shorter trips, focus on one or two regions like Connemara & Clare or Kerry & Cork.

- **Accommodation:** Book ahead in summer months; choose a mix of boutique guesthouses, farm stays, and seafront B&Bs.
- **Food:** Coastal towns boast amazing seafood—try chowder, oysters, and freshly caught fish in harborside eateries.

Causeway Coastal Route: Northern Ireland's Scenic Jewel

The Causeway Coastal Route is Northern Ireland's most iconic drive, a 190-kilometre stretch of breathtaking coastline between Belfast and Derry/Londonderry. Hugging the rugged North Atlantic coast, this route blends natural wonder, cultural heritage, and cinematic drama. From towering cliffs and ancient castles to myth-laden stones and quiet seaside towns, every mile delivers a sensory feast. Whether it's the geological marvel of the Giant's Causeway, the windswept ruins of Dunluce Castle, or the glens and forests that inspired folklore, this journey offers a richly layered Irish experience.

Major Highlights Along the Route

1. Carrickfergus Castle

Start your journey in Belfast and make your first stop at Carrickfergus Castle, a well-preserved Norman fortress overlooking Belfast Lough.

With over 800 years of history, this medieval stronghold tells the story of sieges, invasions, and strategic maritime defense.

2. The Glens of Antrim

Nine lush, steep-sided valleys carve through the Antrim Plateau, each with its charm. Glenariff, known as the "Queen of the Glens," features woodland trails, waterfalls, and a scenic park ideal for hiking and picnicking. The glens are steeped in myth, music, and traditional Irish culture.

3. Cushendun & Cushendall

These postcard-perfect villages offer a window into quiet coastal life. Cushendun, with its Cornish-style cottages, has connections to the Game of Thrones series, as do the caves nearby. Cushendall, nestled between sea and mountain, is a hub for exploring the glens and enjoying local pubs with live music.

4. Torr Head Scenic Route

A thrilling detour, this narrow, cliff-edge road offers sweeping views of Scotland on clear days. It's a white-knuckle drive in places, but also one of the most exhilarating and photogenic segments of the entire route.

5. Carrick-a-Rede Rope Bridge

Originally used by salmon fishermen, this dramatic rope bridge spans a 30-metre deep and 20-metre wide chasm. Walking the swaying bridge to the tiny island of Carrick-a-Rede delivers heart-pounding views and incredible photo opportunities. Pre-booking is recommended in peak months.

6. Giant's Causeway (UNESCO World Heritage Site)

The undisputed highlight of the route, the Giant's Causeway is a surreal landscape of about 40,000 interlocking basalt columns, the result of ancient volcanic activity—or, as legend claims, the handiwork of the giant Finn McCool. Walk the trails, explore the stones, and absorb the coastal energy of this mythical place.

7. Dunluce Castle

Perched precariously on a cliff edge, the haunting ruins of Dunluce Castle have witnessed centuries of battles and storms. Once home to the MacDonnell clan, it offers stunning sea views and a dramatic backdrop for exploring Northern Ireland's turbulent history.

8. Bushmills Distillery

Established in 1608, Old Bushmills Distillery is the oldest licensed whiskey distillery in the world. Take a guided tour to learn about the craft of Irish whiskey-making and enjoy a tasting in its atmospheric bar. The town of Bushmills is also a pleasant stop for artisan shops and cafés.

9. Portstewart & Portrush

These lively seaside towns are popular with surfers, golfers, and families. Portstewart Strand offers a stunning Blue Flag beach, while Portrush is home to Royal Portrush Golf Club, one of the world's great links courses. Both towns are great for dining and nightlife.

10. Mussenden Temple & Downhill Demesne

Set high on a clifftop overlooking the Atlantic, the circular Mussenden Temple is inspired by Rome's Temple of Vesta and is part of the Downhill Demesne, an 18th-century estate with sweeping gardens and ruins. The views stretch for miles along the coast, offering a sublime, romantic finale to the drive.

Route Planning Tips

Start or End in Belfast/Derry: The route works well in either direction, depending on your flight or travel plans.

Allow 3–5 Days: While it's possible to drive in one long day, spacing it over several days allows time to explore, hike, and linger in scenic spots.

Stay Overnight: Consider charming B&Bs or boutique stays in Ballycastle, Bushmills, or Portrush.

Game of Thrones Fans: Locations like Ballintoy Harbour, the Dark Hedges, and Cushendun Caves are all part of the journey, perfect for a themed stop or full-day tour.

Time of Year: Spring and early autumn are ideal for fewer crowds and vibrant colors; summer has the longest daylight but also the most tourists.

The Ring of Kerry: Emerald Peninsula Drives

The Ring of Kerry is one of Ireland's most legendary and visually spectacular routes—a 179-kilometre circuit through County Kerry that unfolds like a moving postcard. Traversing rugged coastlines, rolling green pastures, medieval ruins, colorful villages, and mountainous national parkland, this drive is a quintessential Irish experience. The journey typically starts and ends in Killarney, and moves clockwise or counterclockwise through charming towns like Kenmare, Sneem, Cahersiveen, and Killorglin, skirting along the Atlantic coast and dipping into valleys carved by glaciers. What makes the Ring of Kerry exceptional isn't just the landscapes—it's the seamless blend of nature, history, and traditional life. Expect dramatic ocean views, sheep-dotted hillsides, ancient stone forts, and the enduring spirit of the Irish countryside.

Key Highlights Along the Ring

1. Killarney National Park

At the heart of the Ring lies Killarney National Park, a UNESCO Biosphere Reserve. Home to the Lakes of Killarney, Ross Castle, Torc Waterfall, and the 15th-century Muckross Abbey, this vast expanse of forest, mountain, and lake is ideal for hiking, cycling, and horse-drawn carriage rides. Don't miss the Gap of Dunloe, a glacial valley surrounded by peaks.

2. Ladies' View

Named after Queen Victoria's ladies-in-waiting, who admired the vista during a royal visit, Ladies View offers a sweeping panorama over the Lakes of Killarney. The viewpoint is especially breathtaking at sunrise and sunset.

3. Moll's Gap

This high mountain pass provides a stunning contrast of lush valleys and rocky terrain. With dramatic switchbacks and wide-open views, it's a favourite among photographers and cyclists. A café with local crafts offers a pleasant break.

4. Kenmare

This colourful heritage town is known for its lively atmosphere, artisan shops, and fine dining. Kenmare makes an excellent base for exploring both the Ring of Kerry and the Beara Peninsula. The town's stone circle—a Bronze Age relic—is worth a visit.

5. Sneem

Set on the banks of the River Sneem, this tranquil village is marked by winding streets and painted cottages. It's a great place for a peaceful stroll, fresh seafood, and a connection with slower-paced village life.

6. Staigue Fort

Dating from around 300–400 AD, Staigue Fort is one of Ireland's best-preserved ring forts. Its 4-metre-high dry stone walls once defended a wealthy chieftain and his clan. Reachable by a narrow lane, it evokes Ireland's ancient, tribal past.

7. Derrynane House & National Historic Park

The ancestral home of Daniel O'Connell, a key figure in Irish political history, Derrynane House is set among lush gardens near the sea. The adjacent beach is a hidden gem for walking and picnicking.

8. Cahersiveen

Overlooking the River Fertha, Cahersiveen offers a quiet charm and access to Ballycarbery Castle and two ancient stone forts: Cahergal and Leacanabuaile. The area is a stepping stone to Valentia Island and the Skellig Ring.

9. Skellig Ring & Valentia Island

An extension of the Ring, this detour offers views of the Skellig Islands, a UNESCO World Heritage Site and filming location for Star Wars. Valentia Island features the Bray Head loop walk, tetrapod fossil tracks, and lush cliffside drives.

10. Glenbeigh & Rossbeigh Strand

As the route nears its return to Killarney, the quiet village of Glenbeigh offers beautiful beach walks and views across Dingle Bay. Rossbeigh Strand, with its wide, golden sands, is ideal for a picnic or horseback ride.

Driving Tips & Planning

- **Driving Direction:** Tour buses typically go counterclockwise—so if you're self-driving, going clockwise avoids traffic delays.
- **Duration:** While it's possible to drive in one day, spreading it across 2–3 days allows for unhurried exploration and overnight stays.
- **Best Bases:** Killarney and Kenmare are excellent starting points with ample accommodations and services.
- **Time of Year:** Late spring to early autumn offers the best conditions. Summers bring vibrant greenery and festivals, though also more traffic.
- **Weather Preparedness:** Sudden rain or fog is common; dress in layers and plan some indoor stops like museums or cafés.

Insider Tips

- **Start early** in the day to beat the tour buses and get quieter moments at scenic spots like Torc Waterfall or Staigue Fort.
- **Don't skip the Skellig Ring**, especially if you're interested in less touristy views and dramatic cliffside drives. It's narrower, but stunning.
- **Stay overnight** in a rural B&B or farmhouse along the route to experience local hospitality, traditional Irish breakfasts, and real countryside charm.

Hiking in the Wicklow Mountains & Beyond

Ireland's landscape is a hiker's dream—lush valleys, craggy peaks, windswept cliffs, and ancient trails steeped in myth and history. At the heart of this natural tapestry lies the Wicklow Mountains, a haven for walkers and ramblers of all skill levels. Just a short drive from Dublin, this mountainous region unfolds with dramatic vistas, heather-cloaked moors, hidden lakes, and centuries-old monastic ruins. But beyond Wicklow, Ireland's hiking trails stretch from the rugged Wild Atlantic Way to the serene lakelands of the midlands and the volcanic spines of the north.

The Wicklow Mountains: Ireland's Natural Cathedral

The Wicklow Mountains offer a diverse network of trails within Wicklow Mountains National Park, the country's largest. Whether you're chasing waterfalls, glacial valleys, or panoramic ridgelines, Wicklow delivers.

1. The Spinc & Glendalough Trail

This iconic hike begins at the 6th-century monastic settlement of Glendalough and climbs above the Upper Lake via wooden boardwalks and stone steps. The trail skirts the cliff edge known as "The Spinc," with breathtaking views of the valley. It's a must-do for visitors seeking a mix of heritage and highland.

- **Distance:** 9.5 km loop
- **Time:** 3–4 hours
- **Start Point:** Upper Lake Car Park, Glendalough

2. Lugnaquilla Summit

Lugnaquilla, Wicklow's highest peak (925m), is for experienced hikers. The climb crosses remote bogland and open ridges, with dramatic views stretching as far as the Mourne Mountains and Snowdonia on clear days. Navigational skills are essential, especially in low visibility.

- **Distance:** 13–15 km out-and-back
- **Time:** 5–7 hours
- **Start Point:** Glenmalure or Fenton's Pub

3. Djouce Mountain via Powerscourt

This moderate trail offers views of the Great Sugar Loaf, Powerscourt Waterfall, and Lough Tay (also known as the Guinness Lake). It's wind-swept and dramatic, with rewarding summit views and less foot traffic than Glendalough.

- **Distance:** 7–8 km
- **Time:** 2.5–3 hours
- **Start Point:** Ballinastoe Woods

Beyond Wicklow: Ireland's Best Regional Hikes

The Kerry Way (County Kerry)

Ireland's longest waymarked trail, the Kerry Way, traces the Ring of Kerry inland, through ancient woodlands, remote valleys, and lakeside paths. For those not ready for the full walk, sections from Kenmare to Sneem or Waterville to Caherdaniel offer stunning day hikes. The trail blends natural beauty with deep cultural roots.

- **Distance:** 214 km loop
- **Time:** 9–11 days
- **Start Point:** Killarney

Croagh Patrick (County Mayo)

This conical mountain is Ireland's most famous pilgrimage site, where St. Patrick is said to have fasted for 40 days. Though steep and rocky, the climb is short and spiritual, with sweeping views over Clew Bay. Many hike barefoot on Reek Sunday in July.

- **Distance:** 7 km out-and-back
- **Time:** 3–4 hours
- **Start Point:** Murrisk

Slieve League Cliffs (County Donegal)

Towering nearly 600 metres, these sea cliffs are among the highest in Europe. A clifftop trail leads along narrow paths and rolling highlands to One Man's Pass, a thrilling (though exposed) ridge that's best tackled by seasoned hikers. Clear days offer Atlantic views as far as Sligo.

- **Distance:** 4–5 km (depending on route)
- **Time:** 2–3 hours
- **Start Point:** Bunglass Viewpoint

The Burren Way (County Clare)

This haunting limestone landscape, known for its otherworldly karst formations, unique wildflowers, and ancient ring forts, offers gentle hiking with moments of dramatic elevation. Shorter walks from Carran, Kilfenora, or Ballyvaughan provide accessible day treks.

- **Distance:** 123 km
- **Time:** 5–6 days
- **Start Point:** Lahinch

Mount Errigal (County Donegal)

A steep ascent up Donegal's highest peak, Errigal, offers a short, exhilarating challenge. Its quartzite summit glows pink at sunset and provides cinematic views over the Derryveagh Mountains and Poisoned Glen.

- **Distance:** 4.5 km out-and-back
- **Time:** 2–3 hours
- **Start Point:** Errigal Car Park near Dunlewey

Tips for Safe & Rewarding Hikes in Ireland

- **Weather Changes Fast:** Even summer days can bring wind, fog, and rain. Waterproof gear, warm layers, and sturdy boots are essential. Always check the Met Éireann forecast.
- **Navigation Matters:** Many upland trails are unmarked. A map (OSI Discovery Series), compass, or GPS device is essential for higher elevations and longer treks.
- **Leave No Trace:** Respect the natural and archaeological landscape. Stick to paths, pack out your rubbish, and avoid disturbing livestock or wildlife.
- **Wild Camping Rules:** Legal in many places but not everywhere. Always seek landowner permission and follow Leave No Trace guidelines.

- **Local Knowledge Helps:** Visitor centres and local hikers' clubs offer up-to-date trail conditions, especially after storms or heavy rain.

Hidden Gems & Lesser-Known Walks

- **Sheep's Head Way (County Cork):** A quiet, cliff-hugging peninsula walk with cozy pubs and timeless views.
- **Arigna Miners' Trail (County Roscommon):** Blends industrial history with rolling hills and lake views.
- **Cuilcagh Boardwalk Trail (County Fermanagh):** Nicknamed the "Stairway to Heaven," this raised boardwalk ascends to a high peat plateau overlooking Lough Atona.

Cliffs of Moher, Skellig Michael & Other Natural Icons

Ireland's natural icons are more than scenic landmarks—they are elemental expressions of the island's identity, etched by time, weather, and myth. From sheer sea cliffs and dramatic offshore islands to basalt wonders and lush inland valleys, these landscapes inspire awe, imagination, and pilgrimage. These are not just places to visit, but places to feel.

Cliffs of Moher (County Clare)

Towering 214 meters above the Atlantic at their highest point and stretching over 8 kilometers along the west coast, the Cliffs of Moher are Ireland's most iconic natural attraction. Their jagged grandeur offers a visceral encounter with the raw power of nature. From O'Brien's Tower, the panorama reveals the Aran Islands, Galway Bay, and even the mountains of Connemara on a clear day. Puffins and peregrine falcons nest along the crags, while the waves crash far below. Walking the Cliffs Coastal Trail from Doolin to Liscannor offers an immersive perspective far from the crowded visitor center.

Location: Liscannor, County Clare

Insider Tips:

- Visit at sunrise or sunset for golden light and fewer crowds.
- Use the Doolin or Liscannor entry points for a more serene experience.
- Bring binoculars for seabird and dolphin spotting.

Skellig Michael (County Kerry)

Rising steeply out of the Atlantic Ocean 12 kilometers off the Kerry coast, Skellig Michael is a remote, mystical island once home to 6th-century Christian monks. Its stone-beehive huts, clinging 200 meters above sea level, are accessible only by climbing over 600 ancient stone steps. Designated a UNESCO World Heritage Site, this craggy monastic settlement offers a glimpse into a life of spiritual isolation, battered by wind and sea.

It also captured global imagination as a Star Wars filming location. The journey itself—by boat across rough waters—is a rite of passage.

Location: Off the coast of Portmagee, County Kerry

Insider Tips:

- Book boats well in advance; landings are limited and weather-dependent.
- Wear sturdy shoes and be prepared for no shelter, water, or toilets.
- Learn about the monks before you go—it deepens the awe.

Giant's Causeway (County Antrim)

A surreal landscape of 40,000 interlocking basalt columns formed by volcanic activity some 60 million years ago, the Giant's Causeway is Northern Ireland's geological crown jewel. Legend credits the mythical giant Finn McCool for its creation, lending the site a rich folklore alongside its natural beauty. Visitors can clamber over the polygonal stones, explore the Causeway's trails, and take in the views of the wind-swept Antrim coast.

Location: Near Bushmills, County Antrim, Northern Ireland

Insider Tips:

- Use the cliff-top trail from Dunseverick Castle for a dramatic approach.

- Skip the shuttle and walk down to the stones for the full experience.
- Visit off-season or early morning for quieter conditions and better photos.

The Burren (County Clare)

This otherworldly limestone karst landscape stretches over 250 square kilometers and contrasts sharply with the green image of Ireland. Its cracked grey pavements conceal rich biodiversity—rare alpine, Mediterranean, and arctic plants coexist here—and ancient tombs like Poulnabrone Dolmen rise from the stone. Walking or biking through the Burren reveals hidden caves, dry valleys, and centuries-old farming traditions.

Location: North County Clare

Insider Tips:

- Explore on foot via the Burren National Park or the Green Roads.
- Time your visit for May or early June when wildflowers bloom.
- Try a local walking tour to learn about geology, archaeology, and folklore.

Slieve League Cliffs (County Donegal)

Often overlooked in favor of the Cliffs of Moher, Slieve League offers an even higher and arguably more dramatic cliff experience, reaching up to 601 meters.

These remote cliffs in County Donegal present wild Atlantic vistas with far fewer crowds. The panoramic One Man's Path is not for the faint-hearted but offers unmatched views for the adventurous.

Location: Teelin, County Donegal

Insider Tips:

- Drive up to the upper car park to start closer to the summit.
- Take the Bunglass Loop Walk for safe, moderate hiking with epic views.
- Pack windproof clothing—the gusts are fierce even in summer.

Glendalough (County Wicklow)

Nestled in a glacial valley surrounded by the Wicklow Mountains, Glendalough combines serene lakes, ancient monastic ruins, and scenic hiking trails. Founded by Saint Kevin in the 6th century, the site became a major pilgrimage destination and remains a place of spiritual and natural beauty. Boardwalks, trails, and shaded paths make it ideal for both casual walks and longer hikes like the Spinc Loop.

Location: County Wicklow

Insider Tips:

- Avoid weekends for a quieter experience—early morning visits are magical.

- Bring a picnic and take time by the Upper Lake's shore.
- Combine with a Wicklow Way hike for a full-day adventure.

Connemara National Park (County Galway)

A mosaic of bog, mountain, and coast, Connemara National Park covers nearly 3,000 hectares of untamed beauty. The Twelve Bens mountain range forms its dramatic backbone, with trails ranging from the easy Lower Diamond Hill Loop to challenging full-day hikes. The visitor center in Letterfrack provides insights into the landscape, which remains largely unspoiled and sheep-grazed.

Location: Letterfrack, County Galway

Insider Tips:

- Climb Diamond Hill for panoramic views over the Atlantic and Inishbofin Island.
- Spring and autumn offer milder weather and vibrant colors.
- Visit Kylemore Abbey nearby for a cultural and natural combination.

The Aran Islands (County Galway)

Composed of three starkly beautiful islands—Inis Mór, Inis Meáin, and Inis Oírr—the Aran Islands embody Ireland's ancient heritage and seafaring resilience. Their dry-stone walls, windswept cliffs, and preserved Gaelic culture make for an immersive step back in time. Inis Mór's cliff-edge Dún Aonghasa fort is particularly spellbinding.

Location: Off the coast of Galway Bay

Insider Tips:

- Rent a bike to explore the islands' winding lanes.
- Pack layers—even summer days can feel brisk and damp.
- Learn a few words of Irish (Gaeilge)—locals still speak it daily.

National Parks & Outdoor Escapes

Ireland's national parks are sanctuaries of natural drama, offering glimpses into a landscape shaped by glaciers, wind, and time, and still alive with wildlife, folklore, and solitude. From mist-wrapped mountains to serene lakes, vast peat bogs to coastal headlands, each park tells its own story. Whether walking among ancient oaks or trekking through alpine ridges, these spaces invite visitors to disconnect, breathe deeply, and experience Ireland's raw, unfiltered beauty.

1. Killarney National Park (County Kerry)

Ireland's first national park is a place of superlatives—mountains, lakes, forests, and waterfalls all converging in a sweeping valley beneath MacGillycuddy's Reeks. At its heart lies Muckross House and Gardens, while further in, the Gap of Dunloe beckons with highland drama and pony-drawn carts. Hiking trails traverse old-growth oak woodlands and skirt the shores of Lough Leane.

Torc Waterfall and Ladies View remain two of the most iconic spots, particularly in autumn when the foliage burns gold and crimson.

Insider Tips:

- Rent a bike and ride through the Gap of Dunloe to Lord Brandon's Cottage.
- Explore lesser-known trails like the Old Kenmare Road for solitude.
- Take a boat trip across the lakes to Ross Castle for a memorable afternoon.

2. Glenveagh National Park (County Donegal)

Tucked in the heart of the Derryveagh Mountains, Glenveagh is a place of poetic isolation. Peat bogs stretch endlessly, deer roam freely, and Glenveagh Castle stands in romantic solitude by the lake. Unlike other parks, this one is steeped in Victorian design with a wilderness spirit. Walking trails fan out from the castle, including lakeside paths, hill walks, and access to some of Ireland's most untouched highlands.

Insider Tips:

- Take the shuttle from the visitor center or enjoy the scenic 4 km walk to the castle.
- Watch for golden eagles—reintroduced here after a century-long absence.
- Plan a picnic by Lough Veagh's peaceful shoreline.

3. The Burren National Park (County Clare)

The Burren defies expectations. Instead of green pastures, it presents a vast limestone pavement, cracked and weathered, yet teeming with rare alpine and Mediterranean flora. Walking here feels like stepping onto another planet—one with ancient ring forts, cave systems, and dolmens dotting the silent expanse. Trails range from gentle loops to steep climbs like Mullaghmore Mountain, where the entire alien-like landscape unfolds below.

Insider Tips:

- Visit in spring when orchids, gentians, and primroses bloom among the rocks.
- Take a Burren Ecotour to deepen your understanding of its biodiversity.
- Don't miss nearby Aillwee Cave and its underground river system.

4. Connemara National Park (County Galway)

Connemara is a symphony of granite peaks, windswept bogs, heather-strewn hills, and shimmering lakes. The Twelve Bens dominate the skyline, offering challenging climbs and wide-open panoramas. Diamond Hill is the most popular trek, a manageable climb with boardwalk sections and thrilling views over the Atlantic and Inishbofin. The visitor center in Letterfrack acts as a gateway to these highlands, with family-friendly trails and cultural exhibits.

Insider Tips:

- Start early to summit Diamond Hill before clouds roll in.
- Combine hiking with a visit to Kylemore Abbey, just minutes away.
- Keep an eye out for Connemara ponies grazing in the distance.

5. Wicklow Mountains National Park (County Wicklow)

Just south of Dublin, the Wicklow Mountains offer both accessibility and wildness. Its glacial valleys, heather moors, and deep lakes are laced with walking trails ranging from gentle paths to rugged mountain climbs. Glendalough Monastic Site is the park's spiritual and visual centerpiece—its two lakes framed by towering cliffs and forested trails. The Wicklow Way, a long-distance trail, runs through it, offering multi-day hiking options.

Insider Tips:

- Hike the Spinc and Glenealo Loop for waterfall views and mountaintop solitude.
- Explore on weekdays for quieter paths and better photography opportunities.
- Visit Powerscourt Waterfall nearby for a quieter nature escape.

6. Ballycroy National Park (County Mayo)

Among Ireland's newest and most underexplored parks, Ballycroy protects 11,000 hectares of Atlantic blanket bog, mountainous terrain, and rare wetland ecosystems. The Nephin Beg Range lies at its core, offering a wilderness experience free from crowds. This park is also a certified International Dark Sky Reserve, making it one of the best places in Ireland for stargazing. Boardwalk trails, including the Claggan Mountain Coastal Trail, offer accessible options for visitors of all abilities.

Insider Tips:

- Visit at night during a new moon for a dazzling Milky Way display.
- Take the Nature Loop Walk for a family-friendly stroll through the bog.
- Pair your trip with a visit to Achill Island for dramatic sea cliffs and sandy beaches.

7. Wild Nephin National Park (County Mayo)

Formerly part of Ballycroy, Wild Nephin is now officially recognized as its entity and represents one of Europe's largest intact peatland ecosystems. This vast expanse has little infrastructure, making it ideal for those seeking solitude and self-guided adventure. Backpacking and backcountry camping are allowed in designated areas, and hiking trails like the Bangor Trail trace historical routes through the mountains.

Insider Tips:

- Plan for no mobile signal—carry maps and be self-sufficient.
- Bring waterproof gear; weather changes quickly and dramatically.
- Watch for otters, foxes, and whooper swans in wetland areas.

8. Other Notable Outdoor Escapes

1. Slieve Bloom Mountains (Laois/Offaly)

Ideal for quieter hiking with a mix of forested trails and open hills.

Insider Tip: Combine with the Slieve Bloom Way for a 70 km loop trail.

2. The Mourne Mountains (County Down)

Dramatic granite peaks, often shrouded in mist, inspiration for Narnia.

Insider Tip: Hike the Brandy Pad, a trail used by 18th-century smugglers.

3. The Cooley Peninsula (County Louth)

Home to the legendary Táin Bó Cúailnge and a hidden gem for hikers.

Insider Tip: Walk the Táin Way to trace ancient warrior footsteps.

4. The Beara Peninsula (Cork/Kerry)

Wilder and less touristy than Kerry, with incredible coastal views.

Insider Tip: Take the cable car to Dursey Island—the only one in Ireland.

Whether hiking across a windswept ridge or picnicking by a reflective lake, Ireland's national parks offer immersive, soul-stirring connections to land and legend.

Golf Courses, Spas & Relaxation

Ireland offers more than misty cliffs, green hills, and storybook villages—it also promises world-class indulgence for travelers who seek serenity and leisure. The island is home to some of the most iconic golf courses in the world, acclaimed spa retreats that blend ancient healing with luxury, and wellness escapes that pair ocean air with soulful calm.

Whether you're swinging on championship greens or unwinding in a thermal suite overlooking a rugged coast, Ireland provides restorative moments wrapped in natural beauty and warm hospitality.

Ireland's Premier Golf Courses

Ireland's golfing pedigree is legendary, with over 400 golf courses across the country. From historic links shaped by wind and sea to parkland greens framed by castle ruins, playing golf in Ireland is as much about the setting as the game itself.

1. Royal County Down (County Down)

Often ranked the number one golf course in the world, Royal County Down lies at the foot of the Mourne Mountains. This links course, founded in 1889, boasts heather-lined fairways and sweeping views of Dundrum Bay. The challenging terrain and unpredictable winds make it a favorite among professionals and purists alike.

Highlights:

- Dramatic coastal location
- Narrow fairways and strategic bunkering
- Hosts numerous championships, including the Irish Open

2. Ballybunion Golf Club (County Kerry)

Renowned for its wild Atlantic backdrop and rolling dunes, Ballybunion's Old Course is rugged, remote, and revered. It's a test of skill with natural undulations and coastal winds dictating every shot. A true bucket list course.

Highlights:

- Raw, untamed link experience
- Signature par-3 11th hole above a beachside cliff
- Frequented by legends like Tom Watson

3. Lahinch Golf Club (County Clare)

Overlooking Liscannor Bay and redesigned by Alister MacKenzie, Lahinch combines scenic beauty with unique challenges. Herds of goats still roam the course—a quirky local tradition.

Highlights:

- Blind par-3s and towering dunes
- Proximity to the Cliffs of Moher
- Wind conditions can shift dramatically, requiring adaptability

4. Portmarnock Golf Club (County Dublin)

Just 20 minutes from Dublin city center, Portmarnock is a classic championship course known for its meticulous design and challenging play. It has hosted more Irish Opens than any other venue.

Highlights:

- Elegant layout
- Proximity to Dublin Airport makes it ideal for short visits
- Spectacular sea views on every hole

5. Old Head Golf Links (County Cork)

Dramatically set on a clifftop peninsula that juts into the Atlantic, Old Head is a sensory experience. This newer course, opened in 1997, is as photogenic as it is technically demanding.

Highlights:

- Seven holes played along 300-foot sea cliffs
- Lighthouse landmark within the course
- Luxurious clubhouse with spa and dining options

Spa Experiences Across Ireland

Ireland's spa culture blends ancient Irish traditions—like seaweed baths and herbal infusions—with cutting-edge therapies. Whether tucked inside five-star resorts or cliffside sanctuaries, the country's spas deliver quietude and rejuvenation.

1. The Spa at Ashford Castle (County Mayo)

Voted one of the best spas in the world, Ashford Castle's spa combines old-world opulence with holistic wellness. The interiors shimmer with Donegal quartz crystal and Connemara marble, while treatments use organic Irish products.

Signature Experience:

- Restorative thermal suite and rainforest showers
- VOYA seaweed facials and reflexology
- Tranquil views over Lough Corrib

2. Monart Destination Spa (County Wexford)

Ireland's only true destination spa, Monart, is adults-only and fully immersive. Guests wear robes throughout their stay and enjoy personalized programs that balance body and mind.

Signature Experience:

- Thermal suite with saunas, hydrotherapy pool, salt grotto
- Nature walks and forest meditation
- Award-winning gourmet wellness cuisine

3. The Europe Hotel & Resort (County Kerry)

Overlooking the Lakes of Killarney, this lavish resort offers panoramic views from its lakeside spa. ESPA treatments are combined with tranquil relaxation areas and an indoor/outdoor vitality pool.

Signature Experience:

- Lakeview salt chamber
- Heated loungers with mountain views
- Couples' spa rituals and post-treatment herbal teas

4. Cliff House Hotel Spa (County Waterford)

This five-star boutique hotel clings to a cliff above Ardmore Bay and features an intimate spa that celebrates the elements. With stone therapy, ocean-inspired body rituals, and an outdoor hot tub, it's deeply atmospheric.

Signature Experience:

- Sea salt and seaweed scrubs
- Yoga and cliff-top walks
- Spa with infinity-edge relaxation pool

Natural & Alternative Wellness Retreats

For those seeking a connection to Ireland's land and rhythms, alternative retreats offer something deeper. Think yoga by the sea, wild swimming, digital detoxes, and forest bathing—ways to return to yourself as much as to nature.

1. Burren Yoga Retreat (County Clare)

Nestled in the lunar-like landscape of the Burren, this retreat offers yoga, meditation, and vegetarian meals in a tranquil setting. Weekend and week-long retreats allow guests to dive into practice while exploring nearby walks and beaches.

2. Creacon Wellness Retreat (County Wexford)

Founded by spiritual teacher Derek O'Neill, this holistic center focuses on healing and emotional wellness through energy therapy, counseling, and clean eating.

3. Wild Atlantic Seaweed Baths (County Sligo & Galway)

Traditional seaweed baths date back generations in Ireland's west coast communities. Hot seawater infusions with locally harvested seaweed are believed to detoxify, nourish the skin, and promote circulation.

Wellness Activities to Try Around Ireland

- **Forest Bathing in Wicklow or Glenstal Abbey** – A sensory immersion in ancient woodlands.
- **Wild Swimming in Glendalough, Lough Ouler, or Keem Bay** – Cold, invigorating, and unforgettable.
- **Hot Tub Under the Stars at Finn Lough (County Fermanagh)** – Transparent forest domes paired with open-air spas.
- **Sea Cliff Yoga at Ballycotton or Howth** – Open-air classes with dramatic views and coastal breeze.
- **Digital Detox Weekends** – Offered at retreats like Dzogchen Beara in County Cork.

Chapter 7: History, Heritage & Mythology

Ancient Ireland: Celts, Druids & Megaliths

Long before medieval castles and Christian monasteries dotted the Irish landscape, a much older civilization left its mysterious mark on the island. Ancient Ireland pulses with a deep, spiritual energy, etched into stone circles, passage tombs, and oral traditions that predate written history. The legacy of the Celts, Druids, and megalith builders continues to shape Ireland's culture, myths, and landscape to this day. From sacred groves and solar-aligned tombs to haunting warrior legends, Ireland's prehistoric and early Celtic eras remain some of its most spellbinding chapters.

The Megalithic Legacy: Stones That Speak of Time

Ireland is home to some of the oldest manmade structures in the world. The passage tombs, dolmens, and stone circles scattered across the countryside tell stories of astronomical knowledge, ancestor worship, and communal ritual.

Newgrange (Brú na Bóinne, County Meath)

Constructed over 5,000 years ago—older than Stonehenge and the Great Pyramids—Newgrange is a masterpiece of Neolithic engineering.

Its narrow passageway leads to a central chamber aligned with the rising sun on the winter solstice. Each December 21st, a shaft of light travels down the tunnel and illuminates the tomb's heart, connecting life and afterlife in a display of cosmic precision.

Features:

- Spiral carvings and solar motifs
- Part of a larger complex with Knowth and Dowth
- UNESCO World Heritage Site

Poulnabrone Dolmen (County Clare)

Perched in the limestone karst of the Burren, this iconic portal tomb dates back to 4200–2900 BCE. It's believed to have been a burial site for high-status individuals, marked by an otherworldly landscape that mirrors the myths of the sidhe (fairy folk).

Loughcrew Cairns (County Meath)

These hilltop tombs predate Newgrange and offer panoramic views of the surrounding countryside. The carvings inside Cairn T align with the equinox sunrise—another sign of the Neolithic people's advanced understanding of astronomy and spiritual cycles.

Arriving around 500 BCE, the Celts brought with them a rich oral tradition, a pantheon of deities, and a deeply symbolic worldview. Unlike the Neolithic tomb builders, they left few stone monuments—but their influence lives on in language, myth, and visual design.

Language & Legacy

Irish Gaelic, still spoken in Gaeltacht regions, descends directly from Celtic tongues. Place names like "Dún" (fort) and "Lios" (ringfort) speak of ancient settlements and spiritual sites.

Warriors & Heroes

The Ulster Cycle and Fenian Cycle of Irish mythology recount tales of warriors like Cú Chulainn and Fionn mac Cumhaill, whose feats were passed down through generations by bards and poets. These epic stories reflected ideals of bravery, loyalty, and supernatural prowess.

Celtic Art

Intricate knotwork, spiral motifs, and symbolic zoomorphic figures flourished in Celtic design. These patterns continue in modern Irish jewelry, tattoos, and church manuscripts like the Book of Kells.

Druids were the intellectual elite of the Celtic world—philosophers, astronomers, healers, and spiritual leaders. Though none of their teachings were written down, Roman historians and Irish myth preserve their mystique.

Sacred Spaces

Druids held ceremonies in oak groves, stone circles, and liminal places like riverbanks or hilltops. Trees like the oak (daur), yew, and hazel were especially sacred, believed to connect the human realm to the divine.

Seasonal Festivals

- Many modern Irish festivals trace their roots to ancient Druidic observances:
- **Samhain (Oct 31–Nov 1):** The Celtic New Year, when the veil between worlds thinned.

- **Imbolc (Feb 1):** A festival of light and fertility, later Christianized as St. Brigid's Day.
- **Beltane (May 1):** A fire festival welcoming summer and fertility.
- **Lughnasadh (Aug 1):** Celebrating the harvest and the god Lugh.

Ritual Landscapes & Ancient Sites to Explore

Hill of Tara (County Meath)

The traditional seat of Ireland's High Kings, Tara was a political and spiritual center for millennia. It's dotted with burial mounds, ringforts, and the Lia Fáil ("Stone of Destiny"), said to roar when touched by a true king.

Carrowmore Megalithic Cemetery (County Sligo)

One of Europe's largest megalithic complexes, Carrowmore features over 30 tombs in a sacred landscape aligned with the nearby Knocknarea mountain and Queen Maeve's cairn.

Drombeg Stone Circle (County Cork)

This well-preserved stone circle includes a central altar and ancient cooking site, suggesting community feasting and ritual use. Its alignment with the midwinter sunset shows another link to ancient calendrical systems.

1. Visit During the Solstices or Equinoxes: Many ancient sites come alive during these celestial events. For a rare spiritual experience, apply for a chance to witness the winter solstice sunrise inside Newgrange (lottery entry required).

2. Take a Guided Mythology Tour: Local guides—especially those with backgrounds in folklore—bring the past vividly to life with stories, songs, and historical context you won't find in guidebooks.

3. Respect the Land's Energy: Many locals still view ancient sites with reverence. Approach them mindfully—don't climb cairns or remove stones. These sacred places are best experienced in quiet reflection.

Exploring Ireland's Castles & Fortresses

Ireland's landscape is scattered with hundreds of castles, keeps, and ancient fortresses—each a silent sentinel of the island's dramatic history. From imposing medieval strongholds to romantic ruins draped in ivy, these architectural marvels bring tales of chivalry, conquest, and culture to life. Many are open to the public, with opportunities to step inside centuries-old halls, climb crumbling towers, or even stay overnight like royalty.

Bunratty Castle (County Clare)

Dating back to 1425, Bunratty Castle is one of Ireland's most complete and authentically restored medieval fortresses. Originally a Viking trading post and later a Norman stronghold, the current structure belonged to the powerful MacNamara and O'Brien clans. Today, it features period furnishings and hosts lively medieval banquets with costumed performers, harpists, and hearty traditional fare.

Highlights:

- 15th-century tower house with battlements and murder holes
- Folk Park showcases rural Irish life
- Family-friendly with interactive reenactments

Cahir Castle (County Tipperary)

Set on a rocky island in the River Suir, Cahir Castle is a massive fortress with a long military history. Built in the 13th century, it was cleverly designed for defense, with moat systems, arrow slits, and a keep that withstood repeated sieges. It's exceptionally well preserved and often used as a filming location for historical dramas.

Highlights:

- Working portcullis and inner ward

- Interactive audiovisual displays on sieges
- Tower views over the river and town

Trim Castle (County Meath)

As the largest Anglo-Norman castle in Ireland, Trim was a major outpost during the 12th century. Its cruciform keep and vast curtain walls dominate the River Boyne landscape. Fans of film will recognize it from Braveheart, where it stood in for medieval London. Guided tours provide deep insight into its architecture and strategic design.

Highlights:

- 30,000 sq. meters footprint
- Original moat and drawbridge foundations
- Panoramic rooftop tour

Rock of Cashel (County Tipperary)

Also known as St. Patrick's Rock, this dramatic complex of ruins crowns a limestone outcrop and includes a 12th-century round tower, a Gothic cathedral, and a Romanesque chapel. It once served as the seat of the kings of Munster and was where St. Patrick is said to have converted King Aengus. It's a stirring blend of religious, mythological, and military history.

Highlights:

- Cormac's Chapel with intricate carvings
- Frescoes dating back to the 1100s
- Sweeping views across the Golden Vale

Dunluce Castle (County Antrim, Northern Ireland)

Teetering on the edge of a sheer basalt cliff over the North Atlantic, Dunluce Castle is one of the most haunting and romantic ruins in Ireland. First built in the 13th century and rebuilt by the MacDonnell clan in the 16th century, it was abandoned after a portion of the kitchen collapsed into the sea.

Highlights:

- Connected to the mainland by a footbridge
- Linked to the legend of Atlantis and inspiration for C.S. Lewis's Narnia
- Excellent photo opportunities, especially at sunset

Kilkenny Castle (County Kilkenny)

A symbol of Norman authority, Kilkenny Castle was built in 1195 and evolved over the centuries into a graceful residence. Its stately halls, tapestries, and formal gardens reflect the lifestyle of the influential Butler family, who lived there for almost 600 years. It's now a public museum and parkland, ideal for a cultural city stop.

Highlights:

- Restored Victorian interiors
- Rotating art exhibitions
- Family-friendly with expansive lawns and a playground

Ross Castle (County Kerry)

Nestled on the edge of Lough Leane in Killarney National Park, this 15th-century tower house was built by the O'Donoghue clan. It played a key role in the Cromwellian wars and is steeped in ghost stories and local folklore. Boat tours to Innisfallen Island often begin nearby.

Highlights:

- Lakeside views and forested trails
- 17th-century period rooms

- Small guided tours with storytelling charm

King John's Castle (Limerick City)

A fortress with more than 800 years of history, King John's Castle was built by order of King John of England on the site of a Viking settlement. The visitor center uses high-tech exhibitions and 3D models to vividly depict life through Norman, medieval, and Tudor times.

Highlights:

- Modernized exhibits and the excavation site
- Interactive touchscreen experiences
- Family-friendly courtyard with medieval games

Insider Tips for Exploring Ireland's Castles & Fortresses

1. Combine Castles with Scenic Drives: Plan your routes around castle clusters. For instance, a day trip from Dublin could include Trim Castle, Slane Castle, and the Hill of Tara for a historical trifecta.

2. Book a Castle Stay for the Full Experience: Several historic castles like Ashford Castle (County Mayo) or Dromoland Castle (County Clare) now operate as luxury hotels offering gourmet dining, falconry, and spa treatments.

3. Arrive Early for the Best Light & Least Crowds: Many castles are popular with tour groups—visiting early in the morning not only provides soft, golden lighting for photos but also allows for a more tranquil exploration.

Historic Sites: Step Into Ireland's Storied Past

Ireland's rich history stretches back thousands of years, and its landscape is marked by extraordinary sites that chronicle the rise and fall of kingdoms, the spread of Christianity, ancient spiritual beliefs, and national struggle. From Neolithic tombs older than the pyramids to monastic ruins and pivotal battlefields, the island is an open-air museum where every stone has a story to tell.

Newgrange (Brú na Bóinne, County Meath)

Older than the Egyptian pyramids and Stonehenge, Newgrange is a marvel of Neolithic engineering dating back over 5,200 years. This circular passage tomb is precisely aligned with the rising sun during the winter solstice, flooding the chamber with light in a cosmic display of prehistoric ingenuity. Intricate spirals, megalithic art, and stone corridors whisper the sacred rituals of early Irish civilization.

Highlights:

- UNESCO World Heritage Site
- Solar-aligned passage chamber
- Interpretive visitor center with guided access

Glendalough Monastic Settlement (County Wicklow)

Tucked within a glacier-carved valley, Glendalough's 6th-century monastic site is a spiritual retreat founded by St. Kevin. Towering round towers, carved crosses, and crumbling churches emerge from the forested terrain, giving a mystical atmosphere to this place of pilgrimage and peace. Nature trails and lakes frame the ruins, inviting reflection and exploration.

Highlights:

- Early Christian round tower (30 meters high)
- Twin lakes and medieval structures
- Scenic trails connecting sacred ruins

The Rock of Dunamase (County Laois)

Perched dramatically atop a rocky outcrop, the ruins of Dunamase Castle date to the 12th century, although the site has older roots in early Christian fortification. Once the stronghold of Norman lords, the crumbling walls and broken towers offer panoramic views of the plains of Laois and serve as a powerful symbol of medieval defense.

Highlights:

- Atmospheric ruins are ideal for photography
- Overlooks fertile midlands countryside
- Free entry and open access

The Hill of Tara (County Meath)

Once the ceremonial seat of Ireland's High Kings, the Hill of Tara is steeped in myth and legend. This grassy hill is marked by ancient ring forts, burial mounds, and standing stones, including the Lia Fáil (Stone of Destiny), believed to roar when touched by the rightful king. The site was sacred in both pagan and Christian eras.

Highlights:

- Royal inauguration site and sacred place
- Burial mounds like the Mound of Hostages
- Rich mythology and sweeping views

Kilmainham Gaol (Dublin)

Ireland's struggle for independence echoes through the somber corridors of Kilmainham Gaol. Built in 1796, the prison housed many leaders of Irish rebellions, including those executed after the 1916 Easter Rising. Today, its guided tours offer a moving, immersive experience into the nation's turbulent road to freedom.

Highlights:

- Historic cell blocks and courtyards
- Stories of Irish revolutionaries
- Filming location for In the Name of the Father

Christ Church Cathedral (Dublin)

One of Dublin's most iconic landmarks, Christ Church Cathedral has dominated the city's spiritual and political life since its founding in the 11th century.

Its architectural blend of Norman and Gothic styles is striking. The vast crypt below houses medieval relics, a mummified cat and rat, and rare manuscripts.

Highlights:

- 1,000-year-old crypt
- Evocative choral acoustics
- Viking history and ancient relics

The Burren (County Clare)

While not a conventional historic "site," the Burren's karst landscape is dotted with over 90 megalithic tombs, Bronze Age forts, and ancient stone walls. Poulnabrone Dolmen is the most iconic—a portal tomb dating to 4200 BC. These limestone plains hold thousands of years of human history carved into nature.

Highlights:

- Archaeological gems are scattered across the terrain
- Ideal for self-guided explorations
- Rich blend of history and wild beauty

Charles Fort (County Cork)

A star-shaped military fort near Kinsale Harbour, Charles Fort represents centuries of conflict from the 17th century onward.

Its robust bastions, thick ramparts, and panoramic sea views tell of sieges, maritime battles, and British occupation. The site is especially dramatic at sunset.

Highlights:

- 17th-century fortification
- Walkable ramparts and sea vistas
- Ghost stories and rich military history

Tips for Exploring Historic Sites in Ireland

- **Advance Tickets:** Popular sites like Newgrange and Kilmainham Gaol often require pre-booking.
- **Layered Clothing:** Many sites are outdoors and exposed to wind and rain.
- **Footwear:** Comfortable, waterproof shoes are recommended for walking on uneven or muddy terrain.
- **Guides vs. Self-Guided:** Local guides often provide rich storytelling and context that enhances the experience.
- **Time of Day:** Visit early in the morning or late afternoon for fewer crowds and better lighting.

The Troubles & Modern History of Ireland

Ireland's modern history is shaped by centuries of colonial tension, national identity struggles, and a transformative journey from conflict to peace. One of the most defining periods in this evolution is The Troubles—a complex and deeply emotional era of sectarian violence that gripped Northern Ireland from the late 1960s to the late 1990s. Understanding this chapter is essential to grasping Ireland's contemporary culture, politics, and resilience.

Background: Ireland's Partition and Political Divide

The roots of The Troubles lie in the early 20th century, when Ireland's push for independence from British rule resulted in a hard-fought partial victory. The Government of Ireland Act (1920) established two self-governing regions—Northern and Southern Ireland. The southern counties would later become the independent Irish Free State (now the Republic of Ireland), while Northern Ireland remained part of the United Kingdom, largely due to the Protestant unionist majority in that region.

This division left a Catholic nationalist minority in Northern Ireland who identified as Irish and felt politically and culturally marginalized under unionist-dominated governance. Decades of unequal representation, restricted voting rights, housing discrimination, and lack of access to employment stoked resentment and unrest.

The Troubles Begin (Late 1960s–1972)

What began as a civil rights movement in the late 1960s quickly devolved into violent conflict. Inspired by global civil rights movements, Catholic communities in Northern Ireland began to peacefully protest discriminatory policies. Marches and demonstrations were often met with hostility by police forces and loyalist counter-protesters.

The situation escalated in 1969 with the Battle of the Bogside in Derry and the subsequent deployment of British troops to Northern Ireland. Initially seen as peacekeepers, British forces became a target of suspicion and animosity, particularly after the events of Bloody Sunday in 1972, when British soldiers killed 14 unarmed Catholic protesters in Derry.

This tragedy intensified nationalist anger and recruitment into militant groups like the Irish Republican Army (IRA), which sought to reunify Ireland by force. Loyalist paramilitaries, such as the Ulster Volunteer Force (UVF) and the Ulster Defence Association (UDA), responded with their violent campaigns to maintain union with Britain.

The Era of Violence and Division (1970s–1990s)

For nearly three decades, Northern Ireland endured bombings, shootings, kidnappings, and political assassinations. The IRA carried out attacks not just in Northern Ireland, but also in England. Loyalist groups retaliated, often targeting Catholic civilians. Entire neighborhoods in Belfast and Derry became no-go zones, divided by walls and policed with military checkpoints. Political efforts to restore peace often stalled due to entrenched mistrust between communities. Civilian casualties mounted, and daily life was marked by surveillance, street patrols, and a climate of fear. By the early 1990s, over 3,500 people had been killed, and tens of thousands injured.

The Peace Process and Good Friday Agreement (1998)

The pathway to peace took decades of negotiation and the commitment of local leaders, British and Irish governments, and international mediators.

The turning point came with the Good Friday Agreement (also known as the Belfast Agreement) in 1998.

This landmark deal established:

A devolved Northern Ireland Assembly with power-sharing between unionists and nationalists

- The decommissioning of paramilitary weapons
- Reforms in policing and human rights legislation
- Cross-border institutions between Northern Ireland and the Republic
- A recognition that Northern Ireland would remain part of the UK unless a majority voted otherwise

The agreement was approved by an overwhelming majority in referendums held both north and south of the border. Though fragile and occasionally strained, the peace has largely held, allowing a new generation to grow up without daily violence.

Modern Ireland: Growth, Identity & Reconciliation

In the decades since, both Northern Ireland and the Republic have undergone profound transformations. Dublin and Belfast have become modern, cosmopolitan cities. The Republic joined the European Union and has experienced rapid economic development, known as the Celtic Tiger era in the early 2000s. Northern Ireland has embraced a new political landscape, although sectarian divisions persist. Murals and peace walls remain visible in Belfast and Derry, but so do cultural initiatives, cross-community schools, and tourism focused on reconciliation and understanding.

Places to Explore the History of The Troubles

Museum of Free Derry (Derry): Captures the civil rights movement, Bloody Sunday, and the community's resilience through firsthand narratives.

Crumlin Road Gaol (Belfast): Offers an immersive look at incarceration during the conflict and the prison's infamous role.

The Belfast Murals (Shankill & Falls Roads): A stark visual expression of the Troubles, best explored on guided walking or black cab tours.

Stormont Parliament Buildings: The home of Northern Ireland's Assembly and a symbol of political evolution.

Titanic Belfast: While not focused on the Troubles, this world-class museum reflects Belfast's industrial heritage and modern renaissance.

Insider Tips for Understanding This Complex History

1. Take a Black Cab Tour in Belfast

These guided drives through the Shankill and Falls neighborhoods are led by locals, often former participants or witnesses, offering personal perspectives that humanize the history.

2. Read and Watch Thoughtful Media

Books like Say Nothing by Patrick Radden Keefe or films like '71, Bloody Sunday, and In the Name of the Father delve into the emotional, political, and personal dimensions of The Troubles.

3. Approach with Sensitivity

Though peace reigns, the memories are fresh and the wounds not entirely healed. Locals may differ in their perspectives, so respect is essential when discussing the past.

Folklore, Fairies & Mythical Legends

Ireland's soul is steeped in myth, its landscapes woven with legends that dance between history and imagination. The mists that roll over its hills, the ancient stones standing solemnly in green fields, and the shadowed glens all whisper stories that have survived for thousands of years. These are tales of shape-shifting warriors, elusive fairies, banshees, and ancient gods—reflections of Ireland's deep spiritual roots and storytelling heritage.

The Aos Sí – Ireland's Fairy Folk

The Aos Sí (pronounced "ees shee") are the supernatural beings of Irish mythology, often translated as the "people of the mounds." Believed to be descendants of the Tuatha Dé Danann, a godlike race driven underground by invading forces, they now dwell in the hollow hills, ancient cairns, and ringforts scattered across the countryside.

The Aos Sí are not the delicate, winged creatures found in children's books. They are powerful, unpredictable, and deeply connected to nature. Some are helpful and benign, others are dangerous and easily offended. Farmers once left offerings of milk and bread on windowsills to appease them, while others avoided disturbing fairy trees or cutting down hawthorn bushes for fear of retribution.

The Banshee – Harbinger of Death

A piercing wail in the night is never taken lightly in Irish tradition. It may be the cry of the Banshee, a female spirit said to forewarn death in a family. Described as a pale woman with long silver hair, dressed in white or grey, she keens (cries mournfully) near the homes of those fated to die. While terrifying, the Banshee is not malevolent. She mourns rather than causes death. Families with ancient Gaelic lineage—especially those with names beginning with "O" or "Mac"—are said to be most likely to receive her eerie visitation.

The Tuatha Dé Danann – Ireland's Old Gods

Before fairies and banshees, there were the gods of the Tuatha Dé Danann, a mystical race who arrived in Ireland "on dark clouds" and brought with them powerful magic. They ruled the land before being defeated by the Milesians (mythical ancestors of the Irish people), after which they retreated into the earth, becoming the Aos Sí.

Many Irish legends center around these divine figures:

- Lugh, the warrior god of many skills, is associated with justice and harvest.
- Brigid, the goddess of healing, poetry, and fertility, was later adapted into Christianity as Saint Brigid.
- The Dagda, a father figure and god of abundance, wielding a massive club that could both kill and resurrect.

These deities were not only worshipped but incorporated into place names and seasonal festivals like Samhain and Imbolc.

Cú Chulainn & The Ulster Cycle

Among Ireland's greatest mythical heroes is Cú Chulainn, a demigod warrior who defended Ulster against overwhelming odds.

Known for his battle frenzy—ríastrad—that transformed him into a monstrous figure in war, Cú Chulainn is a symbol of loyalty, courage, and tragic destiny. His tales, part of the Ulster Cycle, feature epic battles, curses, and prophecy. His story ends with his heroic death, tied to a standing stone, refusing to die upright until all enemies had fled.

Selkies, Merrows & Sea Legends

Irish coastal folklore brims with mystical sea creatures. Selkies, seal-folk who shed their skins to walk as humans, appear in both Irish and Scottish mythology. If their seal skin is hidden or stolen, they are bound to live on land but always long for the sea. Merrows—Irish mermaids—are often portrayed as beautiful, green-haired beings who wear magical caps (called "cohuleens") that allow them to travel between land and water. They could be kind, romantic, or vengeful, depending on the tale.

Changeling Lore & Fairy Abductions

One of the darker strands of Irish folklore involves changelings—fairy beings left in place of human children stolen by the fairies. Families who believed their child had been taken might perform strange or even dangerous rituals to try to bring the real child back. Changelings were thought to be sickly, silent, or odd in behavior. Today, many historians link changeling lore with misunderstood medical conditions in history, though the stories endure as a reflection of mystery and loss in the face of the unexplained.

Sacred Sites & Portal Locations

Certain places in Ireland are viewed as literal entrances to the Otherworld. Ringforts, lone hawthorn trees, and ancient burial mounds—like Newgrange— are all thought to be connected to fairy realms. Superstitions still surround these areas:

- Never damage a fairy ring (a circle of mushrooms).
- Avoid cutting down lone hawthorn trees, often considered fairy trees.
- Burial mounds like Knocknarea or Carrowmore are respected not only as archaeological sites but as thresholds to the mystical.

Storytelling: The Seanchaí Tradition

Irish mythology survived and thrived for generations through the seanchaí (shan-a-key)—traditional storytellers. With no written texts for centuries, the seanchaí passed down epic tales orally by firelight in cottages and halls. Their memory and oratory skills were revered, and they helped keep the legends alive across centuries of invasion, famine, and change. Today, their spirit lives on in pubs, festivals, and folklore centers throughout the island.

Insider Tips for Experiencing Irish Folklore

1. Explore Fairy Trails and Forest Walks

Visit fairy-themed walks like those in Rossmore Forest Park (County Monaghan) or Dromore Woods (County Clare), where carved fairy doors, sculptures, and nature meet to spark the imagination.

2. Attend a Folklore Night in a Local Pub

In places like Doolin, Kilkenny, and Dingle, local pubs host traditional music nights woven with myths and storytelling, often led by seasoned locals.

3. Visit the National Leprechaun Museum (Dublin)

A whimsical and surprisingly deep dive into Irish mythology, fairy tales, and superstition—designed for both children and adults, it brings the island's spirit folklore to life in interactive ways.

Chapter 8: Irish Culture & Traditions

Gaelic Language and Irish Identity

Ireland's identity is inseparable from its language. Irish Gaelic—Gaeilge—is more than just a means of communication; it is a cultural soul, a poetic expression, and a reflection of the island's ancient roots and resilient spirit. Long before English echoed across the emerald fields, Irish flowed through bardic poetry, tribal law, and the everyday speech of a people deeply attuned to their land, myths, and rhythms.

A Language Older Than Empire

Gaeilge is one of the oldest written languages in Europe, with inscriptions in Ogham script dating back over 1,500 years. Its structure, syntax, and vocabulary carry echoes of a Celtic past that predates even the Roman Empire. It evolved organically, influenced by druidic traditions, Christian monasticism, and oral storytelling that passed from fireside to fireside through generations. Its endurance is remarkable. Though English colonization pushed it to the margins, the Irish never truly disappeared. It survived in the west—rugged, remote, and proud—and re-emerged during the cultural revival of the late 19th century as a symbol of defiance, dignity, and national pride.

More Than Words: The Spirit of Gaeilge

To speak Irish is to think in metaphor, to experience a world rich in nature, mood, and subtle meaning. The language is deeply contextual and inherently poetic. Consider these idioms:

- **"Tá sí ag cur báistí"** — It is raining (literally: "It is putting rain").
- **"Tá tart orm"** — I am thirsty (literally: "Thirst is on me").
- **"Mo ghrá thú"** — You are my love.

In Irish, feelings and states of being happen to you rather than being you, reflecting a worldview that is less about ownership and more about connection to the environment and emotion.

Gaeilge and National Revival

In the early 20th century, Irish Gaelic became a banner of identity for a people reclaiming their cultural sovereignty.

The Gaelic League (Conradh na Gaeilge), founded in 1893, championed the revitalization of Irish through schools, literature, and song. The Irish Constitution (1937) enshrined it as the first official language, affirming its central role in the national consciousness. Today, it is taught in every school, used in government documents, spoken in the Dáil (parliament), and displayed proudly on road signs, passports, and public transport. While English remains dominant, Gaeilge stands as a cultural compass—an unbroken chain to Ireland's ancestral voice.

The Gaeltacht: Heartlands of the Irish Language

The Gaeltacht regions—primarily in counties Galway, Donegal, Mayo, Kerry, Cork, and Waterford—are strongholds of daily Irish usage. These communities speak Irish as a first language and nurture their traditions through local schools, media, and festivals. Visiting a Gaeltacht is a linguistic and cultural immersion. Street signs are solely in Irish, conversations in pubs hum with native fluency, and young students attend summer language camps, learning through sports, storytelling, and dance. The Gaeltacht Summer Colleges (Coláistí Samhraidh) are a rite of passage for Irish teens, blending language learning with deep cultural experience.

Gaelic in Music, Song & Modern Media

Irish folk and traditional music serve as an enduring vehicle for the language. From sean-nós singing (an expressive, unaccompanied vocal style) to contemporary artists like Clannad, Enya, and Seo Linn, Gaeilge continues to resonate through melody. Modern radio stations like Raidió na Gaeltachta and television channels such as TG4 have brought the language into the digital age, offering drama, news, and entertainment in fluent Irish. These platforms have helped normalize and celebrate Gaeilge among younger generations.

Learning the Language: Revival in the 21st Century

A renewed enthusiasm for Gaeilge has emerged, not only among Irish citizens but also among members of the diaspora and language lovers worldwide. Apps like Duolingo, podcasts, and immersive online courses have made Irish more accessible than ever. Universities across Ireland and even in the U.S. offer degrees in Irish Studies or Celtic Civilisation. Bilingual signage in cities and a growing trend of Irish-medium schools (Gaelscoileanna) in urban areas like Dublin and Cork reflect a society embracing bilingualism not just as policy, but as pride.

Gaelic and the Irish Psyche

Language shapes identity. It influences how people express time, emotion, relationships, and even memory. Irish carries with it a worldview steeped in community, respect for nature, and a strong spiritual dimension. To speak Irish is to carry centuries of myth, struggle, and creativity in the breath. It is not just a language to be preserved in museums or textbooks. It is a living, breathing art form—adaptable, resilient, and intricately woven into the national character. Whether spoken fluently or known only in fragments, Gaeilge inspires a sense of belonging, of roots, and of something older than memory.

Expressions of Irish Identity Through Language

- **Slogans & Political Activism:** From graffiti on walls to speeches in protest, Gaeilge often appears in moments of cultural resistance.
- **Irish Names:** Many family and place names derive directly from Gaelic origins—O'Neill (Ó Néill), Dún Laoghaire, Baile Átha Cliath (Dublin)—a map written in history.
- **Cultural Events:** The Oireachtas na Gaeilge festival celebrates everything from poetry to dance, uniting speakers of all levels.

Traditional Music & Dance: Where to Experience It Live

Few cultural expressions capture the soul of Ireland more vividly than its traditional music and dance. Born from ancient rhythms, oral storytelling, and centuries of shared history, these living art forms are integral to the Irish identity. Music and dance are not mere performances here—they are rituals of joy, memory, and connection, alive in every village session and festival stage.

The Heartbeat of Ireland: Traditional Music

Irish traditional music (or trad) is a blend of soul-stirring melodies and foot-tapping rhythms, passed down through generations. It centers around acoustic instruments—fiddle, uilleann pipes, tin whistle, bodhrán, concertina, and harp—and is often improvised in informal jam sessions called "céilís" or "sessions." These gatherings aren't confined to grand venues. They unfold in corner pubs, at kitchen tables, or in town squares—wherever musicians gather, tunes rise spontaneously, and onlookers join with claps or steps.

Irish Dance: From Riverdance to the Village Hall

While Riverdance helped launch Irish dancing onto the global stage in the 1990s, the dance form itself is centuries old. With fast, precise footwork and an upright upper body, Irish dance is deeply rhythmic and theatrical. There are solo styles like step dancing and group dances known as céilí—the latter is social, joyful, and often community-driven. You'll see dancers of all ages participating, from polished performances in theatres to lively sets in rural halls where everyone's welcome to try a step.

Where to Experience Live Traditional Music & Dance

1. Doolin, County Clare

A coastal village famed for its intimate pub sessions. McDermott's, McGann's, and O'Connor's Pub offer nightly trad music featuring local legends and touring talent. Nearby, the Burren's otherworldly landscape adds to the magic.

- **Location:** West coast, near the Cliffs of Moher
- +353 65 707 4328 (O'Connor's Pub)
- Most sessions start around 9 PM

2. The Cobblestone, Dublin

An authentic Dublin pub in Smithfield, offering raw, spontaneous sessions every night of the week. Musicians of all levels gather to play, with audiences encouraged to listen, tap along, and enjoy the atmosphere—no frills, just music.

- **Location:** 77 King St N, Dublin 7
- +353 1 872 1799
- Open daily from early afternoon till late

3. Galway City

A hub for bohemian energy and cultural expression. Tigh Neachtain, Taaffes, Crane Bar, and Monroe's are local hotspots offering lively sessions and the occasional dance night. Buskers often spill music onto the streets, especially around Shop Street and Spanish Arch.

- **Location:** Galway City Centre
- +353 91 563 634 (The Crane Bar)
- Sessions daily, especially after 9 PM

4. Glencolmcille Folk Village, Donegal

Offers a more immersive, rural experience. In addition to live music events, the village museum showcases traditional life and occasionally hosts céilí dances, storytelling nights, and cultural workshops in an authentic setting.

- **Location:** Glencolmcille, Co. Donegal
- +353 74 973 0017
- Open April–October, events vary seasonally

5. Siamsa Tíre, Tralee (National Folk Theatre)

A professional venue dedicated to preserving and performing Irish folk traditions through dance, drama, and live music. Its productions offer a theatrical yet deeply authentic experience of rural Irish life and culture.

- **Location:** Town Park, Tralee, Co. Kerry
- +353 66 712 3055
- Shows run from May through September

6. Matt Molloy's, Westport

Owned by the flautist of the Chieftains, this pub is a pilgrimage site for trad lovers. Music spills from its front room nearly every night, and its back venue hosts ticketed performances and céilí-style evenings.

- **Location:** Bridge St, Westport, Co. Mayo
- +353 98 26655
- Live music nightly, walk-ins welcome

7. Kilkenny Tradfest (March)

A major annual festival featuring concerts, street performances, céilís, and workshops. Set in one of Ireland's most picturesque medieval towns, the festival draws top musicians and dance troupes from across the country.

- **Location:** Kilkenny City
- www.kilkennytradfest.com
- Held over St. Patrick's weekend

8. The Fleadh Cheoil (Various Cities, August)

Ireland's largest traditional music competition and celebration. Musicians compete by day and fill the streets by night with live performances, impromptu sessions, and open-air céilí dancing. A full-blown cultural explosion.

- **Location:** Rotates annually (e.g., Mullingar, Ennis)
- www.fleadhcheoil.ie
- Early August

Tips for the Best Experience

- **Arrive Early:** Especially in small pubs, seats fill up quickly when a session is expected. Get a pint, settle in, and let the music come to you.
- **Respect the Session:** These are not concerts—musicians often play for each other. Listen quietly, avoid talking loudly, and applaud respectfully.
- **Ask About a Céilí:** Locals love it when visitors join the dancing. Ask the bartender or a musician if there's a céilí happening nearby—it's often how magical nights begin.

Festivals & Events (2025 Calendar Highlights)

Ireland's calendar is steeped in tradition, music, art, and vibrant community spirit. From ancient Celtic celebrations and cultural showcases to internationally acclaimed music and literary festivals, 2025 promises a year of unforgettable experiences for travelers. Each event reflects the island's rich heritage, deep creativity, and warm sense of community.

TradFest Temple Bar (Dates: January 22–26, Temple Bar, Dublin)

TradFest is a powerful celebration of Irish traditional and folk music, transforming the cobbled streets and intimate venues of Temple Bar into a stage for both heritage and innovation. The lineup includes renowned Irish acts and emerging global talent. Concerts unfold in historic buildings like St. Patrick's Cathedral and City Hall, adding grandeur and acoustical brilliance to the performances. Beyond music, TradFest hosts cultural walking tours, family-friendly events, and showcases of Irish crafts and food, creating a complete sensory immersion into Dublin's cultural heartbeat during winter.

Cúirt International Festival of Literature (April 22–28, Galway City)

Cúirt brings together writers and readers from around the world in a celebration of words and ideas. With a strong focus on contemporary literature, the festival includes readings, interviews, panel discussions, and writing workshops.

Events take place in Galway's theatres, libraries, and intimate pubs, creating a deeply engaging literary atmosphere. Authors span genres from poetry and memoir to fiction and political writing, providing space for diverse voices and thought-provoking conversation. It's a literary pilgrimage for book lovers in one of Ireland's most creative cities.

Dublin Dance Festival (May 14–25, Dublin)

This internationally acclaimed festival is dedicated to the art of contemporary dance. It showcases pioneering choreography and innovative performances by leading artists and ensembles from Ireland and abroad. With events held in theatres, public spaces, and outdoor venues, audiences witness everything from solo performances to multidisciplinary collaborations blending dance with film, sound, and sculpture. The festival also includes masterclasses and post-show talks, encouraging dialogue between performers and audiences. It's a kinetic, thought-provoking celebration of movement and storytelling.

Bloomsday Festival (June 16, Dublin)

Bloomsday is a joyful homage to James Joyce and his modernist masterpiece Ulysses, set on a single day—June 16, 1904. Fans dress in Edwardian costumes and retrace Leopold Bloom's route through Dublin, visiting real-life locations from the novel.

The day is filled with dramatic readings, musical performances, lectures, walking tours, and Joycean breakfasts. Museums and bookshops participate, and cafés serve traditional fare mentioned in the book. It's a uniquely immersive literary event, blending scholarship with street theatre and Dublin's enduring charm.

St. Patrick's Festival (March 14–17, Nationwide)

The St. Patrick's Festival is Ireland's most globally recognized celebration, transforming cities, towns, and villages into stages of green-clad revelry. Dublin hosts the largest festivities, featuring a grand parade with floats, dancers, musicians, and dramatic visual installations. Throughout the weekend, visitors enjoy street performances, storytelling, craft markets, and light shows. While rooted in religious tradition, the festival has evolved into a joyous celebration of Irish identity and global cultural unity.

Galway International Arts Festival (July 14–27, Galway)

This multi-disciplinary arts festival draws performers and audiences from across the world. Galway becomes an open-air stage for visual arts, avant-garde theatre, world music, circus acts, and experimental dance. Streets fill with lively pop-up shows while theaters and galleries present internationally acclaimed works. Visitors will find everything from intimate poetry readings to large-scale outdoor spectacles, all set against the bohemian charm of Galway's historic streets. It's a cultural pilgrimage for lovers of creativity and imagination.

Cork Midsummer Festival (June 12–22, Cork City)

Celebrating contemporary arts in all forms, Cork Midsummer Festival brings together local talent and international acts in theatre, music, literature, dance, and street performance. Events take place in both traditional and unconventional venues—galleries, abandoned warehouses, and even on the River Lee. The festival's open, collaborative spirit invites audiences to experience the city's creative pulse while encouraging fresh interpretations of place and story. It's a favorite among those who appreciate boundary-pushing art and vibrant urban energy.

Fleadh Cheoil na hÉireann (August 10–17, Wexford)

The Fleadh Cheoil is the world's largest celebration of traditional Irish music. It's not just a festival but a competitive gathering where musicians of all ages compete in every imaginable traditional Irish instrument and form. The host town, Wexford, in 2025, transforms into a sea of fiddles, bodhráns, tin whistles, and ceili dancing. Street sessions spring up in every pub and corner, making it an immersive experience in the living heritage of Irish music and storytelling.

Puck Fair (August 10–12, Killorglin, County Kerry)

One of Ireland's oldest festivals, dating back over 400 years, the Puck Fair is an eccentric and joyful rural event that blends ancient Celtic tradition with modern merrymaking.

A wild mountain goat is crowned "King Puck" and reigns over the town during the festivities. The fair includes horse and cattle markets, traditional music, dancing, fireworks, and family entertainment. The quirky symbolism, historical roots, and strong sense of community give this festival a one-of-a-kind atmosphere.

Lisdoonvarna Matchmaking Festival (September 1–30, Lisdoonvarna, County Clare)

This unique month-long event in the Burren region draws singles from across the world, making it one of Europe's most renowned matchmaking festivals. What began as a traditional rural courtship fair now includes modern dating events, music sessions, and dancing every night in local pubs and halls. Ireland's last traditional matchmaker still takes part, offering advice and introductions in his small office. Whether looking for love or simply entertainment, the energy of Lisdoonvarna is infectious.

Dublin Theatre Festival (September 26 – October 13, Dublin)

A leading international festival dedicated to the dramatic arts, the Dublin Theatre Festival showcases both contemporary and classical productions. From celebrated Irish playwrights like Samuel Beckett and Brian Friel to cutting-edge new voices, the program spans large-scale performances in major venues and intimate premieres in hidden city spaces.

It's a cornerstone of Dublin's literary and theatrical identity, reflecting the capital's deep storytelling tradition and its role as a global stage for performance.

Halloween Festival at Derry~Londonderry (October 25–31, Derry)

Widely considered the best Halloween celebration in Europe, this spectacular event honors the ancient Celtic festival of Samhain. Derry's walled city becomes a fantastical playground of parades, haunted houses, immersive installations, firework displays, and costume parties. Historical reenactments, ghost tours, and mythological storytelling add a deeper cultural dimension. Visitors are swept into a week-long carnival that fuses ancient tradition with theatrical innovation, making it a must-visit for those seeking a uniquely Irish Halloween.

Wexford Festival Opera (October 17 – November 2, Wexford)

Wexford's internationally respected opera festival is known for reviving rare and often forgotten operatic gems. Set in the atmospheric coastal town, performances take place in the National Opera House and other intimate venues, creating an immersive cultural experience. In addition to its strong musical program, the festival includes lectures, art exhibitions, and late-night performances in unexpected places. It attracts connoisseurs and curious first-timers alike, thanks to its elegant yet welcoming spirit.

New Year's Festival Dublin (December 31, Dublin)

Dublin's New Year's Eve celebration is a visually stunning, high-energy event that welcomes the new year with fireworks, live music, light projections, and street parades. The city center becomes a stage for Irish and international acts, with family-friendly daytime events and late-night revelry. As the countdown begins, the River Liffey glows with color and celebration. The festival's blend of tradition, creativity, and joy makes it a magical way to ring in 2026 in the heart of Ireland.

Literature & the Irish Storytelling Tradition

Ireland's relationship with storytelling is as ancient and enduring as the land itself. From the poetic cadences of early oral tradition to the masterpieces of modern literature, Ireland has gifted the world with a profound and unique literary voice. Storytelling in Ireland is not simply entertainment—it is a deeply rooted cultural tradition that reveals the heart, humor, hardship, and heroism of the Irish people.

The Origins: Oral Tradition and Mythology

Before Ireland's tales were committed to paper, they lived in the breath of the seanchaithe—professional storytellers who served as historians, genealogists, and entertainers.

These storytellers preserved epic narratives like the Táin Bó Cúailnge (The Cattle Raid of Cooley), the Fenian Cycle, and the Mythological Cycle, which recount the feats of heroes such as Cú Chulainn, Fionn mac Cumhaill, and the mystical Tuatha Dé Danann. These stories, passed from generation to generation, reinforced tribal identity, taught moral lessons, and celebrated the landscapes of Ireland with reverent detail. The musicality of Irish speech, combined with a love for rhythm, wit, and irony, formed the foundation of a storytelling culture that thrives to this day. Even in modern times, the tradition of spinning a tale— "having the gift of the gab"—is held in high regard in every corner of the island.

The Monastic Era and the Written Word

With the arrival of Christianity in the 5th century, Ireland entered a golden age of learning. Monasteries became centers of scholarship and the custodians of both Christian doctrine and native lore. Scribes carefully recorded ancient myths, blending pagan legends with Christian theology in manuscripts such as the Book of Leinster, Book of Invasions (Lebor Gabála Érenn), and the exquisitely illustrated Book of Kells. The Irish language flourished, and even Latin texts were infused with Irish poetic sensibilities. This period also gave rise to early saints' lives and the writings of monks such as Saint Patrick, whose Confessio is both a theological document and a deeply personal narrative.

The Anglo-Irish Literary Tradition

The centuries that followed saw both the erosion and transformation of Irish storytelling traditions due to colonization, famine, and political upheaval. Yet literature remained a resilient force. In the 18th and 19th centuries, Irish writers such as Jonathan Swift and Maria Edgeworth shaped the development of the novel in the English language. The late 19th and early 20th centuries witnessed the Irish Literary Revival, a cultural reawakening that drew heavily from Gaelic mythology and folk traditions. Writers such as W.B. Yeats, Lady Augusta Gregory, and John Millington Synge reclaimed Ireland's mythic past and reimagined it for a modern audience. Their work emphasized Irish themes, voices, and landscapes, and they established institutions like the Abbey Theatre, which became a crucible for Irish drama and nationalism.

James Joyce and Modernism

Few writers have transformed literature as radically as James Joyce. His 1922 novel Ulysses redefined the boundaries of fiction, blending the ordinary with the epic in a single day in Dublin. Joyce's use of stream-of-consciousness, linguistic experimentation, and deep symbolic structure made him a towering figure in world literature. Despite its complexity, Ulysses remains a love letter to Ireland, and Dublin itself becomes a living character in the novel. Today, Bloomsday—celebrated each year on June 16—honors Joyce's legacy with public readings, performances, and costumed recreations throughout the city.

20th-Century Giants and Global Voices

Irish literature continued to flourish in the mid-20th century, with Samuel Beckett breaking new ground in existential theatre through works like Waiting for Godot. His sparse, ironic prose reflected the absurdities of modern life and earned him a Nobel Prize in Literature in 1969. Seamus Heaney, also a Nobel Laureate, brought Irish rural life to the fore with lyrical depth and political insight. His poetry, steeped in the soil and soul of Northern Ireland, addressed themes of identity, conflict, and cultural continuity with unmatched grace.

Other towering figures include Edna O'Brien, John Banville, Brian Friel, and Roddy Doyle, each capturing different aspects of Irish experience—whether rural and romantic, urban and gritty, or politically charged and introspective.

Contemporary Voices and the Living Tradition

Today, Irish literature remains as vital and diverse as ever. Authors such as Colm Tóibín, Anne Enright, Emma Donoghue, and Sally Rooney bring new perspectives on Irish identity, gender, family, and modern life. Rooney, in particular, has struck a chord globally with her minimalist, emotionally perceptive novels that explore millennial relationships against the backdrop of contemporary Dublin. Irish storytelling also thrives in festivals, spoken word performances, and community events. The Cape Clear Island International Storytelling Festival, the Yarn Storytelling Festival, and local gatherings in pubs and libraries ensure the oral tradition is passed down in vibrant form.

More Than Words: Storytelling as Irish Identity

In Ireland, storytelling bridges the ancient and the modern, the personal and the political. It celebrates the beauty of language, the power of imagination, and the resilience of a people who have endured centuries of struggle while preserving their voice. Whether on the page, the stage, or by the fireside, the Irish story remains unbroken—a thread that binds generations and continues to inspire the world.

Sports & Passion: Gaelic Games, Rugby, Football

Sport in Ireland is more than competition — it's culture, community, and identity. Whether you're standing in a packed stadium in Dublin or watching a local club on a rural pitch, Irish sports deliver unmatched energy and pride. Three games dominate the national conversation: Gaelic games, rugby, and football (soccer). Each holds a unique place in Irish hearts.

1. Gaelic Games – The Heart of Irish Sport

The Gaelic Athletic Association (GAA), founded in 1884, is the soul of Irish sport. Its games—especially hurling and Gaelic football—are distinctly Irish, played by amateurs with the dedication of professionals. These sports are not just about athletic competition; they are a living link to heritage and identity.

- **Gaelic Football** is a fast-paced hybrid of soccer and rugby, played with a round ball that can be kicked or hand-passed. Teams of 15 compete to score goals (3 points) or points over the bar (1 point). Matches are high-energy, tactical, and fiercely local.
- **Hurling**, often dubbed "the fastest field sport in the world," uses a wooden stick called a hurley and a small ball known as a sliotar. Combining speed, skill, and sheer bravery, hurling is over 3,000 years old and remains a symbol of Irish resilience.
- **Camogie** is the women's version of hurling and showcases extraordinary athleticism and finesse.
- **The All-Ireland Championships**, held each summer, are the pinnacle of the GAA calendar, culminating in epic finals at Croke Park in Dublin—an 82,300-seat stadium and sacred ground for Irish sport.
- Every parish has its GAA club, fostering talent from grassroots to greatness. These clubs are community pillars, often supporting music, language, and cultural programs alongside athletics.

2. Rugby – Pride in the Green Jersey

Irish rugby enjoys a global reputation for excellence and heart. The national team represents the entire island—the Republic of Ireland and Northern Ireland—offering a unique symbol of unity.

- **The Six Nations Championship** is the highlight of the rugby year, with Ireland competing against England, France, Wales, Scotland, and Italy. Ireland has claimed Grand Slam titles and consistently ranks among the world's top teams.
- **The Rugby World Cup** sees passionate Irish support at home and abroad. While elusive, the quarterfinals remain a high benchmark, and anticipation for future victories fuels national enthusiasm.
- **Provincial Rugby** is also fiercely supported. Ireland has four professional teams: Leinster, Munster, Ulster, and Connacht. Leinster, in particular, has become a powerhouse in European rugby.
- Legendary players like Brian O'Driscoll, Paul O'Connell, Ronan O'Gara, and, more recently, Johnny Sexton, have etched their names into rugby history, embodying both grit and grace.

3. Football (Soccer) – A Growing Passion

While traditionally overshadowed by Gaelic games and rugby, football has deep roots and a growing influence in Ireland. The country boasts a long-standing league system and a national team that has made memorable appearances on the international stage.

- **The Republic of Ireland National Team** gained fame during the late 1980s and 1990s, with standout moments including their run to the quarterfinals in the 1990 FIFA World Cup under Jack Charlton. The emotional highs of penalty shootouts and dramatic goals live vividly in the national memory.
- **The UEFA Euro 2016** tournament brought another wave of pride, with Irish fans earning accolades for their spirited and friendly presence.
- **The League of Ireland**, despite modest facilities, showcases raw local talent and loyal followings. Clubs like Shamrock Rovers, Bohemians, and Dundalk FC compete with passion and pride.
- **Irish players abroad** have long made their mark in the English Premier League and other top competitions. Roy Keane, Robbie Keane, Damien Duff, and more recently, Evan Ferguson, have flown the flag for Ireland on the global stage.

4. Community, Identity & Celebration

In Ireland, sport binds generations. It's how towns define themselves and how friendships are forged.

Children learn early what wearing their county or school colors means, and local rivalries can be as intense as national competitions. Watching a match in a rural pub or cheering from the Hill 16 terrace at Croke Park becomes more than sport—it becomes shared memory.

- **Sporting events** often coincide with local festivals and holidays, bringing people together in celebration.
- **School programs and local clubs** ensure nearly every child has access to sport, whether competitively or casually.
- **Inclusivity is growing**, with increasing support for women's teams in all disciplines and greater investment in youth and community engagement.

From the ash of a hurley to the green of a rugby jersey to the roar of a football chant, sport in Ireland is a vibrant, dynamic celebration of what it means to belong. Whether you're a lifelong fan or a curious visitor, experiencing sport in Ireland offers a profound and passionate connection to its people, past, and future.

Chapter 9: Dublin: The Heartbeat of Irish Culture

Overview of the Capital: Dublin

Dublin is Ireland's capital and largest city, located on the country's eastern coast along the River Liffey. It serves as the Republic's political, cultural, economic, and historical core. Despite its status as a capital, Dublin retains a surprisingly human scale. Its walkable streets, friendly locals, and relaxed rhythm give it the feel of a large town rather than a sprawling metropolis. The city's roots date back to the 9th century when Viking settlers established a trading post near the dark tidal pool that gave the area its name—Dubh Linn. Since then, it has evolved through Norman rule, British colonization, revolution, and independence into a vibrant, modern European city with a distinctly Irish identity.

Geography and Layout

The River Liffey divides Dublin into the Northside and Southside. While the Northside has traditionally been more working class, and the Southside more affluent, the city has undergone significant development, and both sides now offer a diverse mix of attractions and neighborhoods. Key areas include the historic Liberties, the commercial centers around Grafton Street and Henry

Street, the redeveloped Docklands, and the residential charm of places like Ranelagh and Clontarf.

Cultural Foundations

Dublin is internationally recognized for its literary legacy. Writers such as James Joyce, Samuel Beckett, W.B. Yeats, and Seamus Heaney all lived or were born in the city. The literary tradition continues through institutions like the Dublin Writers Museum and Trinity College Library, home to the Book of Kells. Dublin's role as a UNESCO City of Literature is not ceremonial—it's deeply tied to daily life. Bookstores, libraries, poetry readings, and literary festivals are deeply embedded in the city's rhythm. Music and theatre also play central roles. Traditional Irish music can be found in pubs across town, while classical performances and modern productions take place in venues like the National Concert Hall and the Abbey Theatre. Film, contemporary art, and dance have strong representation as well, especially in the Temple Bar Cultural Quarter.

Historical and Political Significance

Many of Ireland's pivotal moments unfolded in Dublin. The General Post Office (GPO) on O'Connell Street served as the headquarters for the 1916 Easter Rising. Kilmainham Gaol, now a museum, held many of the rebellion's leaders. Dublin Castle was once the center of British rule in Ireland, while today it hosts state functions. The city's political evolution is also reflected in its architecture—from medieval churches to Georgian townhouses to modern government buildings. Visitors interested in Irish identity, independence, and diaspora will find meaningful experiences at the EPIC Irish Emigration Museum, the Glasnevin Cemetery Museum, and the Jeanie Johnston famine ship.

Urban Character and Contemporary Life

Today, Dublin balances tradition with change. It's home to major tech companies and startups, particularly in the Grand Canal Dock area, which has earned the nickname "Silicon Docks." Yet traditional elements remain—family-run shops, old-school pubs, outdoor markets, and historic buildings still shape the streetscape. Food and drink have gone through a transformation. Once dominated by basic fare, Dublin's culinary landscape now includes Michelin-starred restaurants, artisan bakeries, and international cuisine alongside pub staples like fish and chips or Irish stew. Coffee culture is strong, especially in neighborhoods like Stoneybatter, Ranelagh, and Portobello.

Dubliners themselves are perhaps the city's most memorable feature. Known for their warmth, wit, and storytelling prowess, locals bring humor to everyday conversation and pride to their hometown, even as they navigate the challenges of rising costs and urban change.

Top Attractions & Historic Sites in Dublin

1. Trinity College & The Book of Kells Exhibition

Trinity College Dublin, founded in 1592, is Ireland's most prestigious university and home to the renowned Long Room library and the treasured Book of Kells. This 9th-century illuminated manuscript is one of the finest examples of medieval Christian art. Visitors are led through an informative exhibition before entering the Long Room, a stunning, wood-paneled chamber lined with over 200,000 ancient books. The experience of walking through the library is both scholarly and atmospheric, offering a tangible connection to the intellectual heart of Ireland. The college's historic cobbled campus, with its blend of Georgian and classical architecture, adds further depth to the visit.

- **Location:** College Green, Dublin 2
- **Opening Hours:** Mon–Sat: 8:30 AM–5 PM; Sun: 9:30 AM–5 PM (hours may vary by season)

- **Must Experience:** Standing beneath the barrel-vaulted ceiling of the Long Room
- **Entrance Fee:** €18 (includes Book of Kells and library access)
- **Pro Tip:** Arrive early in the morning to avoid crowds, especially in summer; book online to save time.

2. Dublin Castle

Dublin Castle has been a symbol of British rule in Ireland for over 700 years and is now used for state functions and presidential inaugurations. The site has seen everything from Viking settlements to royal banquets and modern government ceremonies. Visitors can explore the State Apartments, the Viking Excavation site, and the Chapel Royal. The blend of medieval, Georgian, and modern architecture reflects Ireland's layered history. As you walk through its lavish halls and atmospheric crypts, you get a strong sense of Dublin's political and colonial past.

- **Location:** Dame Street, Dublin 2
- **Opening Hours:** Daily: 9:45 AM–5:45 PM (last admission at 5:15 PM)
- **Must Experience:** The opulent Throne Room and the undercroft remain from the Viking settlement
- **Entrance Fee:** €8 adults; guided tours available for €12

- **Pro Tip:** Join the guided tour for full access, including restricted medieval areas not available on self-guided visits.

3. Kilmainham Gaol

A deeply moving and essential visit for anyone interested in Irish independence, Kilmainham Gaol (jail) was the holding place for many leaders of Irish rebellions, most famously the 1916 Easter Rising. The prison was operational from 1796 to 1924 and is now a museum offering guided tours through stark corridors, cells, and the execution yard. Each corner tells a somber yet important story of resistance, oppression, and the birth of the modern Irish state. The tour also contextualizes the social history of Irish incarceration and the broader fight for civil liberties.

- **Location:** Inchicore Road, Dublin 8
- **Opening Hours:** Daily: 9:30 AM–5:30 PM (guided tours only)
- **Must Experience:** Standing in the Stonebreaker's Yard, where 14 Easter Rising leaders were executed
- **Entrance Fee:** €8 adults; booking in advance is essential
- **Pro Tip:** Tours fill up fast—reserve online at least a week ahead, especially in peak seasons.

4. St. Patrick's Cathedral

Founded in 1191 and named after Ireland's patron saint, St. Patrick's Cathedral is the largest church in Ireland and a magnificent example of Gothic architecture. Its soaring nave, detailed stained glass windows, and historical monuments tell stories of faith, literature, and Irish national identity. Jonathan Swift, author of Gulliver's Travels and a former dean of the cathedral, is buried here. The cathedral also hosts choral performances and exhibitions that illuminate its 800-year legacy.

- **Location:** St. Patrick's Close, Dublin 8
- **Opening Hours:** Mon–Fri: 9:30 AM–5 PM; Sat: 9 AM–6 PM; Sun: 9 AM–10:30 AM & 12:30 PM–2:30 PM
- **Must Experience:** The grave of Jonathan Swift and the Lady Chapel
- **Entrance Fee:** €9 adults
- **Pro Tip:** Attend an evensong choral performance in the late afternoon to enjoy the acoustics and spiritual ambiance.

5. The Guinness Storehouse

More than just a brewery, the Guinness Storehouse is one of Ireland's most popular attractions, telling the story of Ireland's most iconic beer. Spread over seven floors inside a converted fermentation plant, the interactive experience walks visitors through the brewing process, branding, global impact, and heritage of Guinness. The tour culminates in the Gravity Bar, offering a panoramic view of Dublin while sipping a pint of the black stuff. The entire presentation is sleek, immersive, and proudly Irish.

- **Location:** St. James's Gate, Dublin 8
- **Opening Hours:** Daily: 9:30 AM–7 PM (last admission 5 PM); extended hours in summer
- **Must Experience:** Pour your pint or enjoy one in the Gravity Bar overlooking the city
- **Entrance Fee:** From €26 online
- **Pro Tip:** Book online for the best price and earliest access—try to go midweek to avoid peak crowds.

6. Christ Church Cathedral

Christ Church Cathedral, founded circa 1030, is the oldest of Dublin's two medieval cathedrals and a stunning fusion of Romanesque and Gothic styles. Inside, vaulted ceilings and historical tombs set the scene for centuries of religious and political history. The cathedral's crypt, one of the largest in Britain and Ireland, houses a fascinating collection of artifacts, including a mummified cat and rat famously trapped inside an organ pipe. The cathedral also played a central role in the Anglo-Norman period and remains an active place of worship.

- **Location:** Christchurch Place, Dublin 8
- **Opening Hours:** Mon–Sat: 9:30 AM–6 PM; Sun: 12:30 PM–2:30 PM
- **Must Experience:** The medieval crypt and the 12th-century stonework
- **Entrance Fee:** €10 adults
- **Pro Tip:** Attend a sung service or organ concert if you enjoy sacred music—the acoustics are phenomenal.

7. EPIC The Irish Emigration Museum

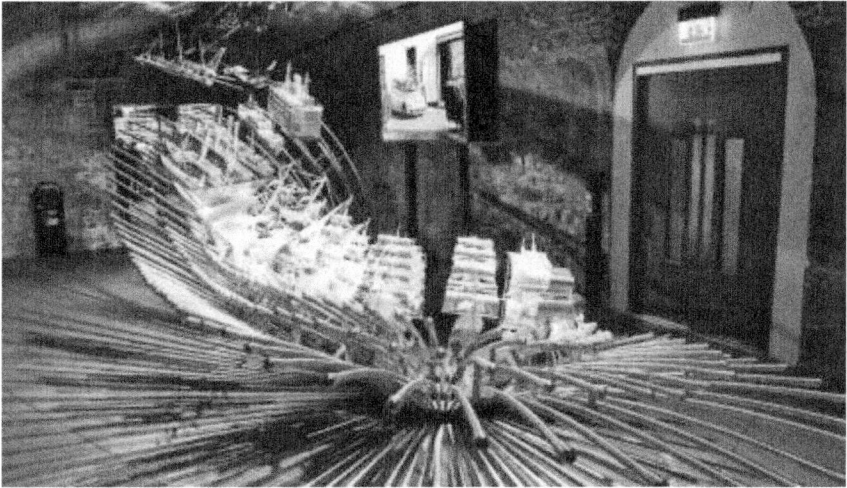

EPIC is an immersive, interactive museum that tells the story of Irish emigration across centuries. Housed in the historic CHQ Building on the River Liffey, this digital museum doesn't rely on artifacts, but on cutting-edge technology to explore the journeys of over 10 million Irish people who left the island for all corners of the globe. Through engaging galleries, visitors trace the global impact of Irish culture in music, politics, science, literature, and more. Rather than being a passive museum experience, EPIC is fully engaging, perfect for all ages, and ideal for those seeking a deeper understanding of Irish identity worldwide.

- **Location:** CHQ Building, Custom House Quay, Dublin 1
- **Opening Hours:** Daily: 10 AM–6:45 PM (last entry at 5 PM)
- **Must Experience:** The "Leaving Home" gallery, simulating a dark ship's hold
- **Entrance Fee:** €19.50 adults
- **Pro Tip:** Pair your visit with the Irish Family History Centre next door if you're researching your ancestry.

8. Glasnevin Cemetery & Museum

Glasnevin Cemetery is Ireland's national cemetery and final resting place of over 1.5 million people, including key figures in the country's turbulent path to independence. Established in 1832, it is both a moving historical site and a beautifully landscaped park filled with impressive monuments. Guided tours reveal gripping stories of figures like Michael Collins, Daniel O'Connell, Éamon de Valera, and Constance Markievicz. The adjacent museum offers interactive displays that delve into Irish funerary customs, politics, and social change. The cemetery's peaceful grandeur offers a solemn yet fascinating look into Ireland's soul.

- **Location:** Finglas Road, Dublin 11
- **Opening Hours:** Daily: 10 AM–5 PM
- **Must Experience:** The Tower over Daniel O'Connell's crypt, offering views and history
- **Entrance Fee:** Cemetery grounds free; museum and tour €14 adults
- **Pro Tip:** Join the General History Tour for the most powerful and complete overview of Ireland's revolutionary history.

9. The Little Museum of Dublin

Tucked into a Georgian townhouse on St. Stephen's Green, this delightful museum offers an intimate and often humorous portrait of Dublin from 1900 to the present. What sets it apart is its focus on ordinary citizens and everyday life. From JFK's visit and U2's rise to quirky advertisements and household relics, the museum is packed with charm. Guided tours, led by witty and knowledgeable locals, make the experience feel more like a conversation than a lecture. It's a perfect introduction to Dublin's heart and wit.

- **Location:** 15 St. Stephen's Green, Dublin 2
- **Opening Hours:** Daily: 9 AM–5 PM
- **Must Experience:** The "U2 Room" chronicling the band's global journey from Dublin streets
- **Entrance Fee:** €15 adults (includes guided tour)
- **Pro Tip:** Entry is free with the Dublin Pass, and booking is strongly recommended due to the museum's small size.

10. National Museum of Ireland – Archaeology

Step into the world of Ireland's ancient past at this treasure trove of archaeological wonders. Located on Kildare Street, this museum is part of Ireland's national museum system and is free to enter.

The exhibits span from the Stone Age through the Celts and Vikings, but the most extraordinary are the eerily preserved "bog bodies"—Iron Age individuals whose remains were naturally mummified in peat bogs. Other highlights include the stunning gold artifacts of prehistoric Ireland and intricately designed Celtic metalwork. It's an awe-inspiring and sometimes haunting journey into early Irish civilization.

- **Location:** Kildare Street, Dublin 2
- **Opening Hours:** Tue–Sat: 10 AM–5 PM; Sun–Mon: 1 PM–5 PM
- **Must Experience:** The "Kingship and Sacrifice" exhibit featuring the bog bodies
- **Entrance Fee:** Free
- **Pro Tip:** Visit early to enjoy the quiet atmosphere and spend time studying the exquisite Tara Brooch and Ardagh Chalice.

Best Areas and Neighborhoods to Stay

1. Temple Bar – For Nightlife & Culture Enthusiasts

Temple Bar is Dublin's cultural quarter and arguably the city's most iconic neighborhood. Known for its cobbled streets, vibrant pubs, and artistic flair, this area thrives with energy day and night. While some parts may be touristy and noisy, it offers unmatched proximity to Dublin's nightlife, live music venues, galleries, and riverside charm. Staying here puts you within walking distance of many top attractions, including Dublin Castle and the Ha'penny Bridge.

Best For: Night owls, solo travelers, culture lovers

Accommodation Options

- **The Morgan Hotel** – Chic and modern with a boutique vibe; stylish rooms and a cocktail bar
- **Temple Bar Inn** – Mid-range hotel with contemporary design and excellent soundproofing
- **Abigail's Hostel** – Budget-friendly and clean with a social, youthful vibe and river views

2. St. Stephen's Green & Grafton Street – For Elegant Comfort & Shopping

A refined and leafy area known for its Georgian architecture, upscale shops, and proximity to the peaceful expanse of St. Stephen's Green.

Grafton Street is Dublin's premier shopping boulevard, with boutiques, street performers, and elegant cafés. This neighborhood is perfect for travelers who want a central location without the chaotic nightlife of Temple Bar.

Best For: Couples, first-time visitors, upscale leisure travelers

Accommodation Options

- **The Shelbourne, Autograph Collection** – Dublin's historic luxury hotel with old-world charm and park views
- **The Fitzwilliam Hotel** – Modern luxury with stylish interiors and doors opening right onto St. Stephen's Green
- **Travelodge Dublin City Centre** – A more affordable, clean, and central option with minimalist comfort

3. Ballsbridge – For Peace, Affluence & Local Life

Located just south of the city center, Ballsbridge is a leafy, embassy-lined neighborhood known for its quiet streets, elegant homes, and relaxed atmosphere. It's ideal for those seeking a slower pace while still being within easy reach of central Dublin. Home to the RDS, Aviva Stadium, and excellent dining, it's popular with business travelers and families alike.

Best For: Families, business travelers, repeat visitors

Accommodation Options

- **InterContinental Dublin** – A five-star experience with lush gardens and spa facilities
- **Herbert Park Hotel** – Comfortable and well-situated near the park and local cafés
- **Pembroke Townhouse** – A charming Georgian guesthouse with personality and boutique touches

4. Docklands (Grand Canal Square & IFSC) – For Modern Luxury & Business

Dublin's Docklands have undergone a sleek transformation, now home to tech headquarters, contemporary architecture, and modern art spaces. Grand Canal Dock, often dubbed "Silicon Docks," is lively with waterfront restaurants and theatres like the Bord Gáis Energy Theatre. The IFSC area is more corporate, ideal for business travelers.

Best For: Business trips, modern aesthetics, urban explorers

Accommodation Options

- **The Marker Hotel** – Stylish, modern, with a rooftop bar offering stunning city views
- **The Spencer Hotel** – Sleek rooms, a spa, and easy access to the Convention Centre
- **The Mayson** – Boutique flair meets industrial design near the riverfront

5. Smithfield & Stoneybatter – For Artsy Vibes & Local Living

Just west of the city center, these neighboring districts are emerging as Dublin's hipster haven. Smithfield features large open plazas, independent cinemas, and the Jameson Distillery, while Stoneybatter is a tight-knit, quirky community with vintage shops, gastropubs, and brunch spots. It's a great area for those who want to experience Dublin like a local.

Best For: Creative travelers, foodies, independent spirits

Accommodation Options

- **Generator Dublin** – Trendy hostel in the heart of Smithfield with private room options
- **The Hendrick Smithfield** – Ireland's first "street art hotel" with compact, stylish rooms
- **Staycity Aparthotels Dublin City Centre** – Spacious, modern apartments with kitchenettes for longer stays

6. Rathmines & Ranelagh – For Laid-Back Vibes & Extended Stays

South of the Grand Canal, these residential areas blend Victorian charm with an active café culture and buzzing nightlife in a more relaxed, suburban setting. Ranelagh, in particular, is loved for its wine bars and gourmet dining scene. Rathmines has a youthful vibe thanks to its student population and indie cinema scene.

Best For: Digital nomads, long-stay visitors, casual urban explorers

Accommodation Options

- **Uppercross House Hotel (Rathmines)** – Welcoming, classic hotel in the heart of the village
- **Donnybrook Hall (near Ranelagh)** – Family-run guesthouse with homely comfort and excellent hospitality
- **Premier Suites Plus Dublin Leeson Street** – Upscale serviced apartments ideal for extended stays

7. Drumcondra – For Budget-Friendly Comfort & Local Charm

Located north of the River Liffey and close to Croke Park stadium, Drumcondra offers excellent transport connections and a quieter, local experience. It's popular among budget travelers and sports fans, with easy access to the airport and city center.

Best For: Budget-conscious travelers, sports enthusiasts, authentic Dublin experience

Accommodation Options

- **The Croke Park Hotel** – Modern, comfortable, and just across from the stadium
- **Egans Guest House** – Cozy B&B with classic Irish hospitality
- **Ashling House B&B** – Affordable, simple, and friendly with quick bus links to the center

Best Pubs, Live Music & Nightlife Scene

1. The Cobblestone – For Traditional Irish Music Aficionados

The Cobblestone is one of Dublin's most authentic venues for traditional Irish music. Tucked into the historic Smithfield district, this pub has a lived-in charm and places music front and center. Every night, skilled musicians gather for informal, impromptu sessions featuring fiddles, bodhráns, and uilleann pipes. The back room hosts gigs, storytelling, and poetry evenings, offering a cultural depth rarely found in a nightlife venue.

- **Location:** 77 King Street North, Smithfield, Dublin 7
- **Opening Hours:** Mon–Thu: 4 PM–11:30 PM, Fri: 3 PM–12:30 AM, Sat: 1 PM–12:30 AM, Sun: 1 PM–11 PM

- **Must Experience:** Unamplified, organic trad sessions where locals and musicians mingle freely
- **Pro Tip:** Arrive early — seats fill up fast, especially on weekends.

2. Whelan's – Iconic Live Music Venue

A legendary name in Dublin's live music scene, Whelan's has hosted everyone from Ed Sheeran and Arctic Monkeys to Irish folk heroes. This multi-room venue includes an intimate main stage, a bar area with vintage vibes, and smaller side rooms for rising acts and DJ nights. Its warm wood interiors and community feel make it a beloved spot for locals and travelers alike.

- **Location:** 25 Wexford Street, Portobello, Dublin 2
- **Opening Hours:** Daily: 5 PM–late
- **Must Experience:** Live indie or folk set with a pint in hand, standing shoulder-to-shoulder with true music lovers
- **Pro Tip:** Check the gig calendar online and book tickets in advance for major acts.

3. The Long Hall – Victorian Charm Meets Pints of Perfection

Stepping into The Long Hall is like stepping into a perfectly preserved 19th-century pub, complete with red velvet seats, ornate mirrors, and old-world elegance. While it doesn't offer live music, its atmosphere is pure Dublin soul. The Guinness pours are expertly crafted, the conversation is genuine, and the experience is timeless.

- **Location:** 51 South Great George's Street, Dublin 2
- **Opening Hours:** Mon–Thu: 12:30 PM–11:30 PM, Fri–Sat: 12:30 PM–12:30 AM, Sun: 12:30 PM–11 PM
- **Must Experience:** Order a pint, grab a snug seat, and watch the rhythm of Dublin life pass by
- **Pro Tip:** Visit during daylight to fully appreciate the preserved interior details.

4. The Palace Bar – Literary Spirits & Classic Pints

One of the few authentic pubs within the Temple Bar area, The Palace Bar dates back to 1823 and has long been a favorite of Irish journalists, writers, and poets. Its upstairs whiskey bar is a sanctuary for connoisseurs, and its old-school charm contrasts sharply with the tourist bustle outside.

- **Location:** 21 Fleet Street, Temple Bar, Dublin 2
- **Opening Hours:** Mon–Thu: 10:30 AM–11:30 PM, Fri–Sat: 10:30 AM–12:30 AM, Sun: 12:30 PM–11 PM
- **Must Experience:** Sampling a fine Irish whiskey in the upstairs snug
- **Pro Tip:** Ask the barman for recommendations from their rare whiskey selection — many aren't on the printed menu.

5. O'Donoghue's – Heartbeat of Irish Folk Music

O'Donoghue's is synonymous with traditional Irish folk, having launched the careers of iconic groups like The Dubliners. Still today, you'll find nightly music in the front bar where the session often spills out onto the footpath. The pub's historic black-and-white photos, dark wood interiors, and passion for live music create a moving, truly Irish atmosphere.

- **Location:** 15 Merrion Row, Dublin 2
- **Opening Hours:** Daily: 10:30 AM–late
- **Must Experience:** Singing along to "The Wild Rover" shoulder-to-shoulder with locals
- **Pro Tip:** Weeknights can be just as lively as weekends, and easier to find a seat.

6. The Workman's Club – Hip & Eclectic Nights Out

A favorite among Dublin's young and creative crowd, The Workman's Club is a multi-level venue offering indie, electronic, alt-pop, and acoustic gigs across its many rooms. It also hosts spoken word events, open-mic nights, and club nights. The rooftop terrace has fantastic river views and a laid-back bar feel.

- **Location:** 10 Wellington Quay, Dublin 2
- **Opening Hours:** Mon–Thu: 5 PM–2:30 AM, Fri–Sat: 3 PM–2:30 AM, Sun: 3 PM–1:30 AM
- **Must Experience:** A DJ set or live gig followed by rooftop drinks with new friends
- **Pro Tip:** Keep an eye out for surprise acts and pop-up parties announced last-minute on their socials.

7. The Brazen Head – Ireland's Oldest Pub

Dating back to 1198, The Brazen Head is an atmospheric pub steeped in history and folklore. While it's certainly on the tourist map, it still retains its character, serving hearty meals, local ales, and nightly traditional Irish music in its dark-wood, candle-lit setting. A great place to absorb storytelling and history along with a Guinness.

- **Location:** 20 Lower Bridge Street, Dublin 8
- **Opening Hours:** Daily: 12 PM–11:30 PM
- **Must Experience:** Evening storytelling and song in the courtyard or main room
- **Pro Tip:** Make a dinner reservation if you plan to visit around 7–8 PM — it's often full.

8. The Bernard Shaw – Creative Vibes & Open-Air Nights

The Bernard Shaw blends pub culture with street art, food markets, and community spirit. After relocating from South Richmond Street, its new home by the Royal Canal continues the tradition of live DJs, spoken word, art installations, and one of the most creative atmospheres in the city. The large yard and Big Blue Bus (serving pizzas) create a mini-festival feel year-round.

- **Location:** Cross Guns Bridge, Drumcondra, Dublin 9
- **Opening Hours:** Mon–Thu: 12 PM–11 PM, Fri–Sat: 12 PM–12:30 AM, Sun: 12 PM–11 PM
- **Must Experience:** Evening DJ sets and alfresco drinks in the yard
- **Pro Tip:** It's dog-friendly, eclectic, and one of the best Sunday hangout spots in the city.

Shopping Districts & Markets

Grafton Street – Dublin's Premier Pedestrian Shopping Boulevard

Grafton Street stands at the heart of Dublin's upscale shopping scene. With its polished red-brick pavements and elegant Victorian facades, this famous thoroughfare is a delight for both seasoned shoppers and casual strollers. Home to prestigious Irish department store Brown Thomas—stocking luxury fashion labels like Chanel, Louis Vuitton, and Hermès—Grafton Street is also lined with flagship boutiques from international brands like Ted Baker, Massimo Dutti, and

& Other Stories. Street performers, florists, and live musicians add an electric yet charming atmosphere.

- **Location:** Dublin 2, stretching from Trinity College to St. Stephen's Green
- **Opening Hours:** Most shops open Mon–Sat: 9 AM–7 PM, Sun: 11 AM–6 PM
- **Must Visit:** Brown Thomas, for curated designer collections and Irish fashion icons
- **Pro Tip:** Visit early on weekday mornings to enjoy peaceful browsing before the crowds arrive.

Powerscourt Centre – Georgian Elegance with Independent Charm

A hidden architectural gem just off Grafton Street, Powerscourt Centre is a boutique shopping destination housed within an 18th-century Georgian townhouse. Inside, cascading wrought-iron staircases and sun-drenched atriums lead to a variety of artisan stores and designer showrooms. You'll find unique Irish jewelry, sustainable fashion, antiques, art galleries, and hand-crafted home goods. It also hosts cafés and wine bars tucked beneath vaulted stone ceilings.

- **Location:** 59 South William Street, Dublin 2
- **Opening Hours:** Mon–Sat: 10 AM–6 PM, Sun: 12 PM–6 PM
- **Must Visit:** Article, for Irish design-forward home décor and lifestyle goods
- **Pro Tip:** Don't miss the rooftop garden and courtyard cafés for a serene shopping break.

Henry Street – Bustling High Street Shopping in the Northside Core

Henry Street is the heart of mainstream high street shopping in Dublin's Northside. It's home to local fashion staples like Arnotts (Ireland's oldest department store), alongside familiar global retailers like Zara, Penneys (Primark), and River Island. The street pulses with foot traffic, street vendors, musicians, and buskers, making it ideal for shoppers who thrive in lively environments. Arnotts offers everything from luxury skincare and accessories to furniture and fine food halls.

- **Location:** Dublin 1, between O'Connell Street and Jervis Street
- **Opening Hours:** Mon–Sat: 9 AM–7 PM, Sun: 11 AM–6 PM
- **Must Visit:** Arnotts for its mix of designer labels, Irish brands, and curated giftware

- **Pro Tip:** Visit on weekday mornings for fewer crowds, and consider Jervis Shopping Centre nearby for even more variety.

George's Street Arcade – Vintage, Vinyl, & Local Designers

This red-brick Victorian indoor market, dating back to 1881, is a blend of bohemian flair, indie design, and retro treasures. At George's Street Arcade, you'll find a vibrant mix of stalls and small shops selling everything from vintage clothes and handmade jewelry to rare vinyl records, books, and tarot cards. It's the perfect place to pick up gifts, curiosities, and quirky fashion pieces.

- **Location:** South Great George's Street, Dublin 2
- **Opening Hours:** Mon–Sat: 9:30 AM–6 PM, Sun: 12 PM–6 PM
- **Must Visit:** Lucy's Lounge, for eclectic vintage wear and second-hand finds
- **Pro Tip:** Grab a coffee and people-watch in the arcade's central atrium — it's as much a social hub as a shopping space.

Temple Bar Food & Book Markets – Culture Meets Commerce

Temple Bar isn't just for nightlife—it hosts vibrant cultural markets that reflect Dublin's artisanal spirit. On Saturdays, the Food Market fills Meeting House Square with stalls offering Irish cheeses, organic produce, artisanal breads, chutneys, and global street food. On certain Sundays, the space transforms into a haven for rare books, records, retro fashion, and vintage prints. It's a mecca for the curious collector or gourmet grazer.

- **Location:** Meeting House Square, Temple Bar, Dublin 2
- **Opening Hours:** Sat: 10 AM–4:30 PM (food), select Sun: 11 AM–5 PM (books & vintage)
- **Must Visit:** McNally Family Farm's produce stall and Blazing Salads for vegetarian bites
- **Pro Tip:** Arrive around 11 AM for the freshest options and the best brunch atmosphere.

Moore Street Market – Traditional Dublin Market Life

A slice of old Dublin with deep historical roots, Moore Street has long been home to a working-class market culture. Fruit and vegetable vendors line the pavement, selling seasonal produce with an unmistakably Dublin flair. You'll hear thick local accents, witness bartering traditions, and get a genuine taste of community life.

The side streets are dotted with multicultural grocers, halal butchers, and Afro-Caribbean and Eastern European specialty shops, making it a hub of global flavors and local tradition.

- **Location:** Parallel to Henry Street, Dublin 1
- **Opening Hours:** Mon–Sat: 9 AM–6 PM
- **Must Visit:** Bang Bang Asian Supermarket and nearby bakeries for an international twist
- **Pro Tip:** Carry cash and bring your bargaining spirit—many vendors offer better deals with a bit of charm.

Creative Quarter – Dublin's Trendiest Indie Scene

The Creative Quarter is Dublin's epicenter for boutique fashion, local design, artisan crafts, and forward-thinking lifestyle concepts. Independent Irish designers like Helen Steele and Om Diva thrive here, along with stores specializing in handmade leather goods, minimalist jewelry, curated vintage collections, and artful stationery. It's where design-savvy shoppers go for items you won't find anywhere else. Chic coffee shops, concept stores, and craft cocktail lounges give the neighborhood a distinctly modern edge.

- **Location:** Centered around South William Street, Drury Street, and Exchequer Street, Dublin 2
- **Opening Hours:** Varies by shop, typically 10 AM–6 PM
- **Must Visit:** Irish Design Shop and Om Diva for emerging Irish fashion
- **Pro Tip:** Combine your shopping spree with brunch or cocktails at nearby hangouts like Peruke & Periwig or Kaph Café.

Dublin's Food Scene & Where to Eat

Dublin's Culinary Landscape: A Rich Mix of Old & New

Dublin has transformed from a city of humble stews and pub grub into one of Europe's most exciting food destinations. While the deep roots of traditional Irish cooking remain, today's Dublin thrives with international flavors, creative chefs, and a renewed emphasis on fresh, local ingredients. Whether you're looking for a cozy pub meal, an avant-garde tasting menu, or global street food, Dublin serves it all with flair and friendliness. From Michelin-starred restaurants to casual neighborhood bistros, from fresh farmers markets to smoky gastropubs, there's a seat and a plate for every appetite and budget.

Traditional Irish Fare: Hearty, Local, Soulful

To understand Dublin through food, start with its traditional cuisine. Irish stews simmered with lamb and potatoes, crisp battered fish with hand-cut chips, and boxty (a type of potato pancake) are staples still served with pride. Look for dishes like coddle (a Dublin favorite with sausages, bacon, and onion), colcannon (mashed potatoes with kale), and soda bread slathered with creamy Kerrygold butter. Many pubs and heritage restaurants offer modern twists, using seasonal ingredients and creative presentations.

Top Picks for Traditional Irish Cuisine:

- **The Woollen Mills (Ormond Quay)** – Iconic dishes with a view of the Ha'penny Bridge
- **The Brazen Head (Usher's Quay)** – Dublin's oldest pub with historic charm and stews worth traveling for
- **Gallagher's Boxty House (Temple Bar)** – A shrine to the Irish boxty and potato culture

Fine Dining & Michelin Stars

Dublin is home to several Michelin-starred restaurants and fine dining venues that showcase Ireland's gourmet evolution. Expect intricate tasting menus, hyper-local sourcing, and wine lists curated with international sophistication.

- **Unmissable Fine Dining Destinations:**
- **Chapter One by Mickael Viljanen (Parnell Square)** – Two Michelin stars, modern Irish cuisine in a stylish Georgian setting
- **Liath (Blackrock Market)** – Inventive dishes and artistic plating in an intimate 22-seat space
- **Patrick Guilbaud (Merrion Street)** – Dublin's grand dame of French-influenced haute cuisine, with two Michelin stars and timeless elegance

Booking is essential, and many tasting menus run between €120–€250 per person.

Contemporary Casual & New Irish Cuisine

Not all high-caliber food comes with a white tablecloth. A new wave of casual eateries and chef-led bistros is driving Dublin's culinary revival, offering innovative Irish dishes without the formality.

Expect sourdough everything, fermented flavors, charcuterie, and seafood platters served in airy, design-forward spaces.

Beloved Modern Spots:

- **Forest Avenue (Sussex Terrace)** – Bright, Nordic-inspired bistro with seasonal Irish ingredients
- **Etto (Merrion Row)** – Small plates with big flavor and one of the best wine lists in the city
- **Host (Ranelagh)** – Minimalist interiors, wood-fired dishes, and impeccable cooking without fuss

Global Flavors & Culinary Diversity

Dublin's international dining scene has flourished over the past decade, thanks to its multicultural population and growing demand for global cuisines. Whether you're after ramen, tacos, Korean barbecue, or Palestinian street food, you'll find authenticity and flair.

Global Gems in the City:

- **Masa (Drury Street)** – Inventive tacos and mezcal cocktails with a cool interior vibe
- **Shouk (Drumcondra)** – Middle Eastern flavors bursting from open pitas and sharing plates
- **Big Fan Bao (Aungier Street)** – Modern Chinese small plates, bao buns, and clever cocktails
- **Kimchi Hophouse (Parnell Street)** – Korean staples in a casual pub-meets-BBQ setup

Cafés, Brunch, & Bakeries

Coffee culture is booming, and Dubliners take their flat whites seriously. You'll find third-wave cafés, minimalist bakeries, and brunch spots offering everything from sourdough waffles to mushroom lattes.

Don't Miss:

- **Two Boys Brew (Phibsborough)** – One of the city's most beloved brunch destinations

- **Bread 41 (Pearse Street)** – Organic bakery with cult-status pastries and grain-forward brunch dishes
- **Network (Aungier Street)** – Sleek interiors and specialty coffee with creative small plates

Pub Grub & Gastropubs

The line between pubs and restaurants continues to blur in Dublin, thanks to a surge in gastropubs that take their food seriously. Expect local ingredients, generous portions, and menus that go far beyond the usual pies and chips.

Exceptional Gastropubs:

- **The Old Spot (Bath Avenue)** – Refined pub fare with steaks, oysters, and Sunday roasts
- **The Legal Eagle (Chancery Place)** – Nose-to-tail dishes, craft beers, and creative sides in a cozy space
- **L. Mulligan Grocer (Stoneybatter)** – An ever-changing Irish menu with incredible craft beer pairings

Food Markets & Street Eats

Markets are an essential part of Dublin's food ecosystem, offering everything from artisan cheese and fresh oysters to ethnic street food and baked goods. Whether you're picnicking in a park or looking for lunch on the go, the city's markets are full of local flavor.

Market Highlights:

- **Dublin Food Co-op (Kilmainham)** – Organic produce, eco-conscious snacks, and vegan treats
- **Temple Bar Food Market (Saturdays)** – A compact but essential showcase of Irish farm-to-table offerings
- **Eatyard (Drumcondra)** – Trendy shipping container market with rotating food trucks, DJs, and craft beer stalls

Vegetarian & Vegan Scene

Dublin's plant-based options are no longer just an afterthought. Many restaurants offer creative vegetarian and vegan dishes, and several are fully meat-free.

Top Spots for Plant-Based Dining:

- **Cornucopia (Wicklow Street)** – Dublin's original vegetarian restaurant with a cult following
- **Veginity (Parnell Street)** – Globally inspired vegan dishes with flair and zero compromise on flavor
- **Sova Vegan Butcher (Camden Street)** – Hearty, indulgent plates that satisfy meat-lovers and vegans alike

Day Trips from Dublin

1. Howth: Seaside Village & Coastal Cliff Walks

Just a 30-minute DART ride from Dublin, Howth is a picturesque fishing village on a rugged peninsula that offers a perfect blend of seafood, history, and nature. The highlight is the Howth Cliff Walk, a loop trail that skirts the dramatic coastline with panoramic views of the Irish Sea and Baily Lighthouse. Wander through the harbor, explore Howth Castle, and feast on freshly caught seafood at local favorites like Aqua or Octopussy's Tapas.

Must Experience: Cliff walk at golden hour, followed by a harborfront seafood dinner.

Getting There: DART from Dublin city center, approx. 30 minutes.

Pro Tip: Visit early on weekends to avoid crowds, especially in spring and summer.

2. Glendalough & Wicklow Mountains National Park

Set in the "Garden of Ireland," Glendalough is a magical glacial valley known for its early medieval monastic settlement, serene lakes, and forested trails. It is located in Wicklow Mountains National Park and makes for a soul-refreshing escape just 1.5 hours from Dublin. Hike the Spinc trail for views over Upper Lake or walk the quiet wooded paths by the Round Tower and ancient ruins.

Must Experience: A hike through the Upper Lake trail in the early morning mist.

Getting There: Car or guided day tour; Bus Éireann also serves the area.

Pro Tip: Dress in layers; Wicklow weather shifts quickly even in summer.

3. Kilkenny: Medieval Charm & Castle Beauty

A compact, walkable city with cobbled lanes, Kilkenny is famous for its striking castle, well-preserved medieval core, and vibrant artisan scene. The 12th-century Kilkenny Castle is the star, but don't miss St. Canice's Cathedral and the climbable Round Tower. Explore local craft studios along the Medieval Mile and enjoy a pint at Kyteler's Inn, dating back to 1324.

Must Experience: Touring Kilkenny Castle, followed by lunch at Zuni or Petronella.

Getting There: Irish Rail from Heuston Station, approx. 1.5 hours.

Pro Tip: Combine the trip with the Smithwick's Experience Brewery Tour for a cultural twist.

4. Newgrange & the Boyne Valley

Step back over 5,000 years at Newgrange, one of the world's oldest prehistoric monuments—older than Stonehenge and the pyramids of Giza. This UNESCO World Heritage site is a masterpiece of Neolithic engineering, aligned with the winter solstice sunrise. Nearby attractions include the Hill of Tara, ancient seat of the High Kings of Ireland, and the battlefields of the Boyne.

Must Experience: Entering the narrow stone passage of Newgrange and witnessing the simulated solstice light.

Getting There: Car or guided tour; not easily accessible by public transport.

Pro Tip: Book tickets in advance through Brú na Bóinne Visitor Centre—walk-ins often miss out.

5. Belfast & the Titanic Quarter

A journey north to Belfast is a deep dive into history, innovation, and post-conflict renewal. Visit the world-renowned Titanic Belfast museum, walk through the politically-charged murals of the Falls and Shankill Roads, or admire the grandeur of City Hall. The train from Dublin takes just over two hours, making this Northern Ireland capital an ambitious but doable day trip.

Must Experience: Titanic Experience and a Black Cab political tour.

Getting There: Irish Rail from Connolly Station, approx. 2.15 hours.

Pro Tip: Bring a passport or ID just in case, as Northern Ireland uses GBP.

6. Trim Castle & the River Boyne

Film buffs may recognize Trim Castle as the backdrop for Braveheart, but this massive 12th-century fortress is more than a movie set. It's one of Ireland's largest Anglo-Norman castles, and its medieval architecture is beautifully preserved. The charming town of Trim, perched along the River Boyne, is also ideal for riverside walks and slow-paced discovery.

Must Experience: A guided tour of Trim Castle's keep with panoramic town views.

Getting There: Car is best; approx. 50 minutes from Dublin.

Pro Tip: Combine with a visit to the Hill of Tara for a full Meath heritage day.

7. Rock of Cashel

A bit further afield but doable with an early start, the Rock of Cashel rises from the Tipperary landscape like a fortress of myth. This majestic limestone outcrop is crowned by medieval buildings, including a round tower, a Gothic cathedral, and Cormac's Chapel with rare frescoes. It's a place where Celtic legends, saints, and kings converge.

Must Experience: Sunset views over the golden fields from the rock's edge.

Getting There: Car (approx. 2 hours) or day tours available.

Pro Tip: Pair it with lunch and a pint in the charming town of Cashel.

8. Malahide Castle & Coastal Walks

Only 40 minutes north of Dublin, Malahide is a genteel coastal town with an impressive 800-year-old castle set in a manicured park. Tour the castle's furnished interior, stroll through botanical gardens, then walk or cycle the scenic route to Portmarnock's Velvet Strand. The town center has elegant cafés, boutiques, and seafood bistros.

Must Experience: The castle tour and walk through the private gardens.

Getting There: DART or Irish Rail, approx. 35 minutes.

Pro Tip: Stop by Avoca café in the castle grounds for a memorable brunch.

Chapter 10: Galway: The Bohemian Soul of Ireland's West Coast

Overview of Galway

Woven into Ireland's rugged western edge, Galway is more than a destination—it's a rhythm, a heartbeat, a city alive with language, lore, and the salt-swept voice of the Atlantic. From ancient stone to modern stage, Galway wears its contradictions with grace: youthful yet historic, energetic yet laid-back, grounded yet imaginative.

A City Shaped by Water and Word

Galway's soul is tethered to the sea. The River Corrib flows fast and clear through the city's heart, meeting Galway Bay at the Spanish Arch—a centuries-old sentinel to the city's medieval maritime roots. In the 13th century, Galway grew into a thriving port under the stewardship of the 14 merchant families known as the "Tribes of Galway." Their legacy lingers in the names etched into buildings, the narrow lanes of the Latin Quarter, and the defiant spirit of a city that has always danced to its tune.

Cultural Core of the West

Music pours out of doorways, from fiddles and bodhráns played by musicians who seem as much a part of the cityscape as the cobblestones themselves. Galway's role as a cultural stronghold is not accidental. It sits on the edge of Ireland's largest Gaeltacht (Irish-speaking region), and Irish is spoken not as a formality but as a first language in surrounding communities. The preservation of language, tradition, and folklore is embedded in everyday life. Each year, the Galway International Arts Festival transforms the city into a kaleidoscope of color, performance, and thought-provoking expression. At the Galway Races, fashion and festivity mix with the thunder of hooves and the roar of crowds. Even in quieter months, galleries, theatres, and bookshops pulse with a quiet kind of brilliance.

Food, Flavor, and the Flow of Life

The culinary scene mirrors the landscape—coastal, earthy, and deeply rooted. Oysters pulled from the bay find their way to menus citywide. Casual markets, seafood taverns, and Michelin-recognized kitchens coexist with ease.

The Galway Market, held near St. Nicholas' Church, offers everything from fresh crab to artisan cheese and vegan tarts. Pubs aren't merely watering holes— they're storytelling venues, gathering places, homes of impromptu sessions that go long into the night.

Gateway to the Wild

Galway stands at the threshold of Ireland's most breathtaking landscapes. To the north, Connemara's mountains ripple toward the sky; to the west, the Aran Islands rise from the sea like relics of another world. Scenic drives, ferry crossings, and cliff walks radiate from the city, making it an ideal hub for nature-bound adventurers. Yet it's often the simple pleasures that define time in Galway: a stroll along the Salthill Promenade with the wind in your face, a late-night bowl of chowder in a candlelit bistro, the crackle of a peat fire beneath the strains of a ballad.

Top Attractions & Historic Sites in Galway

1. Galway Cathedral – A Fusion of Faith and Art

Galway Cathedral, officially known as the Cathedral of Our Lady Assumed into Heaven and St Nicholas, is one of the youngest stone cathedrals in Europe, completed in 1965.

Its architecture is a dramatic blend of Renaissance, Gothic, and Romanesque styles—an unusual mix that somehow works beautifully. Inside, the high stone arches, mosaic art, and stained glass windows create a reverent, awe-inspiring atmosphere. A mosaic of JFK, Ireland's beloved American president, is particularly noteworthy. The cathedral's riverside setting offers peaceful views and photo opportunities.

- **Location:** Gaol Road, Galway City
- **Opening Hours:** Daily, 8:30 AM – 6:30 PM
- **Must Experience:** Stand under the massive dome and observe the intricate mosaics
- **Entrance Fee:** Free (donations welcome)
- **Pro Tip:** Visit around noon when natural light filters through the stained glass, illuminating the interior in brilliant color.

2. Eyre Square – The City's Social and Historical Heart

Eyre Square, officially known as John F. Kennedy Memorial Park, is a central urban space that seamlessly blends history, community, and leisure. It has been a gathering place for centuries, once a bustling market square and now a vibrant hub for locals and tourists.

Modern sculptures and stonework reference Galway's past, including the Quincentennial Fountain and the Browne Doorway—a relic from a 17th-century merchant house. In summer, live music and pop-up festivals fill the park with energy and charm.

- **Location:** City Centre, Galway
- **Must Experience:** View the Browne Doorway and relax on the grassy lawns
- **Pro Tip:** Grab takeaway food from nearby cafés and enjoy a picnic with a view of the square's historical monuments.

3. Spanish Arch – A Portal to the Past

The Spanish Arch, part of Galway's medieval city wall, was built in 1584 to protect the quays and ships of the bustling port. Despite its name, the arch doesn't have Spanish origins—it was dubbed so due to Galway's robust trade with Spain during the 16th and 17th centuries. Today, it stands as one of the last visible remnants of the old wall, with a backdrop of the River Corrib and Claddagh Basin. It's a popular meeting spot and starting point for riverside walks.

- **Location:** On the River Corrib, near Galway City Museum
- **Must Experience:** Walk through the arches and explore the surrounding quayside

- **Pro Tip:** Visit in the golden hour before sunset when the light hits the river and the stone beautifully—perfect for photos.

4. Galway City Museum – Stories Through Time

This modern museum explores Galway's layered history, from its prehistoric roots to its status as a thriving medieval port and a contemporary cultural capital. The exhibits cover everything from archaeology and war to local fishing traditions, trade, and Galway's relationship with the sea. The museum's architecture incorporates sweeping glass walls that offer stunning views of the Spanish Arch and the Claddagh. It's both educational and atmospheric, ideal for visitors of all ages.

- **Location:** Spanish Parade, Galway
- **Opening Hours:** Tuesday to Saturday, 10:00 AM – 5:00 PM (closed Sundays and Mondays)
- **Must Experience:** The "Galway Hooker" maritime exhibit and panoramic windows overlooking the harbor
- **Entrance Fee:** Free
- **Pro Tip:** Combine your visit with a stroll along the Long Walk right behind the museum for one of Galway's most scenic routes.

5. Lynch's Castle – A Medieval Banking Legacy

In the middle of Galway's bustling shopping streets stands Lynch's Castle—a four-story fortified townhome dating back to the 15th century. Once the residence of one of Galway's influential "Tribes" (merchant families), this impressive limestone building now houses a modern bank. Yet its exterior retains richly carved stone windows, gargoyles, and coats of arms, offering a glimpse into the city's feudal past. Plaques and exhibits inside provide insight into Galway's power structure during the Middle Ages.

- **Location:** Shop Street, Galway
- **Opening Hours:** Monday to Friday, 9:30 AM – 4:30 PM (limited public access inside)
- **Must Experience:** Admire the façade and learn about the Lynch family legacy
- **Entrance Fee:** Free
- **Pro Tip:** If you're on a walking tour of Galway's Tribes, Lynch's Castle is a must-see stop for understanding the city's elite past.

6. The Claddagh – From Fishing Village to Symbol of Love

Just across the River Corrib lies The Claddagh, once a self-governing fishing village with its own customs and elected king. While many of the old cottages are gone, the area remains a powerful symbol of Galway's heritage, especially because of the iconic Claddagh Ring, which originated here.

The ring, featuring hands, heart, and crown, represents friendship, love, and loyalty. Stroll along the promenade or visit local shops selling traditional rings and crafts.

- **Location:** West bank of the River Corrib, adjacent to the Spanish Arch
- **Opening Hours:** Always accessible
- **Must Experience:** Walk along the Claddagh Quay and learn the ring's history in local jewelry stores
- **Entrance Fee:** Free
- **Pro Tip:** Visit in the early morning for a peaceful walk with views of Galway Bay and the distant Burren hills.

7. Galway Atlantaquaria – Discover the Ocean's Wonders

Galway Atlantaquaria, Ireland's largest native species aquarium, is a fascinating stop for those keen on marine life. Located on the scenic Salthill Promenade, it showcases the rich aquatic biodiversity of Galway Bay. Exhibits feature native species like sea anemones, starfish, and Irish marine life, offering an interactive and educational experience for families, couples, and ocean enthusiasts alike. It also has a section dedicated to Galway's coastal environment, including the preservation of local species.

- **Location:** Salthill, Galway
- **Opening Hours:** Monday to Saturday, 10:00 AM – 5:30 PM (Sunday 12:00 PM – 5:30 PM)
- **Must Experience:** The touch pool, where you can interact with sea creatures like starfish and crabs
- **Entrance Fee:** Adults €10, Children €5, Family tickets available
- **Pro Tip:** Visit early in the day to avoid crowds and enjoy the aquariums at a more relaxed pace.

8. The Galway Arts Centre – A Hub of Creativity

For art lovers, the Galway Arts Centre is a must-visit. It is a leading contemporary arts venue that hosts a range of visual arts exhibitions, performances, and community events. Located near the city center, the arts center also runs educational programs for all ages. Whether you're visiting for a gallery exhibition or a theatre production, it offers a space to appreciate both emerging and established Irish artists.

- **Location:** 47 Dominick Street, Galway
- **Opening Hours:** Tuesday to Saturday, 11:00 AM – 5:00 PM

- **Must Experience:** Visit during the Galway International Arts Festival for the best collection of performances and shows
- **Entrance Fee:** Free (most exhibitions)
- **Pro Tip:** Check the event schedule ahead of time to catch performances or talks that offer deeper insights into Irish art and culture.

9. Salthill Promenade – Scenic Views and Relaxation

Stretching along Galway Bay, the Salthill Promenade offers one of the most stunning views in the city. Ideal for a stroll or bike ride, the promenade is lined with beaches, cafés, and spectacular views of the Atlantic Ocean. It's also a popular spot for locals to swim and relax, with the iconic Blackrock Diving Tower offering a thrilling plunge into the bay for the adventurous.

- **Location:** Salthill, Galway
- **Opening Hours:** Always accessible
- **Must Experience:** Walk the full length of the promenade for panoramic views of the bay and the surrounding coastline
- **Pro Tip:** Visit at sunset for breathtaking views of the horizon as the sky changes color over the Atlantic Ocean.

10. Knockma Hill – Galway's Hidden Gem for Nature Lovers

For those seeking outdoor tranquility and panoramic views of Galway, Knockma Hill offers an escape from the city buzz. Also known as the Hill of the Fairies, Knockma Hill is steeped in Irish folklore and history, said to be the burial site of Queen Maeve of Connacht. The hill provides breathtaking views of the surrounding countryside and Galway Bay. A short hike will take you to the summit, where you can enjoy the serene natural beauty of the area.

- **Location:** Near Balla, County Galway
- **Must Experience:** Visit the ancient fairy ring at the top and take in the panoramic views of the surrounding areas
- **Pro Tip:** It's best to visit during early spring or autumn when the weather is mild and the landscape is most colorful.

Best Areas and Neighborhoods to Stay

Galway is a charming, vibrant city known for its rich history, coastal beauty, and artistic culture. When selecting where to stay in Galway, the best areas depend on your interests—whether you're looking for a lively city atmosphere, a quieter, scenic retreat, or something in between. Here's a breakdown of the best areas and neighborhoods to stay in, along with accommodation options for each.

1. Galway City Centre (Latin Quarter) – Heart of the Action

The Galway City Centre, particularly the Latin Quarter, is the city's heartbeat. This bustling district is known for its cobbled streets, vibrant pubs, traditional Irish music, and lively atmosphere. Staying here means you'll be within walking distance of some of Galway's top attractions, including Eyre Square, the Spanish Arch, and the Galway Cathedral. The Latin Quarter also offers plenty of shopping, dining, and entertainment options.

Accommodation Options:

- **Luxury:** The Dean Galway – A stylish, contemporary hotel with top-notch amenities, located in the heart of the city.
- **Mid-range:** The House Hotel – An elegant boutique hotel with a great location near the Spanish Arch.
- **Budget:** Snoozles Hostel – A popular, budget-friendly option offering both dormitory-style and private rooms.

2. Salthill – Coastal Relaxation

If you're seeking a more relaxed, coastal atmosphere with easy access to the beach, Salthill is the place to stay. Located just a short drive or a pleasant 30-minute walk from the city center, Salthill offers stunning views of Galway Bay and is famous for its long promenade and local swimming spots. It's ideal for families or those looking to unwind by the sea while still being close to the city's attractions.

Accommodation Options:

- **Luxury:** The Galway Bay Hotel – A premium hotel located right on the seafront, with excellent views and high-end facilities like a spa and leisure center.
- **Mid-range:** The Claddagh Guesthouse – A cozy, family-run guesthouse with modern amenities and a welcoming atmosphere, just a short walk from the seafront.
- **Budget:** Salthill Hostel – An affordable option that provides basic yet comfortable accommodation, perfect for backpackers and solo travelers.

3. The Claddagh – Historic Charm

The Claddagh is a historic neighborhood just across the River Corrib from the city center. Once an independent fishing village, it's now a tranquil part of Galway with a deep connection to local culture, especially thanks to its association with the Claddagh Ring. Staying here means you'll be surrounded by traditional cottages, riverside views, and the opportunity to explore Galway's heritage at a slower pace.

Accommodation Options:

- **Luxury:** The g Hotel & Spa – A luxurious, contemporary hotel offering exceptional service, located a short distance from the Claddagh and the city center.
- **Mid-range:** Claddagh Guesthouse – A quaint guesthouse offering great comfort and proximity to both the city and the tranquil Claddagh area.
- **Budget:** Galway City Hostel – A great budget option within walking distance of the Claddagh, with basic facilities and a friendly vibe.

4. Knocknacarra – Peaceful Suburb with Local Charm

For a quieter stay, Knocknacarra is a residential area on the outskirts of Galway, known for its family-friendly vibe and proximity to Barna Woods and Silverstrand Beach. This neighborhood offers a peaceful escape from the city while still being well-connected by public transport to the city center. It's ideal for nature lovers and those who want to enjoy Galway's surrounding beauty.

Accommodation Options:

- **Luxury:** Clybaun Hotel – A luxurious hotel offering excellent facilities, located in Knocknacarra with great access to beaches and parks.
- **Mid-range:** The Oranmore Lodge Hotel – Situated in the nearby village of Oranmore, this charming lodge provides a welcoming atmosphere with easy access to both nature and the city.
- **Budget:** The Corrib Village – A budget-friendly option offering self-catering accommodation with the comfort of hotel-style amenities, perfect for longer stays.

5. The West End – Artsy & Hip

The West End is a vibrant, artsy neighborhood known for its independent cafés, boutiques, and lively atmosphere. It has a youthful energy with a creative flair, making it a great spot for those interested in exploring Galway's artistic side. The West End is also a popular nightlife district with a wide selection of pubs offering traditional Irish music and contemporary beats.

Accommodation Options:

- **Luxury:** The House Hotel – A chic boutique hotel offering modern amenities and a prime location near the West End's cafes and bars.
- **Mid-range:** The Townhouse – A cozy yet stylish guesthouse offering an intimate setting with comfortable rooms and easy access to both the West End and the city center.
- **Budget:** Kinvara Guesthouse – A charming, budget-friendly guesthouse located a short distance from the West End, ideal for those who want a quiet stay close to the action.

6. Taylor's Hill – Quiet Residential Area with Green Spaces

For a more residential stay surrounded by green parks and gardens, Taylors Hill offers a peaceful atmosphere while still being relatively close to the city center. This area is ideal for those who prefer a more laid-back setting with easy access to outdoor activities like walking or cycling in nearby parks. Taylor's Hill is also home to several upscale homes and elegant streets.

Accommodation Options:

- **Luxury:** Glenlo Abbey Hotel – A luxury 5-star hotel set within a 17th-century estate, offering a beautiful location with views of Lough Atalia and a private golf course.
- **Mid-range:** Taylors Hill Guesthouse – A welcoming and homely guesthouse, offering comfortable and spacious rooms with easy access to Galway's green spaces.
- **Budget:** The Claddagh House – A budget-friendly option offering simple, comfortable rooms and a warm, friendly atmosphere.

Best Pubs, Live Music & Nightlife

Galway, known as Ireland's "Cultural Heart," delivers an electric blend of traditional Irish pubs, lively music sessions, bohemian bars, and unforgettable nights out. Unlike larger cities, Galway's nightlife feels deeply personal and unfiltered, where a cozy pub session might suddenly erupt into a communal sing-along, and every street corner seems to pulse with music. The city's compact size makes it easy to wander between venues, letting the night unfold naturally. Whether you are after a roaring trad session, a storytelling pint in a candlelit bar, or a vibrant DJ set, Galway has perfected the art of an unforgettable night.

Tigh Neachtain

Set within a historic 17th-century building on Cross Street, Tigh Neachtain embodies the soul of Galway's pub scene. Inside, a maze of snug, wood-paneled rooms and roaring fires offers the perfect backdrop for pint-sipping and conversation. Expect an ever-changing rotation of live traditional Irish music, indie folk, and even poetry nights. It's a favorite haunt for artists, musicians, and old souls seeking an authentic Galway atmosphere.

- **Location:** Cross Street Upper, Galway
- **Opening Hours:** Daily, 10:30 AM – 11:30 PM
- **Must Experience:** Settle into a snug with a Galway Hooker ale while enjoying an impromptu trad session.
- **Pro Tip:** Arrive early in the evening to secure one of the coveted nooks, especially on weekends.

The Crane Bar

Regarded as a pilgrimage site for lovers of traditional Irish music, The Crane Bar is an institution. The downstairs bar offers an intimate setting where casual sessions ignite organically among local musicians. Upstairs, a dedicated listening room hosts scheduled performances, featuring some of the finest fiddlers, pipers, and balladeers in Ireland. This is a place where storytelling and song live on in every corner.

- **Location:** 2 Sea Road, Galway
- **Opening Hours:** Daily, 5:00 PM – 12:30 AM
- **Must Experience:** Attend an upstairs trad concert for an intense and unforgettable musical immersion.

- **Pro Tip:** Bring cash for the upstairs room—small cover charges often apply for headline acts.

Taaffes Bar

Situated right on Shop Street, Taaffes Bar might seem unassuming from the outside, but step inside and you'll find nightly traditional music sessions bursting with life. Small and always packed, this pub is known for authentic, foot-stomping Irish music. Patrons crowd into every available space, pints in hand, joining in chorus to old ballads.

- **Location:** 19 Shop Street, Galway
- **Opening Hours:** Daily, 10:30 AM – 12:30 AM
- **Must Experience:** Stand shoulder-to-shoulder with locals during a lively session of jigs and reels.
- **Pro Tip:** Visit mid-week for a slightly less crowded, but equally passionate, music experience.

O'Connell's Bar

A blend of vintage charm and urban buzz, O'Connell's on Eyre Square is a historic pub with a modern twist. Once a traditional grocery-pub, it now offers an expansive beer garden with food stalls, craft beers, and DJs spinning on weekends. Inside, old-world décor preserves its heritage, with stained glass windows and vintage memorabilia telling the story of its long past.

- **Location:** 8 Eyre Square, Galway
- **Opening Hours:** Daily, 12:00 PM – Late
- **Must Experience:** Grab a gourmet burger from the outside stalls and enjoy a pint under fairy-lit skies.
- **Pro Tip:** Sundays often feature chilled live music sets in the beer garden.

Róisín Dubh

Galway's definitive live music venue, Róisín Dubh, is the place to experience everything from indie rock to comedy to late-night DJ sets. A cornerstone of the city's alternative scene, it hosts both local legends and major touring acts. The energy here is magnetic—young crowds, flowing drinks, and a feeling that anything could happen next.

- **Location:** 8 Dominick Street Upper, Galway
- **Opening Hours:** Daily, 5:00 PM – 2:00 AM
- **Must Experience:** Catch a live gig followed by an after-hours indie DJ set.
- **Pro Tip:** Check their schedule ahead; popular nights sell out fast, and pre-booking tickets is wise.

Monroe's Tavern

Combining a traditional pub atmosphere with a dynamic live music venue, Monroe's Tavern offers a little bit of everything. Downstairs is a warm, welcoming pub perfect for enjoying hearty Irish meals and a pint. Upstairs, Monroe's Live showcases an eclectic program of acts, from traditional bands to indie stars and lively ceilí dances.

- **Location:** 14 Dominick Street Upper, Galway
- **Opening Hours:** Daily, 10:30 AM – Late
- **Must Experience:** Participate in a céilí night—no dance skills required, just enthusiasm.
- **Pro Tip:** Book a table if planning dinner before a show, especially on weekends.

Tig Coili

An emblematic Galway institution, Tig Coili is a family-run pub known for its relentless dedication to live Irish music. With musicians playing twice daily, it's almost guaranteed you'll stumble into a session in full swing. The atmosphere is relaxed and spirited, with a constant ebb and flow of musicians joining in.

- **Location:** 24 Mainguard Street, Galway
- **Opening Hours:** Daily, 11:00 AM – 11:30 PM
- **Must Experience:** Join the crowd during an evening session, tapping along to reels and hearty ballads.
- **Pro Tip:** Stand near the musicians for the best energy and best acoustics.

Electric Garden & Theatre

For those seeking a vibrant late-night venue, Electric Garden offers a multi-space nightlife experience: rooftop garden parties, house beats, and retro-themed dance floors. It's a bold, creative space that feels entirely different from Galway's traditional pubs yet remains true to the city's spirit of music and revelry.

- **Location:** 36 Abbeygate Street Upper, Galway
- **Opening Hours:** Thursday to Sunday, 6:00 PM – 2:00 AM
- **Must Experience:** Dancing in the open-air rooftop garden under the Galway night sky.
- **Pro Tip:** Thursday nights often feature discounted entry and special drinks promotions.

Shopping Districts & Markets

Galway may be compact, but its shopping scene is a vibrant blend of artisan crafts, independent boutiques, vintage curiosities, and locally produced goods. Whether you're hunting for handwoven Aran knitwear, contemporary Irish design, rare books, or handmade jewelry, Galway offers a deeply satisfying retail experience rooted in its cultural heritage. The pedestrian-friendly layout of the city center makes it easy to explore at your own pace, while the laid-back atmosphere ensures that browsing never feels rushed.

Shop Street & William Street

This bustling pedestrian thoroughfare is the heart of Galway's retail scene. Stretching from Eyre Square through William Street and onto Shop Street, it's lined with a vibrant mix of international fashion outlets, traditional Irish stores, bookstores, jewelers, and street performers that add a lively soundtrack to your stroll. Heritage shops selling Claddagh rings, tweeds, and woolens sit side-by-side with boutiques and global brands like Zara and Brown Thomas. The historic buildings and cobblestone paths lend a sense of timeless charm.

Must Explore: Don't miss Thomas Dillon's Claddagh Gold, the original makers of the Claddagh ring since 1750, and McCambridge's, a gourmet food store that's a paradise for Irish culinary gifts.

Pro Tip: Visit in the morning or early evening for a quieter shopping experience and easier photo opportunities along the colorful shopfronts.

Latin Quarter

Charming and historic, the Latin Quarter combines old-world ambiance with bohemian flair. Tucked away in narrow lanes and historic stone buildings are independent shops selling handmade crafts, organic skincare products, vinyl records, and Galway-made pottery.

The emphasis here is on originality and quality, with many shopkeepers directly connected to the products they sell. This area is ideal for finding unique souvenirs that reflect the creative soul of the city.

Must Explore: Step into Twice as Nice for vintage fashion treasures or Cloon Keen for artisan perfumery inspired by the Irish landscape. The Galway Woollen Market offers authentic Aran sweaters and tweeds.

Pro Tip: Spend time chatting with the shop owners; many are artists, weavers, or designers themselves and love to share the stories behind their goods.

Galway Market (Church Lane)

Set against the backdrop of St. Nicholas' Collegiate Church, this open-air weekend market is one of Galway's most beloved traditions. Vibrant, eclectic, and packed with character, it's a treasure trove of locally made crafts, artisanal foods, handmade soaps, organic produce, jewelry, and street food. You'll find everything from carved wood bowls and stained-glass pieces to second-hand books and Japanese dumplings. The atmosphere is unhurried and creative, often accompanied by street musicians and storytellers.

Opening Days: Saturdays and Sundays, with extended stalls during festivals and holidays.

Must Explore: Sample goat cheese from local producers, grab a steaming falafel wrap, and browse handcrafted Celtic-inspired jewelry from regional artisans.

Pro Tip: Arrive by late morning for the widest selection of goods and to enjoy the freshest produce and food offerings before they sell out.

Eyre Square Centre

Located just off Eyre Square, this indoor shopping mall offers convenience and variety under one roof. With over 70 shops ranging from fashion and beauty to tech and lifestyle, it's ideal for a quick retail fix, especially on rainy days. The center also connects directly to Galway's train and bus stations, making it a good spot for last-minute gifts or travel essentials. Though more mainstream in style, it balances Irish chains with international labels.

Must Explore: Browse Born Clothing for Irish-designed pieces or stop by Art & Hobby for creative souvenirs and gifts.

Pro Tip: Keep an eye out for seasonal pop-up stalls during the holidays or festivals offering handcrafted goods and local art.

Middle Street & Abbeygate Street

A quieter alternative to Shop Street, these parallel streets are home to niche boutiques and specialty stores that reward the curious shopper. You'll find bookstores, vintage clothing shops, local galleries, and gift stores that lean toward the quirky and eclectic. This is also where many small cafés and bakeries are tucked between storefronts, making it a lovely area to shop and relax.

Must Explore: Discover hidden literary gems at Charlie Byrne's Bookshop, Galway's beloved independent bookstore, or browse ethical Irish fashion and accessories at Public Romance.

Pro Tip: Take your time to explore the courtyards and hidden lanes branching off these streets—they often lead to independent studios and art collectives.

Galway's Food Scene & Where to Eat

Galway's food scene has blossomed into one of the most exciting and celebrated in Ireland, fusing old traditions with bold innovation. As a coastal city, Galway is synonymous with outstanding seafood, but the culinary offering goes far beyond the bounty of the Atlantic. From rustic pubs serving hearty Irish classics to Michelin-starred restaurants redefining contemporary Irish cuisine, and from lively cafés to world-class markets, Galway offers an incredibly diverse, deeply flavorful experience. Creativity and passion are the driving forces behind the city's dining culture, with a strong emphasis on local ingredients, artisanal producers, and seasonal menus.

Michelin-Starred Excellence: Aniar

Under the leadership of Chef JP McMahon, Aniar is a flagship for Irish fine dining, proudly awarded a Michelin star. The menu draws exclusively on seasonal West of Ireland produce, showcasing native ingredients through modern techniques. Diners embark on a tasting journey that captures the essence of the rugged Connemara landscape — think Atlantic fish, wild herbs, heirloom vegetables, and sustainably sourced meats, transformed into delicate, imaginative plates. Each dish is a poetic tribute to place and season.

- **Location:** 53 Lower Dominick Street, Galway

- **Opening Hours:** Tuesday–Saturday from 6:00 PM
- **Reservations:** Essential (often booked months in advance)
- **Pro Tip:** Opt for the full tasting menu paired with Irish and natural wines for the ultimate experience.

Quintessential Galway: Ard Bia at Nimmos

Tucked beside the Spanish Arch, Ard Bia at Nimmos captures everything Galway is about: history, atmosphere, and a profound love for local food. Housed in a historic stone building, this charming restaurant and café feels both bohemian and timeless. Its menus offer hearty, imaginative dishes influenced by Irish and Mediterranean traditions — think slow-roasted lamb shoulder, chickpea tagines, homemade cakes, and rich seafood chowders. Ingredients are seasonal and largely sourced from nearby farms and fisheries.

- **Location:** Long Walk, Galway
- **Opening Hours:** Daily from 9:30 AM (brunch and dinner service)
- **Reservations:** Strongly recommended for dinner
- **Pro Tip:** Visit during brunch for a more relaxed experience; the scones and coffee are among the best in Galway.

Seafood Royalty: Oscar's Seafood Bistro

Seafood lovers will find paradise at Oscar's Seafood Bistro. With a menu that changes daily depending on what's freshest from the boats, it's no surprise this bistro is a local favorite. Expect dishes like pan-fried scallops, Galway Bay oysters, crab claws dripping in garlic butter, and whole roasted fish prepared with minimal intervention to let the quality of the catch shine through. The casual setting is warm, welcoming, and utterly unpretentious.

- **Location:** Dominick Street Upper, Galway
- **Opening Hours:** Monday–Saturday from 5:30 PM
- **Reservations:** Highly recommended
- **Pro Tip:** Start with the seafood chowder; it's considered one of the best in Ireland.

Global Flavors: Kai

Meaning "food" in Maori, Kai is a bright, energetic bistro that consistently ranks among Ireland's best places to eat. Led by New Zealand-born chef Jess Murphy, Kai offers bold, flavor-packed dishes inspired by international cuisines while grounded in local Irish ingredients. Expect unexpected combinations such as Irish goat cheese gnocchi with wild greens, or spiced lamb flatbreads with house-made pickles. The décor — all rustic wood, art, and hanging plants — matches the food's organic spirit.

- **Location:** Sea Road, Galway
- **Opening Hours:** Monday–Saturday for lunch, Thursday–Saturday for dinner
- **Reservations:** Advised for dinner
- **Pro Tip:** Come early for lunch to grab one of their wildly popular, freshly baked pastries.

Traditional Pubs with Hearty Fare: Tigh Neachtain

Tigh Neachtain isn't just one of Galway's best-loved pubs — it's also a brilliant place to enjoy traditional Irish pub food made with real care. Established in 1894, this colorful, character-filled spot serves up generous plates of Irish stew, fish pie, beef and Guinness casserole, and creative vegetarian dishes. Craft beers and whiskeys flow freely, and live traditional music fills the air several nights a week. It's the ultimate cozy Galway experience.

- **Location:** 17 Cross Street Upper, Galway
- **Opening Hours:** Daily from noon
- **Reservations:** Not needed — arrive early for a good table
- **Pro Tip:** Pair a hot plate of stew with a locally brewed ale and linger through a music session.

Sweet Stops: Cupán Tae

For an afternoon treat straight out of a storybook, Cupán Tae serves traditional afternoon tea in a vintage tearoom setting. Think lace tablecloths, antique china, towering stands of delicate sandwiches, buttery scones with clotted cream, and an extensive tea menu. The vibe is intentionally whimsical and nostalgic, making it perfect for a relaxed indulgence away from the busy streets.

- **Location:** 8 Quay Lane, Galway
- **Opening Hours:** Daily from 10:00 AM to 6:00 PM
- **Reservations:** Recommended for afternoon tea service
- **Pro Tip:** Their signature Galway Bay Tea blend is worth bringing home as a souvenir.

Casual Favorites: The Dough Bros

What started as a humble food truck has grown into one of Ireland's best-loved casual dining experiences. The Dough Bros specializes in wood-fired pizza made with local and organic ingredients. Their dough is slow-fermented for maximum flavor, and toppings range from the classic Margherita to inventive options featuring Irish lamb, wild mushrooms, or local cheeses. The vibe is laid-back, cool, and family-friendly.

- **Location:** 1 Middle Street, Galway
- **Opening Hours:** Daily from 12:00 PM
- **Reservations:** Not needed
- **Pro Tip:** Their seasonal specials often feature collaborations with local farmers and brewers — don't miss them.

Galway's Food Markets: A Taste of Everything

Galway Market beside St. Nicholas' Church remains the city's most enduring food destination. On weekends, stalls overflow with artisanal cheeses, fresh oysters, handmade chocolates, spice-laden curries, organic vegetables, and every imaginable baked good. Sampling your way through the market offers an unbeatable introduction to Galway's dynamic and proudly local food culture.

- **Location:** Church Lane, Galway City
- **Opening Hours:** Saturday and Sunday, with extra days during festivals
- **Pro Tip:** Bring cash, as many small vendors may not accept cards, and try the famous Madras curry wrap.

Day Trips from Galway

Galway's location on Ireland's west coast makes it the perfect base for unforgettable day trips into some of the most breathtaking and culturally rich areas in the country. From dramatic coastal cliffs and ancient stone landscapes to charming villages and serene islands, the surroundings offer an extraordinary variety. Each journey reveals another facet of the Ireland that captures the imagination — wild, lyrical, and deeply authentic.

The Cliffs of Moher

Rising more than 700 feet above the roaring Atlantic Ocean, the Cliffs of Moher are among Ireland's most iconic natural wonders.

A visit here offers awe-inspiring views that stretch to the Aran Islands and the mountains of Kerry on a clear day. Well-maintained pathways lead to multiple viewing platforms, and the Visitor Centre inside the hillside blends naturally with the environment while offering educational exhibits about the geology, history, and wildlife of the cliffs. Standing at the edge, with the sea spray in the air, captures the rugged spirit of Ireland like few other places.

- **Location:** County Clare
- **Travel Time:** Approximately 1.5 hours by car or tour bus
- **Highlights:** O'Brien's Tower, the Cliffs Coastal Trail, Atlantic Edge Exhibition
- **Pro Tip:** Visit early in the morning or late in the afternoon to avoid crowds and capture the cliffs in the best light for photography.

The Aran Islands (Inis Mór)

The Aran Islands feel like a step back in time, offering a glimpse into a traditional Irish way of life largely untouched by modern development. Inis Mór, the largest of the three, is home to the prehistoric fort of Dún Aonghasa, perched dramatically on a cliff edge. Explore the island by bike or horse-drawn carriage, passing tiny stone-walled fields, ancient churches, and windswept beaches.

Irish (Gaelic) remains the first language of the locals, and the island's handmade woolen crafts and warm hospitality add to the unique experience.

- **Location:** Off the coast of Galway Bay
- **Travel Time:** 40-minute ferry ride from Rossaveal Port (about a 45-minute drive from Galway City)
- **Highlights:** Dún Aonghasa, Kilmurvey Beach, The Wormhole (Poll na bPéist)
- **Pro Tip:** Book ferry tickets in advance and rent a bike upon arrival to explore at your own pace.

Connemara National Park

Connemara National Park showcases Ireland's wild beauty at its most untamed and poetic. Covering over 2,000 hectares, it encompasses mountains, bogs, heaths, grasslands, and woodlands. The park is famous for the Twelve Bens mountain range, offering superb hiking trails of varying difficulty. The Visitor Centre provides fascinating insights into the park's ecology and history, and the scenic Diamond Hill trail rewards hikers with panoramic views of Connemara's lakes and coastline. The raw, ever-changing light and weather give the landscape an ethereal quality.

- **Location:** Letterfrack, County Galway

- **Travel Time:** Approximately 1.5 hours by car
- **Highlights:** Diamond Hill trails, Connemara ponies, Wild Atlantic Way viewpoints
- **Pro Tip:** Bring layers and waterproof clothing, as the weather can shift dramatically within minutes.

Kylemore Abbey & Victorian Walled Garden

Nestled against a backdrop of wooded mountains and mirrored in a tranquil lake, Kylemore Abbey is one of Ireland's most romantic and photogenic sites. Originally built as a private home in the 19th century, it later became a Benedictine monastery. The abbey's Gothic Church, Victorian Walled Garden, and beautifully restored rooms are steeped in history and craftsmanship. Walking through the estate feels like wandering through a real-life fairytale, complete with secret gardens and dramatic landscapes.

- **Location:** Connemara, County Galway
- **Travel Time:** About 1 hour and 20 minutes by car
- **Highlights:** Gothic Church, Victorian Walled Garden, scenic lake walk
- **Pro Tip:** Allocate at least 3–4 hours to fully explore the estate, and don't miss a stop at the lovely café, which uses produce grown in the gardens.

The Burren

The Burren is a fascinating and surreal landscape of limestone pavements, dotted with rare flora, ancient dolmens, ring forts, and medieval ruins. Though it can appear barren at first glance, it is a rich ecosystem harboring over 70% of Ireland's native plant species. Walking across its lunar-like surface, visiting places like the Poulnabrone Dolmen and Caherconnell Stone Fort, or hiking in Burren National Park, offers visitors a glimpse into both Ireland's deep geological history and ancient human settlement.

- **Location:** County Clare
- **Travel Time:** About 1 hour by car
- **Highlights:** Poulnabrone Dolmen, Burren National Park trails, Aillwee Cave
- **Pro Tip:** Stop at Burren Perfumery, a hidden gem crafting natural perfumes, soaps, and teas from local botanicals.

Kinvara and Dunguaire Castle

The picturesque fishing village of Kinvara sits on the edge of Galway Bay, marked by brightly painted buildings, lively pubs, and the striking silhouette of Dunguaire Castle. Built in 1520, the castle has been lovingly restored and offers a glimpse into medieval life in Ireland. In the summer, medieval banquets bring the castle to life with traditional music, storytelling, and feasts inspired by historical recipes.

Kinvara's harbor area is perfect for a gentle stroll, with traditional Galway Hooker boats adding to the old-world charm.

- **Location:** County Galway
- **Travel Time:** Approximately 40 minutes by car
- **Highlights:** Dunguaire Castle, Kinvara Harbour, traditional music sessions
- **Pro Tip:** Plan your visit around the Kinvara Fleadh or Cruinniú na mBád Festival for a truly unforgettable cultural experience.

Roundstone and Dog's Bay

The tiny fishing village of Roundstone captures the quiet magic of Connemara. Its main street is lined with craft shops and pubs, and just a short drive away lies Dog's Bay and Gurteen Bay — twin crescent beaches of dazzling white sand and turquoise waters that feel almost tropical. It's one of the most stunning seaside spots in Ireland, perfect for a swim on a warm day or a peaceful coastal walk any time of year.

- **Location:** County Galway
- **Travel Time:** About 1.5 hours by car
- **Highlights:** Dog's Bay Beach, Roundstone Harbour, O'Dowd's Seafood Bar
- **Pro Tip:** Pack a picnic and a swimsuit, especially if visiting in summer when the beaches are at their most beautiful.

Chapter 11: Cork: Culinary Hub & Rebel County

Overview of Cork

Cork, Ireland's second-largest city, proudly refers to itself as the "real capital" of Ireland—and with good reason. It's a vibrant, culturally rich city known for its independent spirit, friendly locals, dynamic food scene, and deep historical roots. Nestled on the River Lee and built on a series of islands, Cork's unique waterways and bustling city center create a lively yet relaxed atmosphere, blending history with modern urban life.

Key Features of Cork:

Historic Significance: Dating back over a thousand years, Cork was founded by Saint Finbarr and developed into a key medieval trading port. Today, its rich past is reflected in historic buildings, old churches, and heritage sites scattered throughout the city.

Cultural Heartbeat: Cork is a cultural powerhouse, hosting world-renowned festivals such as the Cork Jazz Festival and Cork Film Festival. Its vibrant arts scene is visible in its galleries, theaters, and live music venues.

Architectural Blend: Walking through Cork reveals a mix of Georgian avenues, Victorian houses, medieval laneways, and modern glass structures. The city's character shines through its colorful buildings and quirky side streets.

Food Lover's Paradise: Home to the famous English Market, Cork is a haven for food enthusiasts. The market and a growing number of innovative restaurants showcase Cork's commitment to farm-to-table dining, artisanal produce, and culinary creativity.

Young and Dynamic Energy: Thanks to University College Cork (UCC) and several tech industries, Cork enjoys a youthful, energetic vibe. Cafés buzz with students and professionals alike, while nightlife thrives in traditional pubs and contemporary bars.

Why Visit Cork?

Friendly Locals: Corkonians are famously welcoming and proud of their heritage, always ready with a story or recommendation.

Compact and Walkable: Despite its status as a major city, Cork's center is compact enough to explore on foot, with hidden gems around every corner.

Gateway to Adventure: Cork serves as a gateway to some of Ireland's most breathtaking landscapes, including the Wild Atlantic Way, West Cork's coastal villages, and Blarney Castle.

Quick Facts About Cork

- **Province:** Munster
- **Population:** Approx. 220,000
- **Airport:** Cork Airport (15 minutes from the city center)
- **Best Time to Visit:** May to September for the warmest weather and festivals, though Cork's lively atmosphere can be enjoyed year-round.

Top Attractions & Historic Sites in Cork

Blarney Castle & Gardens

No trip to Cork would be complete without a visit to the iconic Blarney Castle, home of the legendary Blarney Stone.

Dating back to 1446, this historic fortress stands amid magnificent gardens and mystical woodlands. Visitors flock from around the world to kiss the stone, said to bestow the "gift of eloquence." Beyond the stone, the castle grounds offer a rich experience with features like the Poison Garden, fern gardens, and hidden waterfalls, creating a fairytale-like atmosphere. Exploring the towers and battlements offers a glimpse into Ireland's medieval history, paired with breathtaking views over the countryside.

- **Location:** Blarney, County Cork (about 8 km northwest of Cork city center)
- **Opening Hours:** Daily, 9:00 AM – 6:00 PM (seasonal changes apply)
- **Must Experience:** Kissing the Blarney Stone and wandering through the mystical Rock Close gardens
- **Entrance Fee:** Approx. €20 for adults, €9 for children (online discounts available)
- **Pro Tip:** Arrive early in the morning to avoid long queues at the stone, especially in summer.

St. Fin Barre's Cathedral

An architectural masterpiece, St. Fin Barre's Cathedral is a stunning Gothic Revival church dedicated to Cork's patron saint. Built between 1865 and 1879, the cathedral features intricate sculptures, striking stained-glass windows, and a golden angel atop its spire. Its intricate interiors, ornate mosaics, and symbolic carvings narrate centuries of Christian tradition and Cork's spiritual history.

The cathedral gardens also provide a peaceful retreat from the bustling city streets, making it both a visual and spiritual highlight.

- **Location:** Bishop Street, Cork City
- **Opening Hours:** Monday–Saturday, 10:00 AM – 5:30 PM; Sunday, 12:30 PM – 5:30 PM
- **Must Experience:** Admire the impressive Great West Window and the organ with over 4,000 pipes
- **Entrance Fee:** Approx. €7 for adults, €5 for seniors/students, free for children under 16
- **Pro Tip:** Join a guided tour to learn about the hidden symbols carved into the building's stonework.

The English Market

An institution in Cork since 1788, the English Market is a vibrant food market renowned for its fresh produce, artisan treats, and friendly banter. Housed under a beautiful Victorian-era vaulted ceiling, this bustling space offers everything from fresh seafood and traditional Irish meats to handmade chocolates and international delicacies. It's a sensory delight, where locals and visitors mingle among the colorful stalls. A visit offers a true taste of Cork's culinary identity and a chance to interact with passionate local traders.

- **Location:** Grand Parade, Cork City

- **Opening Hours:** Monday–Saturday, 8:00 AM – 6:00 PM; closed Sundays and public holidays
- **Must Experience:** Sampling traditional tripe and drisheen (a Cork delicacy) or picking up a handmade Irish cheese
- **Pro Tip:** Visit early for the freshest selections and enjoy lunch upstairs at the Farmgate Café overlooking the market floor.

Cork City Gaol

Step back into Ireland's tumultuous past at Cork City Gaol, an impressive 19th-century prison turned fascinating museum. Once housing both men and women (many incarcerated for political reasons), the gaol showcases life behind bars in the 1800s through lifelike wax figures, restored cells, and haunting audio tours. Visitors gain a vivid understanding of Cork's social and political history. The building's stunning Gothic architecture and peaceful location contrast dramatically with the hardships once endured inside its walls.

- **Location:** Convent Avenue, Sunday's Well, Cork City
- **Opening Hours:** Daily, 10:00 AM – 5:00 PM
- **Must Experience:** Take the self-guided audio tour narrated by former inmates' stories for a deeply immersive experience

- **Entrance Fee:** Approx. €12 for adults, €7.50 for children, family tickets available
- **Pro Tip:** Bring a jacket—parts of the gaol can feel chilly, adding to the authentic atmosphere.

Fitzgerald's Park

Situated along the River Lee, Fitzgerald's Park is Cork's premier urban green space, offering a peaceful retreat filled with sculptures, water features, and playgrounds. Once the site of the Cork International Exhibition in 1902, today it's a local favorite for picnics, strolls, and family outings. The park also hosts the excellent Cork Public Museum, where visitors can delve into Cork's storied past. Shaded pathways, a rose garden, and a whimsical pedestrian bridge ("The Shakey Bridge") make this a must-visit.

- **Location:** Mardyke Walk, Cork City
- **Opening Hours:** Daily, 8:30 AM – dusk
- **Must Experience:** Crossing the Shaky Bridge and visiting the Cork Public Museum
- **Entrance Fee:** Free
- **Pro Tip:** Visit during a sunny afternoon when the park buzzes with locals and street musicians.

Elizabeth Fort

Built in the early 17th century, Elizabeth Fort stands as a fascinating piece of Cork's military past. Originally constructed during the reign of Queen Elizabeth I to defend the walled city, the fort later served as a military barracks, prison, and police station. Its star-shaped ramparts offer stunning panoramic views over Cork's skyline, while walking along the fort walls gives a sense of the city's turbulent history. Regular exhibitions and events add further depth to the visitor experience.

- **Location:** Barrack Street, Cork City
- **Opening Hours:** Monday–Sunday, 10:00 AM – 5:00 PM
- **Must Experience:** Walk the full perimeter of the walls for sweeping views of Cork's historic cityscape
- **Entrance Fee:** Free (small fee for guided tours)
- **Pro Tip:** Visit during late afternoon for beautiful golden-hour photography over the city.

Shandon Bells & Tower (St. Anne's Church)

No landmark in Cork is more iconic than the red and white tower of St. Anne's Church, home to the world-famous Shandon Bells. Dating back to 1722, visitors can climb 132 steps to the top of the tower for spectacular 360-degree views.

Along the way, you're encouraged to ring the bells yourself—an unforgettable and noisy highlight! The church's unique architecture, featuring limestone and red sandstone walls, is a beloved symbol of the city.

- **Location:** Church Street, Shandon, Cork City
- **Opening Hours:** Monday–Saturday, 10:00 AM – 4:00 PM (last admission 3:30 PM)
- **Must Experience:** Ring the ancient bells yourself using the ropes provided at the first level
- **Entrance Fee:** Approx. €6 for adults, €5 for seniors/students, €3 for children
- **Pro Tip:** Bring earplugs or be ready for loud chimes when near the bell tower during busy times!

Nano Nagle Place

Nano Nagle Place is a hidden cultural gem in Cork, blending history, education, and modern community spirit. Dedicated to Nano Nagle, an 18th-century pioneer of Catholic education in Ireland, the beautifully restored convent grounds now house an interactive heritage museum, gardens, and a contemporary café. The museum delves deeply into Ireland's social history and Nano's inspirational mission, making it a thoughtful, moving experience. Its tranquil gardens are perfect for a reflective walk after the museum visit.

- **Location:** Douglas Street, Cork City
- **Opening Hours:** Tuesday–Saturday, 10:00 AM – 5:00 PM; Sunday, 12:00 PM – 5:00 PM

- **Must Experience:** Tour the interactive heritage experience tracing Nano's courageous efforts during Penal times
- **Entrance Fee:** Approx. €7.50 for adults, €5 for seniors/students, children free
- **Pro Tip:** Enjoy lunch at Good Day Deli, a sustainable café on-site, offering organic and locally sourced dishes.

Cobh Heritage Centre

While a little outside Cork city in the harbor town of Cobh, the Cobh Heritage Centre is essential for understanding Ireland's emigration history. Known as the last port of call for the Titanic, Cobh was a departure point for over 2.5 million Irish emigrants. The interactive exhibits tell poignant stories of those who left Ireland behind, as well as detailing Cobh's role in the Titanic and Lusitania tragedies. The center is housed in the beautifully restored Victorian railway station, enhancing its historic atmosphere.

- **Location:** Cobh, County Cork (25 minutes by train from Cork City)
- **Opening Hours:** Monday–Sunday, 9:30 AM – 5:30 PM
- **Must Experience:** Explore the Titanic and Lusitania exhibitions alongside personal emigrant stories
- **Entrance Fee:** Approx. €13 for adults, €9 for students/seniors, €7 for children
- **Pro Tip:** Combine your visit with a short harbor cruise for stunning coastal views of Cobh's colorful waterfront.

Best Areas and Neighborhoods to Stay

Cork, often called the "real capital of Ireland" by locals, is a vibrant, cosmopolitan city that blends rich history with a dynamic arts, culinary, and cultural scene. Choosing the right neighborhood can shape your experience—whether you're looking for lively pubs, waterfront strolls, or serene escapes just outside the urban hum. Each area offers a distinct flavor of Cork's diverse charm.

City Centre (St. Patrick's Street, Grand Parade, and Oliver Plunkett Street)

Cork's beating heart, the City Centre, is ideal for travelers who want to immerse themselves in the action. Cobblestone streets wind past colorful storefronts, historic churches, excellent restaurants, and lively pubs. Staying here means easy access to top attractions like the English Market, Crawford Art Gallery, and Shandon Bells, all within walking distance.

Accommodation Options:

- **The River Lee Hotel:** A stylish riverside property with elegant rooms, an indoor pool, and a trendy bar.
- **Imperial Hotel Cork City:** A historic, luxurious hotel with a rich legacy and modern amenities, perfectly situated for exploring.
- **Maldron Hotel South Mall:** Contemporary comfort in a superb location, great for business and leisure travelers alike.

Why Stay Here: Perfect for first-time visitors who want convenience, nightlife, and a lively atmosphere right outside their door.

Victorian Quarter (MacCurtain Street and Lower Glanmire Road)

On the north side of the River Lee, the Victorian Quarter has blossomed into one of Cork's most charismatic neighborhoods. With a resurgence of independent restaurants, cocktail bars, boutique hotels, and quirky shops, it offers a fresh, creative energy while maintaining its historic elegance. The area is walkable to the city centre yet feels slightly more relaxed.

Accommodation Options:

- **The Metropole Hotel:** A Cork institution offering old-world charm blended with modern luxury.

- **Hotel Isaacs Cork:** A boutique hotel known for its characterful rooms and the famous Greenes Restaurant.
- **REZz Cork:** Budget-friendly and ultra-modern, perfect for younger travelers or those looking for a more casual vibe.

Why Stay Here: Best for foodies, nightlife lovers, and travelers who appreciate a vibrant, yet authentic, local neighborhood feel.

Shandon & Northside

Steeped in history and offering panoramic views of the city, Shandon and the surrounding Northside neighborhood are home to the iconic Shandon Bells and Butter Museum. These neighborhoods retain a traditional Cork charm, with winding streets, colorful houses, and a strong sense of local community.

Accommodation Options:

- **Shandon Bells Guest House:** A charming B&B offering river views and a warm welcome.
- **Ashley Hotel:** An affordable, centrally located hotel close to Shandon's historical sights.

Why Stay Here: Perfect for travelers who love history, photography, and a slightly quieter setting that is still within walking distance of central Cork.

University College Cork (UCC) & Western Road

Set around the picturesque grounds of University College Cork, this leafy area is quieter and ideal for those who prefer a relaxed environment. The beautiful Fitzgerald's Park and the tranquil banks of the River Lee offer scenic walks, while several museums and galleries nearby highlight Cork's cultural sophistication.

Accommodation Options:

- **Hayfield Manor:** A luxurious five-star manor hotel offering impeccable service, fine dining, and an indulgent spa.
- **Garnish House:** An excellent guesthouse known for its outstanding breakfast and welcoming atmosphere.

Why Stay Here: Ideal for luxury travelers, academics, and anyone seeking peace, greenery, and an elegant base close to the city centre.

Douglas

Douglas is a fashionable suburb located about 10 minutes by car from central Cork. Known for its upscale shops, cozy cafés, bustling bars, and leafy parks, it offers a village-like charm while maintaining easy city access. Douglas is an excellent choice for longer stays or travelers looking for a more residential, local feel.

Accommodation Options:

- **Maryborough Hotel & Spa:** A historic mansion set on beautiful grounds with an award-winning spa.
- **Rochestown Park Hotel:** A comfortable, family-friendly hotel offering excellent leisure facilities.

Why Stay Here: Great for families, spa enthusiasts, and visitors who want a suburban retreat with quick access to both Cork city and the countryside.

Blackrock & Mahon

Located southeast of the city centre along the waterfront, Blackrock and Mahon offer scenic river walks, charming cafés, and a laid-back atmosphere. Blackrock Castle Observatory is a highlight, and the area's proximity to Mahon Point Shopping Centre makes it convenient for shopping and dining.

Accommodation Options:

- **The Montenotte Hotel:** Perched on a hilltop with stunning views over Cork, this boutique hotel offers a luxurious experience complete with a private cinema and panoramic terrace.
- **Clayton Hotel Silver Springs**: A modern hotel featuring spacious rooms and easy access to both the city centre and eastern routes.

Why Stay Here: Ideal for travelers who enjoy waterfront scenery, shopping, and easy road access to explore further afield.

Best Pubs, Live Music & Nightlife

Cork's nightlife is an unforgettable blend of cozy, old-world pubs, energetic live music venues, and stylish late-night bars. Locals have a deep passion for good conversation, great Guinness, and lively traditional music sessions.

Whether you are after a pint in a historic pub, an indie gig in a backroom bar, or a late-night DJ set, Cork offers something to match every mood.

Sin É

One of Cork's most iconic traditional pubs, Sin É ("That's it" in Irish), has been pouring pints and hosting unforgettable live sessions since 1889. With its dimly lit interior, timber walls lined with old photographs, and the sound of fiddles and bodhráns filling the air, Sin É captures the spirit of authentic Irish music like few places can. The atmosphere grows especially magical on weekends when local musicians gather spontaneously for lively trad sessions.

- **Location:** 8 Coburg Street, Cork City
- **Opening Hours:** Daily, 12:00 PM – 11:30 PM (12:30 AM weekends)
- **Must Experience:** Traditional live Irish music every night.
- **Pro Tip:** Arrive early if you want a seat; it gets packed quickly, especially after 9:00 PM.

The Crane Lane Theatre

The Crane Lane Theatre stands out with its eclectic live performances that range from swing and jazz to reggae and indie rock. Set in a historic former Gentleman's Club, its vintage décor—with velvet curtains, antique furnishings, and quirky art—is as much a reason to visit as the music. The venue often hosts free gigs earlier in the evening before transitioning into a lively dance floor with DJs spinning late into the night.

- **Location:** Phoenix Street, Cork City
- **Opening Hours:** Daily, 12:00 PM – 2:00 AM
- **Must Experience:** Sunday swing nights or one of their free early evening concerts.
- **Pro Tip:** Explore the outdoor beer garden between sets — it's one of Cork's best-kept secrets.

Rearden's Bar

Rearden's is a cornerstone of Cork's nightlife scene, especially popular with a younger crowd and students. The sprawling venue features multiple bars under one roof, offering everything from live sports screenings to dance floors and live cover bands.

It is particularly famous for its high-energy Friday and Saturday nights, when the dance floor fills with people enjoying chart hits and classic anthems.

- **Location:** Washington Street, Cork City
- **Opening Hours:** Daily, 10:30 AM – 2:00 AM
- **Must Experience:** Catch a live band early and dance the night away in Havana Browns nightclub upstairs.
- **Pro Tip:** Happy hour deals make it a great starting point before heading to late-night venues.

The Oliver Plunkett

A bustling, multi-room venue famous for live music and hearty food, The Oliver Plunkett celebrates Cork's musical heritage. The ground floor fills up with locals enjoying traditional and folk music, while the upstairs area, known as "The Frisky Whiskey," offers an elegant cocktail lounge experience. It has something happening every night, from solo artists to seven-piece bands playing vibrant, foot-stomping tunes.

- **Location:** 116 Oliver Plunkett Street, Cork City
- **Opening Hours:** Monday–Thursday 10:30 AM – 11:30 PM, Friday–Saturday 10:30 AM – 2:00 AM, Sunday 12:00 PM – 11:00 PM
- **Must Experience:** The "Brunch & Trad" Sunday sessions, where music starts from lunchtime.
- **Pro Tip:** Book a table if you want to have dinner while enjoying the show, especially on weekends.

Coughlan's Bar

Award-winning Coughlan's is small in size but immense in reputation. A cozy, atmospheric bar during the day, it transforms at night into one of Cork's finest live music venues. The intimate setting has attracted some big names from the Irish and international folk, jazz, and indie scenes. Artists love performing here for its close-knit, appreciative audiences, making it a firm favorite for live music lovers.

- **Location:** 7 Douglas Street, Cork City
- **Opening Hours:** Monday–Thursday 3:00 PM – 11:30 PM, Friday–Sunday 1:00 PM – Late

- **Must Experience:** An intimate folk gig; Coughlan's hosts some of the best emerging and established artists in Ireland.
- **Pro Tip:** Check the gig calendar ahead—tickets for major acts sell out very quickly.

Other Notable Mentions

- **An Spailpín Fánach (South Main Street):** A cozy, traditional Irish pub with a proud reputation for storytelling sessions and acoustic gigs.
- **Dwyers of Cork (Washington Street):** Perfect for early evening traditional sessions and hearty Irish meals.
- **Cyprus Avenue (Caroline Street):** The go-to place for indie and alternative live gigs featuring both international and Irish acts.

Shopping Districts & Markets

Cork offers a vibrant shopping scene that blends the historic with the contemporary, the boutique with the mainstream. Whether you are hunting for handmade crafts, designer fashion, artisan foods, or quirky antiques, Cork's diverse shopping districts and markets deliver an experience as rich as the city's culture itself. Strolling through its streets, one feels the pulse of a place that values tradition while embracing innovation.

Patrick Street – The Heart of Retail

Patrick Street, affectionately known as "Pana" by locals, is Cork's main shopping artery. Broad and bustling, it is lined with a mixture of high-street favorites, elegant department stores, and independent boutiques. The street's graceful Georgian buildings lend a charming backdrop to a full day of browsing. Shoppers can explore Brown Thomas, Cork's premier luxury department store, which houses brands like Gucci, Chanel, and Irish designers. Further along, popular brands such as H&M, River Island, and Marks & Spencer draw a lively crowd.

Don't Miss: Venture into nearby French Church Street and Opera Lane for more boutique finds and stylish cafés perfect for a mid-shop break.

Pro Tip: Visit early on weekday mornings to enjoy a quieter atmosphere and the best window displays.

English Market – Cork's Culinary Gem

Tucked under an elegant Victorian vaulted roof in the city center, the English Market has been Cork's gastronomic heart since 1788. This covered market is a paradise for food lovers, offering everything from fresh seafood, artisan cheeses, and organic vegetables to handmade chocolates and traditional Irish meats. Generations of families have traded here, and the vendors' passion is evident in every conversation and sample. It is not only a place to shop but a cultural experience.

Don't Miss: Grab a seat upstairs at the Farmgate Café, which sources ingredients directly from the market stalls for an unforgettable meal.

Pro Tip: Engage with the vendors; many are happy to share tips about traditional Irish cooking or offer small tastings.

Oliver Plunkett Street – Stylish Boutiques and Hidden Gems

Just a stone's throw from Patrick Street, Oliver Plunkett Street hums with energy and creativity. Independent shops dominate this pedestrian-friendly stretch, offering everything from quirky Irish gifts and handmade jewelry to bespoke fashion. It's a street that invites exploration, with hidden laneways branching off into delightful artisan stores and small cafés. Its characterful charm and local spirit make it a favorite for visitors seeking something more authentic than mainstream offerings.

Don't Miss: Pay a visit to Kilkenny Shop for premium Irish crafts, clothing, and homewares.

Pro Tip: Stop by in the early evening when the street often features live music performances from local artists, adding a magical soundtrack to your shopping experience.

Marina Market – Cork's New Creative Hub

The Marina Market, located along Centre Park Road in Cork's docklands, has quickly become one of the city's trendiest shopping and eating destinations. Set in a repurposed industrial space, this vibrant, open-plan market bursts with independent food vendors, artisan stalls, lifestyle shops, and rotating pop-up events. From vegan treats to handmade homewares and even yoga classes, it embodies Cork's youthful and creative energy.

Don't Miss: Browse through local art pieces and boutique fashion pop-ups before grabbing a coffee and soaking in the lively atmosphere.

Pro Tip: Visit during weekend mornings when the market buzzes with farmers' produce stalls, craft displays, and live performances.

Paul Street and Carey's Lane – Quaint and Quirky

For those seeking a more relaxed shopping experience, Paul Street and Carey's Lane offer a charming detour. Nestled between the busier shopping hubs, these lanes are rich with independent shops, artisan bookstores, and trendy coffee shops. Expect to find vintage clothing boutiques, rare vinyl records, handcrafted goods, and Irish designer items tucked inside inviting little storefronts.

Don't Miss: Pop into Vibes & Scribes, one of Cork's best independent bookstores, for a treasure trove of books, craft materials, and unique gifts.

Pro Tip: Spend time wandering without a set agenda — many of the best finds in this area are completely unexpected.

Douglas Village Shopping Centre – Suburban Convenience

Just a short drive from the city center, Douglas Village Shopping Centre offers a more relaxed, suburban shopping experience. It blends well-known brands with local businesses and a thriving farmers' market every Saturday. It's an ideal destination if you're looking for easy parking, a family-friendly environment, and a quieter atmosphere away from the city's bustle.

Don't Miss: The farmers' market offers a wonderful selection of organic produce, handmade pastries, and specialty foods.

Pro Tip: Combine a visit to Douglas with a walk along the scenic Douglas Estuary for a refreshing break after shopping.

Cork's Food Scene & Where to Eat

Known as the "Food Capital of Ireland," Cork has a culinary reputation that punches far above its size. With its access to some of Ireland's freshest seafood, organic farms, and artisan producers, the city has developed a food scene that celebrates both heritage and innovation. Cork's chefs are masters at blending traditional Irish comfort foods with creative global influences, ensuring that every palate, from the casual snacker to the gourmet connoisseur, is satisfied.

From lively markets to Michelin-starred restaurants, Cork's dining landscape is vibrant, welcoming, and deliciously diverse.

English Market – A Food Lover's Paradise

At the heart of Cork's food scene is the English Market, operating since 1788. This covered market buzzes with stalls selling local produce, fresh seafood, gourmet cheeses, and handmade chocolates. Browsing through its historic aisles feels like stepping into the very soul of Cork's culinary tradition. Stop by Farmgate Café on the mezzanine level for a plate of traditional Irish stew while overlooking the bustling market activity.

- **Location:** Grand Parade, Cork City
- **Opening Hours:** Monday–Saturday, 8:00 AM – 6:00 PM (closed Sundays)
- **Pro Tip:** Visit early in the morning for the freshest selection and fewer crowds.

Michelin-Starred Excellence: Ichigo Ichie

Chef Takashi Miyazaki's Ichigo Ichie brings a stunning fine-dining experience to Cork with Japanese kaiseki-inspired menus. Delicate, multi-course meals showcase local Irish ingredients prepared with precise Japanese techniques, earning it a Michelin star. Dining here is an immersive experience, blending art, seasonality, and elegance.

- **Location:** Sheares Street, Cork City
- **Opening Hours:** Dinner only, select days (booking essential)
- **Pro Tip:** Book months in advance—Ichigo Ichie's intimate setting fills up quickly.

Casual Dining Favorite: Market Lane

Located just steps from the English Market, Market Lane offers hearty Irish dishes crafted from locally sourced produce. Expect beautifully executed comfort foods like braised beef cheek, fresh seafood chowder, and inventive vegetarian plates. With a stylish yet relaxed atmosphere, it's ideal for a casual dinner without sacrificing quality.

- **Location:** Oliver Plunkett Street, Cork City
- **Opening Hours:** Monday–Sunday, 12:00 PM – 9:00 PM

- **Pro Tip:** Try their early bird menu for great value without compromising on flavor.

Traditional Irish Pub Food: The SpitJack

For a lively but food-focused experience, The SpitJack delivers a menu full of flame-roasted meats, juicy rotisserie chicken, and gourmet burgers. Combining the character of an old Irish pub with a serious kitchen operation, it's a favorite for lunch or a hearty dinner.

- **Location:** Washington Street, Cork City
- **Opening Hours:** Monday–Sunday, 9:00 AM – late
- **Pro Tip:** Their brunch is a local legend—arrive early on weekends to snag a table.

Seafood Delights: Goldie

Goldie offers a casual but sharp seafood experience with a focus on "whole catch cooking." Every part of the fish is used in creative dishes, from crispy collars to sashimi specials. Their menu changes daily based on the morning's catch from Irish waters.

- **Location:** Oliver Plunkett Street, Cork City
- **Opening Hours:** Tuesday–Saturday, from 5:00 PM
- **Pro Tip:** If you love oysters, Goldie's fresh daily specials are a must-try.

Vegan & Vegetarian: Café Paradiso

Founded by Denis Cotter, Café Paradiso is one of Europe's legendary vegetarian restaurants. Their imaginative dishes elevate local vegetables into show-stopping plates, blending global influences with traditional Irish produce. Even non-vegetarians are often stunned by the creativity and depth of flavor here.

- **Location:** Lancaster Quay, Cork City
- **Opening Hours:** Tuesday–Saturday, 5:30 PM – 9:00 PM
- **Pro Tip:** Book early; with limited seating, tables at Café Paradiso are in high demand.

Hidden Gem: Liberty Grill

A cozy American-style bistro, Liberty Grill serves up one of Cork's best brunches with a menu full of buttermilk pancakes, crab cakes, and gourmet eggs benedict.

Its intimate setting and emphasis on local ingredients make it a favorite for casual dining.

- **Location:** Washington Street, Cork City
- **Opening Hours:** Monday–Saturday, 8:00 AM – 9:00 PM; Sunday brunch from 9:00 AM
- **Pro Tip:** Go midweek to avoid long brunch queues on weekends.

Sweet Tooth Stop: O'Conaill Chocolate

For those needing a dessert fix, O'Conaill Chocolate offers handmade chocolates, decadent hot chocolate, and truffles crafted in Cork. Their cozy café near the English Market is a perfect place to recharge between sightseeing.

- **Location:** French Church Street, Cork City
- **Opening Hours:** Monday–Saturday, 9:00 AM – 6:00 PM
- **Pro Tip:** Don't leave without trying their signature hot chocolate with a shot of melted dark chocolate.

Day Trips from Cork

Cork's strategic location in southern Ireland makes it a perfect base for exploring a tapestry of landscapes, charming towns, historic landmarks, and natural wonders. Whether seeking dramatic coastal cliffs, medieval castles, or colorful villages, the day trips from Cork offer memorable experiences filled with culture, history, and scenic beauty. Every journey reveals a different facet of Ireland's soul, making day excursions an essential part of any Cork itinerary.

Blarney Castle and Gardens

A visit to Blarney Castle remains one of the quintessential day trips from Cork. Built nearly 600 years ago by one of Ireland's greatest chieftains, Cormac MacCarthy, the castle today draws visitors eager to kiss the legendary Blarney Stone. Folklore promises that those who kiss the stone receive the gift of eloquence. The surrounding gardens are equally impressive, featuring exotic plants, mystical rock formations at the Rock Close, and serene water gardens. The atmosphere feels timeless, with winding paths leading to fern gardens, waterfalls, and hidden nooks that invite quiet reflection.

- **Location:** Blarney, Co. Cork (15 minutes' drive from Cork City)
- **Opening Hours:** Daily, 9:00 AM – 5:00 PM (extended in summer)

- **Entrance Fee:** €22 for adults, €9 for children
- **Must Experience:** Climbing the narrow stone staircase to the Blarney Stone, exploring the Poison Garden with its collection of dangerous plants
- **Pro Tip:** Arrive early in the morning to avoid long queues at the stone, especially in summer months.

Kinsale

The colorful harbor town of Kinsale is a dream for food lovers, history buffs, and photographers alike. Its pastel-painted buildings, gourmet restaurants, winding streets, and vibrant marina create a captivating setting. Kinsale also holds deep historical significance; it was the site of the pivotal Battle of Kinsale in 1601. A visit to Charles Fort, a massive star-shaped 17th-century fortress overlooking the sea, offers panoramic views and an insightful glimpse into Ireland's past. Kinsale's culinary reputation is legendary, with seafood taking center stage on most menus.

- **Location:** Kinsale, Co. Cork (30 minutes' drive from Cork City)
- **Opening Hours (Charles Fort):** Daily, 10:00 AM – 6:00 PM
- **Entrance Fee (Charles Fort):** €5 for adults, €3 for students/seniors
- **Must Experience:** Walking the Scilly Walk coastal trail between Kinsale town and Charles Fort
- **Pro Tip:** Book a table in advance at a local seafood restaurant such as Fishy Fishy, particularly on weekends.

Cobh

The picturesque port town of Cobh (pronounced "Cove") offers a poignant journey through Irish emigration history. Once known as Queenstown, Cobh was the last port of call for the RMS Titanic and a major departure point for millions of Irish emigrants. The stunning St. Colman's Cathedral towers dramatically above the town, its bells echoing across the harbor. The Titanic Experience, located in the original White Star Line ticket office, provides an immersive exploration of the ship's ill-fated voyage, while the Cobh Heritage Centre recounts the stories of those who left Ireland in search of a new life.

- **Location:** Cobh, Co. Cork (25 minutes by train from Cork City)
- **Opening Hours (Titanic Experience):** Daily, 10:00 AM – 5:30 PM
- **Entrance Fee (Titanic Experience):** €11 for adults, €8.50 for children
- **Must Experience:** Taking the Titanic Trail walking tour through the historic waterfront
- **Pro Tip:** Time your visit to hear the bells of St. Colman's Cathedral, especially in the late afternoon.

Fota Wildlife Park

For those traveling with family or simply seeking an enchanting wildlife encounter, Fota Wildlife Park offers a unique and ethical experience. Unlike traditional zoos, many animals roam freely in expansive habitats, and visitors can walk among kangaroos, lemurs, and exotic birds.

Species from around the globe, including giraffes, cheetahs, and red pandas, thrive in carefully designed environments that prioritize conservation and education. Educational talks and feeding sessions throughout the day deepen the experience.

- **Location:** Fota Island, Co. Cork (20 minutes by train from Cork City)
- **Opening Hours:** Daily, 9:30 AM – 5:00 PM (longer hours in summer)
- **Entrance Fee:** €19.90 for adults, €13.90 for children
- **Must Experience:** Walking the African Savannah trail and the Asian Sanctuary exhibits
- **Pro Tip:** Bring a picnic and enjoy lunch on the expansive park lawns between exhibitions.

Midleton and the Jameson Distillery

Whiskey enthusiasts find paradise in the charming town of Midleton, home to the famous Jameson Distillery. The guided tours explore the old distillery grounds where whiskey has been crafted for centuries, complete with tastings that include special reserve blends not widely available elsewhere. Beyond the distillery, Midleton's Farmers Market, held every Saturday, stands as one of Ireland's best, offering local cheeses, artisan breads, and fresh produce.

- **Location:** Midleton, Co. Cork (25 minutes by train from Cork City)
- **Opening Hours (Jameson Distillery):** Daily, 10:00 AM – 5:00 PM
- **Entrance Fee:** From €23 for the Classic Tour
- **Must Experience:** The Premium Whiskey Tasting and Barrelman's Tour for a more in-depth whiskey experience
- **Pro Tip:** Reserve a late afternoon tour to enjoy the distillery grounds during golden hour, followed by dinner in Midleton town.

Gougane Barra

A hidden gem in the West Cork mountains, Gougane Barra enchants visitors with its fairytale-like setting. A tiny stone chapel sits on an island in the middle of a serene lake, surrounded by pine-clad hills. The peaceful atmosphere invites quiet walks, photography, or simply pausing to absorb the natural beauty. Gougane Barra also houses Ireland's first National Forest Park, with multiple trails ranging from gentle lakeside strolls to vigorous mountain hikes.

- **Location:** Gougane Barra, Co. Cork (1 hour 10 minutes' drive from Cork City)
- **Opening Hours:** Always open for visitors
- **Entrance Fee:** Free, parking €5 per car
- **Must Experience:** Walking the Slí an Easa trail for panoramic views of the valley and waterfall
- **Pro Tip:** Visit early morning or late afternoon for misty, atmospheric photography and to avoid busier periods.

Chapter 12: Belfast & Northern Ireland

Cultural Highlights & Political History

Northern Ireland's culture is a rich tapestry woven from centuries of tradition, art, resilience, and identity. Its story is complex—shaped by both triumphs and tragedies—and today, the region stands as a testament to creative spirit and human endurance. To truly understand Northern Ireland is to appreciate both its vibrant cultural life and the pivotal role history has played in forging its modern identity.

Political History: From Division to Peace

Northern Ireland's political landscape has been profoundly shaped by a period known as The Troubles—a conflict that spanned roughly three decades from the late 1960s to 1998. Rooted in historical tensions between mainly Protestant unionists (who wanted to remain part of the United Kingdom) and largely Catholic nationalists (who sought unification with the Republic of Ireland), the Troubles deeply affected daily life.

Key moments:

Civil Rights Movement (1960s): Inspired by global civil rights movements, protests for equal rights in housing and employment grew, leading to escalating tensions.

Bloody Sunday (1972): A tragic event where British soldiers shot unarmed civil rights protesters in Derry, fueling international outrage.

Good Friday Agreement (1998): A landmark peace accord that largely ended violence, introduced shared governance, and opened the door for reconciliation.

Today, political murals across Belfast and Derry—once stark symbols of division—have evolved into powerful storytelling canvases reflecting hopes for peace, identity, and a shared future.

A City Transformed: Belfast's Cultural Renaissance

Following the peace process, Belfast has undergone a remarkable transformation. Once heavily scarred by conflict, the city now bursts with creativity, innovation, and pride. The Titanic Quarter is a beacon of regeneration, celebrating Belfast's shipbuilding heritage alongside cutting-edge architecture. Neighborhoods like the Cathedral Quarter have flourished with a dynamic arts scene—think buzzing galleries, intimate theaters, independent bookstores, and open-air festivals that showcase a new generation of writers, musicians, and visual artists. Street art is a major part of Belfast's identity, with international artists leaving vibrant marks that reflect the city's layered history and bold future.

Living Traditions: Music, Language, and Storytelling

Northern Ireland's cultural heartbeat can be felt through its enduring traditions:

Traditional Music: Sessions in pubs echo with the sounds of fiddles, flutes, and bodhráns. From lively céilí dances to soul-stirring ballads, music remains a cornerstone of community life.

Irish Gaelic: Though English dominates daily life, efforts to revive the Irish language are growing, especially in areas like Belfast's Gaeltacht Quarter.

Storytelling: A nation of born storytellers, Northern Ireland is rich in folklore, mythology, and literary legacy. Modern authors like Seamus Heaney, Brian Friel, and Lucy Caldwell continue this tradition.

Festivals: Expressions of Identity and Celebration

Festivals in Northern Ireland offer windows into its vibrant culture:

- **Belfast International Arts Festival:** Showcasing theater, dance, music, and visual art from across the world.

- **Derry Halloween:** Europe's largest Halloween festival, blending ancient Celtic traditions with dazzling contemporary celebrations.
- **Fleadh Cheoil na hÉireann:** When hosted in Northern Ireland, it transforms towns into living stages for traditional Irish music.

Museums and Memorials: Honoring Memory

Cultural institutions play a key role in preserving and interpreting Northern Ireland's story:

- **The Ulster Museum (Belfast):** Offers a thoughtful look at the history, art, and natural heritage of the region.
- **Museum of Free Derry:** Provides an unflinching account of the civil rights movement and Bloody Sunday.
- **Titanic Belfast:** Immerses visitors in the city's industrial golden age and its most famous ship.

These spaces encourage dialogue, reflection, and understanding among visitors and locals alike.

Game of Thrones Filming Locations

Northern Ireland's dramatic landscapes, ancient castles, and haunting coastlines provided some of the most iconic backdrops for HBO's legendary series Game of Thrones. With its rugged natural beauty and atmospheric historic sites, Northern Ireland was transformed into Westeros in scenes that captivated millions of viewers worldwide. Travelers today can explore these remarkable filming locations, stepping into the world of dragons, direwolves, and political intrigue.

The Dark Hedges – The Kingsroad

Few images are as unforgettable as the haunting beech trees lining the Kingsroad, where Arya Stark disguised herself as a boy to escape King's Landing. The Dark Hedges near Ballymoney in County Antrim capture this eerie beauty. The gnarled branches twist into a natural tunnel that looks almost supernatural in early morning mist or twilight.

- **Location:** Ballymoney, County Antrim
- **Must Experience:** Visit early in the morning to avoid crowds and capture the dreamlike atmosphere.

- **Pro Tip:** Drone photography is restricted; ground shots at sunrise or sunset offer the most magical light.

Ballintoy Harbour – Lordsport, The Iron Islands

Ballintoy Harbour portrays the rugged port of the Iron Islands, the homeland of House Greyjoy. It was here that Theon Greyjoy returned after years as a ward of House Stark. The rough coastline, ancient rock formations, and crashing waves evoke the harshness and pride of the Ironborn.

- **Location:** Ballintoy, County Antrim
- **Must Experience:** Walk along the coastal paths and visit the nearby Carrick-a-Rede Rope Bridge for additional dramatic views.
- **Pro Tip:** Weather can change rapidly; waterproof clothing and sturdy shoes are recommended.

Cushendun Caves – Birthplace of the Shadow Creature

The Cushendun Caves, formed over 400 million years ago, served as the setting where Melisandre gives birth to the shadow creature in Season 2. Their dark, mysterious interiors and proximity to the rugged coastline made them a perfect setting for one of the show's most chilling moments.

- **Location:** Cushendun, County Antrim
- **Must Experience:** Explore the caves at low tide to venture deeper into the passageways.
- **Pro Tip:** Combine this visit with a stroll through the charming village of Cushendun, known for its picturesque cottages.

Castle Ward – Winterfell

Castle Ward, a stunning 18th-century mansion and farmyard in County Down, was transformed into Winterfell, the ancestral home of House Stark. Many key early scenes were filmed here, including Bran's archery practice and the arrival of King Robert Baratheon. The grounds also feature the Whispering Wood and Robb Stark's camp.

- **Location:** Strangford, County Down
- **Must Experience:** Participate in interactive experiences such as archery lessons, medieval banquets, and costume dress-ups offered onsite.

- **Entrance Fee:** Approximately €12 / $13 per adult for general grounds entry; special experiences cost extra.
- **Pro Tip:** Book experiences in advance, especially during peak seasons, to guarantee availability.

Tollymore Forest Park – The Haunted Forest

Tollymore Forest Park set the stage for several chilling sequences, including the discovery of the direwolf pups and the White Walkers' first appearances. The park's ancient trees, gothic stone structures, and twisting trails create an otherworldly setting that perfectly suited the supernatural aspects of the series.

- **Location:** Near Newcastle, County Down
- **Must Experience:** Follow the designated Game of Thrones trail within the park to find the most recognizable scenes.
- **Entrance Fee:** Small car park fee of about €5 / $5.50.
- **Pro Tip:** Allocate at least half a day to fully explore; Tollymore's beauty extends far beyond the filming sites.

Downhill Strand – Dragonstone

Downhill Strand's sweeping beach, crowned by the cliffside Mussenden Temple, became Dragonstone's shoreline where Stannis Baratheon and Melisandre burn statues of the Seven Gods. The vast, windswept landscape mirrors the intense, brooding atmosphere central to Stannis's story arc.

- **Location:** Castlerock, County Londonderry
- **Must Experience:** Visit Mussenden Temple, perched dramatically atop the cliffs, for breathtaking views of the coastline.
- **Pro Tip:** Check tidal schedules before visiting; low tide reveals the full stretch of the beach.

Murlough Bay – Slaver's Bay and Iron Islands

Murlough Bay's secluded beauty has doubled as both Slaver's Bay and parts of the Iron Islands. Known for its rugged cliffs and panoramic views, this remote location captured the essence of exile and freedom intertwined throughout the series' storylines.

- **Location:** North Antrim Coast

- **Must Experience:** Hike to the high vantage points for sweeping views over the sea and surrounding headlands.
- **Pro Tip:** The access road is steep and narrow; only confident drivers should attempt it, or opt for a guided tour.

Pollnagollum Cave – Beric Dondarrion's Hideout

Hidden deep in County Fermanagh's Marble Arch Caves Global Geopark, Pollnagollum Cave served as the hideout for the Brotherhood Without Banners. This dramatic waterfall cave adds a sense of mystery and adventure, ideal for fans seeking the series' darker, underground locales.

- **Location:** Marble Arch Caves Geopark, County Fermanagh
- **Must Experience:** Guided tours into the geopark reveal not only the filming spot but also fascinating geological wonders.
- **Entrance Fee:** Varies depending on the tour, typically around €15 / $16.
- **Pro Tip:** Tours are seasonal, operating mainly from spring through autumn; pre-booking is essential.

Titanic Belfast, Maritime Heritage, & Political Murals

Belfast, a city of resilience and reinvention, carries its history in every street corner and waterfront. Nowhere is its layered story more vivid than in its maritime roots and the art emblazoned across its walls. From the triumph and tragedy of the Titanic to the deeply personal political murals, the city's spirit is captured in both proud legacies and powerful expressions.

Belfast's Maritime Heritage: A City Built by the Sea

Long before the world heard of the Titanic, Belfast was one of the most important shipbuilding centers globally. Harland & Wolff, the shipyard that birthed the Titanic, symbolized Belfast's industrial might. Walking through the Titanic Quarter, visitors encounter preserved docks, pump-houses, and cranes like Samson and Goliath, towering reminders of a once-thriving shipyard that shaped the city's fortunes and gave Belfast an enduring maritime identity.

- **Location:** Titanic Quarter and Waterfront Area, Belfast
- **Opening Hours:** Public spaces are accessible at all hours; Maritime attractions typically 10:00 AM – 6:00 PM

- **Must Experience:** Visit the historic slipways, Titanic Dock and Pump-House, and the Harbour Office showcasing Belfast's seafaring history.
- **Entrance Fee:** Many sites are free; Pump-House tours and boat rides are priced individually
- **Pro Tip:** Take a Titanic-themed boat tour for a different perspective of the shipyards and the harbor.

Titanic Belfast: A Monument to Innovation and Tragedy

Opened in 2012 to mark the centenary of the Titanic's launch, Titanic Belfast stands at the very site where the legendary liner was built. The building itself, shaped like a ship's prow, rises dramatically from the historic slipways. Inside, visitors move through immersive exhibits featuring life-size reconstructions, cinematic storytelling, and fascinating artifacts that bring to life the ambition, craftsmanship, and heartbreak surrounding the Titanic.

- **Location:** 1 Olympic Way, Queen's Road, Titanic Quarter, Belfast BT3 9EP
- **Opening Hours:** Daily from 9:00 AM to 6:00 PM (last admission at 5:15 PM)
- **Must Experience:** Explore nine interactive galleries that trace Belfast's industrial boom, the construction of the Titanic, and the ship's fateful maiden voyage.
- **Entrance Fee:** Adult £24.95, Child (5-15 years) £11, Family Pass £63
- **Pro Tip:** Book tickets in advance, especially in summer; combine your visit with the SS Nomadic, the last remaining White Star Line ship.

Political Murals: A Living Canvas of Belfast's Struggles and Hopes

The political murals of Belfast are more than street art; they are a vivid record of the city's modern history. Painted on gable walls and buildings, the murals narrate stories of division, conflict, remembrance, and resilience. From the Unionist and Loyalist murals of Shankill Road to the Republican artwork on Falls Road, each brushstroke speaks of the Troubles, a thirty-year conflict that left deep scars on the city. More recently, many murals have shifted to themes of peace, human rights, and international solidarity, showing a city striving toward reconciliation.

- **Location:** Shankill Road, Falls Road, and other parts of West Belfast
- **Opening Hours:** Public spaces; accessible 24 hours
- **Must Experience:** View the Peace Walls, tour Shankill and Falls Roads, and see murals evolving to reflect contemporary issues.
- **Entrance Fee:** Free (guided tours typically around £10–£20 per person)
- **Pro Tip:** Take a Black Taxi Tour for personal stories from drivers who lived through the Troubles.

The Giant's Causeway & Antrim Coast

Northern Ireland's Antrim Coast unfurls in a dramatic sequence of cliffs, beaches, and sweeping vistas, culminating in one of the world's most extraordinary geological wonders: the Giant's Causeway.

Recognized as a UNESCO World Heritage Site, this breathtaking stretch is steeped not only in natural marvels but also in myths and legends that have stirred imaginations for centuries.

The Giant's Causeway: Nature's Masterpiece

Formed around 60 million years ago by volcanic activity, the Giant's Causeway consists of roughly 40,000 interlocking basalt columns that step down into the sea like a colossal staircase. Scientists explain the phenomenon through geology, yet the local legend tells of the giant Finn McCool, who built the causeway to challenge his Scottish rival. The truth, whether myth or magma, is less important than the awe visitors feel standing upon this surreal natural formation. Rugged walking trails of varying difficulty levels offer the chance to explore the cliffs and coastline at your own pace, revealing new perspectives with every step.

- **Location:** Bushmills, County Antrim, Northern Ireland, BT57 8SU
- **Opening Hours:** Visitor Centre - Daily from 9:00 AM to 6:00 PM (seasonal variations)
- **Must Experience:** Walk across the basalt columns, explore the Giant's Boot, the Wishing Chair, and take the cliff-top trail for panoramic coastal views.
- **Entrance Fee:** Access to the causeway itself is free; Visitor Centre entry - Adult £15.50, Child £7.75, Family £38.50

- **Pro Tip:** Arrive early or after 5 PM to avoid peak crowds and capture stunning golden-hour photography.

Antrim Coast Road: A Journey through Coastal Beauty

Dubbed one of the most scenic coastal drives in the world, the Antrim Coast Road hugs the rugged shoreline between towering cliffs and the rolling sea. Each bend offers another postcard-perfect view, from sleepy villages nestled in glens to medieval ruins perched precariously on rocky outcrops. Highlights along the way include the nine Glens of Antrim, rich in folklore, and dramatic sites like Carrick-a-Rede Rope Bridge and the haunting remains of Dunluce Castle. Whether driven in a leisurely day or explored in sections, the journey along the Antrim Coast is as much a destination as any of its stops.

- **Location:** Stretching from Larne to Ballycastle, Northern Ireland
- **Opening Hours:** Public road; accessible at all times
- **Must Experience:** Drive or cycle the Causeway Coastal Route, stop at the Glens of Antrim, Torr Head, and Dunluce Castle.
- **Entrance Fee:** Free (charges apply for specific attractions)
- **Pro Tip:** Allow extra time for impromptu stops — the route is full of hidden gems, quaint villages, and dramatic vistas.

Carrick-a-Rede Rope Bridge: A Heart-Pounding Walk

Originally erected by fishermen over 350 years ago, the Carrick-a-Rede Rope Bridge spans a gaping chasm between the mainland and Carrick-a-Rede Island. Crossing the bridge today is a thrilling experience, offering incredible views of the sea and distant islands, and perhaps a newfound respect for the hardy fishermen who once plied these dangerous waters. For those less daring, the coastal path to the bridge is worth the journey in itself, offering sweeping ocean panoramas and glimpses of seabird colonies nesting along the cliffs.

- **Location:** Ballintoy, County Antrim, BT54 6LS
- **Opening Hours:** 9:30 AM to 5:00 PM (seasonal variations)
- **Must Experience:** Cross the rope bridge suspended 30 meters above sea level to a tiny island once used by salmon fishermen.
- **Entrance Fee:** Adult £14.50, Child £7.25, Family £36.25
- **Pro Tip:** In windy weather, the bridge may close; check ahead and dress warmly.

Derry/Londonderry: Walled City Wonders

Derry, officially known as Londonderry, stands proudly as one of Ireland's most fascinating and historically significant cities.

Known for its beautifully preserved 17th-century city walls, compelling history, thriving cultural scene, and youthful vibrancy, Derry offers travelers a powerful blend of past and present. It is a city where the echoes of medieval times coexist with modern creativity, and where every cobbled street or mural tells a story.

The City Walls: A Walk Through History

Constructed between 1613 and 1618, the Derry city walls are the only completely intact historic city walls in Ireland. Originally built to protect English and Scottish settlers during the Plantation of Ulster, the walls survived the 1689 Siege of Derry — one of the most iconic moments in Irish history. As you stroll along the elevated stone paths, you'll pass cannons, towering gates, and panoramic views of both the old town and the surrounding countryside. The walls offer a living timeline of the city's dramatic story, from its colonial foundations to its pivotal role in the Troubles.

- **Location:** Access from various points around Derry city centre, Northern Ireland
- **Opening Hours:** Accessible at all times (Visitor Information Centre open daily 9:00 AM – 5:30 PM)
- **Must Experience:** Walk the full 1.5-kilometre circuit atop the walls, stopping at the seven gates and historic bastions.

- **Pro Tip:** Join a guided walking tour for expert insights into the sieges, battles, and history that shaped the city.

Guildhall: Heart of Civic Life

Standing proudly beside the River Foyle, the Guildhall is one of Derry's most striking landmarks. Built in 1890 and rebuilt after a fire and bomb damage, it features ornate Gothic-style architecture blended with elements of Tudor design. Inside, the Great Hall dazzles with its stunning stained-glass windows, many depicting the history of the city. The Guildhall also houses exhibitions that tell the story of Derry's founding and its journey through centuries of conflict and change. The building remains a centre for civic events, concerts, and cultural gatherings, embodying the city's resilient spirit.

- **Location:** Guildhall Square, Derry, BT48 6DQ
- **Opening Hours:** Monday to Friday, 10:00 AM – 5:30 PM; Weekends, 11:00 AM – 4:00 PM
- **Must Experience:** Admire the neo-Gothic architecture, the intricate stained-glass windows, and the free exhibition on the Plantation of Ulster.
- **Pro Tip:** Visit in the evening when the Guildhall is beautifully illuminated, creating a magical backdrop for photos.

Bogside Murals & Free Derry Corner: Witness to Change

A short walk from the city walls leads into the Bogside, an area synonymous with Derry's role in the civil rights movement and the conflict known as the Troubles. The murals along Rossville Street, collectively called the People's Gallery, are both haunting and beautiful, portraying scenes like Bloody Sunday and the struggle for peace and equality. Nearby, the Free Derry Corner — a gable wall with the iconic slogan "You Are Now Entering Free Derry" — stands as a potent symbol of resistance and identity. Visiting the Bogside offers a poignant, moving insight into the recent history that shaped modern Northern Ireland.

- **Location:** Bogside neighbourhood, Derry
- **Must Experience:** View the iconic murals known as the "People's Gallery," depicting key moments from the Civil Rights era and the Troubles.
- **Pro Tip:** Consider booking a walking tour with a local guide who lived through the events for a deeply personal perspective.

Peace Bridge: Symbol of a New Era

Opened in 2011, the Peace Bridge is a sleek pedestrian and cycle bridge designed to connect communities divided by decades of sectarian conflict. Its elegant curves symbolize unity and a new chapter for Derry.

Walking across the bridge is not just a scenic experience; it's an emotional one, representing hope, reconciliation, and the power of progress. On one end lies the vibrant city centre, and on the other, the redeveloped Ebrington area, filled with galleries, cafes, and cultural spaces.

- **Location:** Connecting Ebrington Square to the city centre across the River Foyle
- **Must Experience:** Walk or cycle the graceful S-shaped bridge while soaking in panoramic views of the river and city skyline.
- **Pro Tip:** Sunset is the best time for photos as the bridge and river reflect the golden hues of the evening light.

Limerick: A City of Stories and Strength

Limerick: A City of Stories and Strength

Limerick, poised along the broad waters of the River Shannon, pulses with history, resilience, and creativity. As one of Ireland's oldest cities, it wears its scars and triumphs proudly, revealing a compelling narrative woven through medieval walls, Georgian streets, and vibrant modern life. Far more than just a stopover, Limerick is a destination where the past and present coexist with grit and grace.

A City with Deep Historical Roots

Founded by the Vikings in 922 AD, Limerick's strategic position made it a crucial trading port and fortress city. Over centuries, it bore witness to sieges, battles, and shifting empires, particularly during the turbulent Williamite War of the late 17th century. The Treaty of Limerick (1691), signed after a long siege, sought to end hostilities between the Jacobites and Williamites. Although the treaty's promises were later broken, the "Treaty Stone" remains a powerful symbol of the city's fighting spirit and quest for justice.

King John's Castle: A Centerpiece of Strength

Standing proudly on King's Island, King John's Castle is one of Limerick's most iconic sights. Dating from the early 13th century, its thick walls and battle-scarred towers tell stories of medieval sieges and political intrigue. A state-of-the-art visitor center brings the history vividly to life through interactive exhibits, 3D models, and virtual reality experiences, making it an essential stop for anyone seeking to understand Limerick's soul.

Georgian Elegance and Urban Legacy

In the 18th century, Limerick flourished economically, and a wave of elegant Georgian architecture transformed the city. The "Newtown Pery" district is one of Ireland's finest surviving examples of planned Georgian urban development. Wide boulevards, graceful townhouses, and leafy squares speak to a time of ambition and prosperity — remnants of a city striving to redefine itself beyond its turbulent past.

A Cultural Heartbeat

Modern Limerick is a cultural powerhouse. Designated Ireland's first National City of Culture in 2014, the city boasts a dynamic arts scene that thrives in galleries, theaters, and on the streets.

- **Hunt Museum:** Houses an eclectic collection of artifacts, including works by Picasso and Renoir.
- **Limerick City Gallery of Art:** Offers a profound exploration of Irish contemporary and historical art.
- **Dolan's Warehouse:** Revered for live music, Dolan's captures the raw, creative energy that defines Limerick's cultural identity.

Street art flourishes across the city's walls, adding bold color and commentary to everyday life.

Literary Soul: Frank McCourt's Limerick

Limerick's reputation in literature owes much to Frank McCourt, whose Pulitzer Prize-winning memoir Angela's Ashes paints a raw and unforgettable portrait of the city during the Great Depression.

Visitors can explore McCourt's Limerick on guided walking tours that trace his footsteps through the lanes and neighborhoods that shaped his childhood, revealing a story both deeply personal and universally resonant.

Markets, Shops, and Local Flavor

Limerick retains a proud tradition of markets and local commerce:

- **Milk Market:** A bustling Saturday institution where locals gather for artisan foods, crafts, and music.
- **Crescent Shopping Centre:** One of Ireland's largest, offering a full range of retail experiences.

Markets and boutiques across the city blend tradition and trend, making Limerick a rewarding place to explore unique Irish goods.

Riverfront Life and Green Spaces

The rejuvenation of the River Shannon's waterfront has infused the city with new life. The boardwalks, parks, and promenades along the river create ideal settings for strolls, picnics, and relaxation. People's Park in the heart of the city offers colorful gardens, a Victorian bandstand, and space to breathe amid the urban buzz.

Outdoor activities extend beyond the city:

- **Curraghchase Forest Park:** A 30-minute drive brings visitors to wooded trails and lakeside walks.
- **Adare Village:** Just outside Limerick, this picturesque village enchants with thatched cottages and medieval ruins.

Spirit of Strength and Renewal

Limerick's story is not just about surviving hardship; it's about transformation. Over the decades, the city has reinvented itself as a center of education, innovation, and sport.

- **University of Limerick:** With its stunning riverside campus and world-class facilities, UL embodies the city's forward-looking spirit.
- **Thomond Park:** Home to Munster Rugby, Thomond Park is a cathedral of passion where the city's deep love of sport comes vividly alive.

The pride in Limerick's resilience runs deep — locals, affectionately known as "Shannonsiders," embrace their identity with fierce loyalty and warm hospitality.

Why Limerick Leaves a Lasting Impression

Whether walking the ramparts of King John's Castle, savoring coffee at a riverside café, cheering with the Red Army at a Munster match, or losing yourself in the beauty of Milk Market's aromas and colors, Limerick offers an experience textured with authenticity. It is a city that wears its battle scars as badges of honor, continually shaping its future with creativity, resilience, and heart.

Kilkenny: Ireland's Medieval Treasure

Charming, compact, and effortlessly atmospheric, Kilkenny offers an exquisite glimpse into Ireland's medieval past wrapped in a lively modern spirit. Known as the "Marble City" for its distinctive black limestone, Kilkenny is famous for its beautifully preserved architecture, cobbled streets, and artistic heart. Walking its narrow lanes feels like stepping into a living storybook, where medieval cathedrals, craft shops, historic pubs, and vibrant festivals create a city that is as rich in culture as it is in history. Dominating the skyline is the grand Kilkenny Castle, one of Ireland's most iconic historic landmarks, with its sprawling parklands offering a tranquil escape right in the heart of the city. Meanwhile, St. Canice's Cathedral and its 9th-century round tower stand as silent witnesses to over 800 years of faith and resilience. Art and craft thrive here, especially during the renowned Kilkenny Arts Festival, when the city buzzes with creativity.

Kilkenny isn't just about heritage — it's a lively destination with exceptional dining, craft breweries, boutique shopping, and a nightlife scene where traditional music spills from ancient pubs. The city's energy and friendliness make it a must-visit whether you're tracing history, tasting craft beer, or simply soaking up the easygoing, welcoming atmosphere.

Top Experiences in Kilkenny

Kilkenny Castle: Explore opulent rooms, historical exhibits, and 50 acres of serene parkland.

St. Canice's Cathedral & Round Tower: Climb the ancient tower for panoramic views over the medieval rooftops.

Smithwick's Experience: Discover the art of brewing at Ireland's oldest brewery, dating back to 1710.

Rothe House & Garden: Wander through a rare intact 17th-century merchant's townhouse and its restored period gardens.

Medieval Mile Museum: Dive deep into Kilkenny's medieval heritage through fascinating artifacts and stories.

Butler Gallery: Admire a contemporary art collection housed in the beautifully restored Evans' Home.

Best Areas to Explore

The Medieval Mile: Stretching from Kilkenny Castle to St. Canice's Cathedral, this historic trail links the city's top landmarks.

Parliament Street & High Street: Lively shopping streets filled with boutiques, artisan stores, and bustling cafés.

John's Quay & Canal Walks: Scenic riverside paths perfect for relaxed strolls and photography.

Pro Tips

- **Castle Visit:** Arrive early in the morning for Kilkenny Castle tours to avoid the midday crowds and enjoy the grounds in peace.
- **Medieval Mile App:** Download the free "Medieval Mile" app for an interactive, self-guided walking tour with hidden stories and local legends.

- **Craft Shopping:** Visit Kilkenny Design Centre across from the Castle for high-quality Irish crafts, jewelry, and ceramics.

Waterford: Ireland's Oldest City

Founded by Viking settlers in 914 AD, Waterford proudly holds the title of Ireland's oldest city. It is a place where history whispers from medieval walls, Georgian architecture shines with timeless elegance, and the mighty River Suir flows quietly alongside centuries of stories. Waterford blends its rich past with a vibrant, youthful energy, offering visitors a perfect combination of ancient heritage and modern creativity. The historic center, known as the Viking Triangle, is a compact area filled with atmospheric streets, where you can explore treasures like Reginald's Tower, Ireland's oldest civic building still in use, and the fascinating Medieval Museum, home to ancient vestments and medieval masterpieces. Waterford's most famous global export, Waterford Crystal, continues to sparkle in the House of Waterford Crystal, where artisans demonstrate the intricate craft that has dazzled the world for over two centuries.

Beyond its historic roots, Waterford thrives with colorful festivals like Spraoi and Waterford Walls, an annual international street art festival that transforms the city into a living canvas. Its lively cafés, riverside walks, burgeoning dining scene, and easy access to the stunning Copper Coast Geopark make Waterford an essential stop for those looking to experience Ireland's evolution through the ages.

Top Experiences in Waterford

Reginald's Tower: Climb inside a real Viking stronghold, with exhibits that trace Waterford's Norse origins.

House of Waterford Crystal: Witness master craftsmen at work and browse exquisite pieces in the showroom.

Medieval Museum: Discover priceless medieval treasures, including the Great Charter Roll and the stunning 15th-century cloth-of-gold vestments.

Bishop's Palace: Step inside a magnificent Georgian residence filled with 18th-century art, furniture, and stories.

Waterford Greenway: Cycle or walk along this breathtaking 46km trail stretching from Waterford City to Dungarvan, with coastal and countryside views.

The Viking Triangle: Wander the cobblestone streets of this compact historic quarter filled with museums, sculptures, and charming cafés.

Best Areas to Explore

Viking Triangle: Ideal for history lovers; packed with attractions and walkable streets full of charm.

John's Street Quarter: Waterford's lively nightlife district with traditional pubs, live music, and modern eateries.

The Quay: A scenic riverside stretch, perfect for relaxed walks and outdoor dining spots.

Pro Tips

- **Museum Bundle Ticket:** Save money by purchasing a combined ticket that grants access to the Medieval Museum, Bishop's Palace, and Reginald's Tower.
- **Early Tours:** For the House of Waterford Crystal, book the first tour of the day for a quieter, more personal experience.
- **Greenway Adventure:** Rent a bike near the start of the Waterford Greenway and plan a full day to truly savor the scenery.

Logan Matthews Ireland Travel Guide 2025

Chapter 14: Irish Food & Drink Guide

Traditional Irish Dishes & Local Specialties

Irish cuisine, with its deep roots in hearty, comforting flavors, has evolved into a celebration of fresh, local ingredients and rich traditions. From ancient cooking methods to modern interpretations of age-old recipes, food in Ireland tells a delicious story of the land, the sea, and the spirit of its people.

1. Irish Stew

A true emblem of Irish comfort food, Irish stew typically combines lamb or mutton, potatoes, onions, and carrots simmered to create a nourishing and flavorful dish. Originally a humble meal designed for sustenance, today it appears on menus everywhere from cozy pubs to high-end restaurants.

- **Must Try:** Choose a version made with locally sourced lamb for the most authentic taste.
- **Pro Tip:** Look for stews with a clear broth for a more traditional version rather than a thickened modern style.

2. Boxty

Boxty is a beloved Irish potato pancake, crisp on the outside and tender within. Made from a mixture of grated raw potato, mashed potato, flour, and buttermilk, it is often served alongside a hearty breakfast or stuffed with savory fillings for lunch.

- **Must Try:** Sample boxty stuffed with smoked salmon or beef in traditional eateries around the west of Ireland.
- **Pro Tip:** In places like Sligo and Mayo, you'll find regional variations that are worth seeking out.

3. Soda Bread

An essential staple, Irish soda bread relies on baking soda as a leavening agent rather than yeast, producing a dense, crumbly loaf with a slightly tangy flavor. Variations may include sweet versions with raisins or more savory takes with seeds and oats.

- **Must Try:** Freshly baked soda bread slathered with Irish butter at breakfast.
- **Pro Tip:** In rural bed-and-breakfasts, homemade soda bread is often served — don't miss it.

4. Coddle

Particularly associated with Dublin, coddle is a hearty one-pot stew made with sausages, rashers (Irish bacon), potatoes, and onions. Traditionally eaten on Thursdays to use up leftovers before Friday fasting days, coddle has a warm, savory flavor that's perfect for cooler weather.

- **Must Try:** Find a coddle in historic Dublin pubs for the most authentic experience.
- **Pro Tip:** Pair it with a pint of Guinness for a truly local meal.

5. Seafood Chowder

Ireland's coastal bounty shines in a rich, creamy seafood chowder, brimming with fresh fish, mussels, clams, and sometimes smoked salmon. Each restaurant often has its special twist.

- **Must Try:** Sample chowder in seaside towns like Dingle or Kinsale, known for outstanding seafood.
- **Pro Tip:** Always ask if the seafood is locally caught — the fresher, the better.

6. Black and White Pudding

A traditional part of the Irish breakfast plate, black pudding (blood sausage) and white pudding (oatmeal and pork) are savory, flavorful slices often fried until crisp. Though unfamiliar to some, they are beloved in Ireland and worth tasting at least once.

- **Must Try:** Enjoy them as part of a full Irish breakfast at a family-run café.
- **Pro Tip:** Some artisan butchers now offer gourmet versions with spices and herbs.

7. Dingle Pie

A specialty of County Kerry, Dingle pie is a savory lamb pie traditionally made for special occasions. Tender lamb pieces, carrots, and onions are wrapped in flaky pastry, delivering pure comfort with every bite.

- **Must Try:** Seek out family-owned bakeries in Dingle town for the most authentic taste.
- **Pro Tip:** Visit during the Dingle Food Festival to sample freshly made Dingle pies along with other local treats.

8. Barmbrack

Barmbrack is a sweet, yeasted bread dotted with raisins and sultanas, traditionally enjoyed at Halloween. It often contains hidden tokens that predict the future, much like a fortune-telling game.

- **Must Try:** Sample barmbrack toasted with butter alongside an afternoon tea.
- **Pro Tip:** Artisan bakeries offer fresher, less sugary versions than supermarket varieties.

9. Colcannon

A creamy blend of mashed potatoes and kale or cabbage, colcannon is a simple yet deeply satisfying dish tied to old Irish harvest traditions. It pairs beautifully with roasted meats or is sometimes served simply with a knob of butter melting into a well in the center.

- **Must Try:** Enjoy colcannon as a side dish with traditional Irish lamb.
- **Pro Tip:** Some restaurants incorporate wild garlic for an aromatic twist in springtime.

10. Irish Smoked Salmon

Smoked salmon from Ireland, particularly from areas like the Burren and Connemara, is celebrated for its silky texture and delicate smoky flavor. Whether served simply on brown bread or elevated into gourmet dishes, it is a must-try for seafood lovers.

- **Must Try:** Burren Smoked Salmon, recognized for its artisanal quality.
- **Pro Tip:** Farmers' markets often offer tasting samples, perfect for comparing different curing styles.

11. Bacon and Cabbage

A traditional Sunday lunch favorite, this dish pairs salted pork collar with boiled cabbage and creamy parsley sauce. Rooted in simple, rustic cooking, bacon and cabbage symbolize familial gatherings and traditional Irish hospitality.

Pubs, Gastropubs & Local Favorites

Ireland's pub culture is woven into its very soul — a place where conversation flows freely, music fills the corners, and meals are crafted with heart. From ancient watering holes steeped in legend to stylish gastropubs elevating traditional flavors, each establishment offers more than just a pint; it offers a true Irish experience.

The Brazen Head – Dublin

Often cited as Ireland's oldest pub, dating back to 1198, The Brazen Head feels like stepping into a living museum. Stone walls, flickering candlelight, and timber beams create an atmospheric setting where live folk music breathes life into centuries of tales. The menu leans into classic Irish comfort — think beef and Guinness stew or seafood chowder — paired with an impressive selection of whiskeys. It is a favorite not just for its history but for its genuine warmth and authenticity that even locals cherish.

- **Location:** 20 Lower Bridge Street, Dublin 8, D08 WC64, Ireland
- **Opening Hours:** Monday–Sunday, 12:00 PM – 11:30 PM
- **Insider Tip:** Arrive early in the evening to snag a spot near the musicians for the full traditional music experience.

Tigh Neachtain – Galway

At the heart of Galway's vibrant Latin Quarter stands Tigh Neachtain, a beloved pub that perfectly captures the city's creative spirit. The building itself has been a gathering place since 1894, and today, its cozy snugs and art-adorned walls invite a wonderfully eclectic crowd. Renowned for championing local craft beers and ciders, Tigh Neachtain also shines with hearty gastropub fare, especially their artisan cheese boards and lamb sliders. It is an effortless blend of old-world character and modern culinary pride.

- **Location:** 17 Cross Street Upper, Galway, H91 FX30, Ireland
- **Opening Hours:** Monday–Thursday 10:30 AM – 11:30 PM, Friday–Saturday 10:30 AM – 12:30 AM, Sunday 12:30 PM – 11:00 PM
- **Insider Tip:** Ask the bartender for a recommendation from their rotating selection of Galway Bay Brewery specials — they often serve limited-edition releases unavailable elsewhere.

The Locke Bar – Limerick

Overlooking the Abbey River, The Locke Bar combines historical charm with lively energy, making it a cornerstone of Limerick's social scene. The building itself dates back to the 18th century, and the setting feels timeless, with riverside tables and an interior of stone and wood.

Beyond its stunning location, The Locke Bar is famous for its seafood, particularly the creamy chowder and the loaded seafood platter. Regular traditional music and Irish dancing sessions add to its infectious spirit.

- **Location:** 3 George's Quay, Limerick, V94 K3H6, Ireland
- **Opening Hours:** Monday–Thursday 12:00 PM – 11:30 PM, Friday–Saturday 12:00 PM – 12:30 AM, Sunday 12:00 PM – 11:00 PM
- **Insider Tip:** Time your visit for Sunday afternoons when impromptu dance performances often break out alongside live music.

Sean's Bar – Athlone

Holding the Guinness World Record as the oldest pub in Europe, Sean's Bar in Athlone is a must-visit for anyone seeking Ireland's ancient, convivial heart. Its origins trace back to 900 AD, and fragments of wattle and daub from the original walls are still on display. Despite its remarkable history, Sean's is anything but a museum piece — it buzzes with life, pouring excellent pints of Guinness and welcoming all with fireside warmth. Storytelling nights and traditional music are a regular, treasured feature.

- **Location:** 13 Main Street, Athlone, County Westmeath, N37 DW76, Ireland
- **Opening Hours:** Monday–Sunday 10:30 AM – Late (usually around midnight)
- **Insider Tip:** Take a few minutes to ask the bartender about the pub's history; some staff give spontaneous mini-tours if it's not too busy.

The Stag's Head – Dublin

Hidden along a narrow passage off Dame Street, The Stag's Head is a Dublin institution that has barely changed since Victorian times. Dark polished wood, stained glass, a commanding mounted stag — every corner whispers elegance and tradition. While the drinks are exceptional, including a legendary pint of Guinness, it is the atmosphere that leaves the lasting impression: lively but unpretentious, filled with sharp Dublin wit. The upstairs room occasionally hosts brilliant comedy nights, showcasing rising stars of the Irish scene.

- **Location:** 1 Dame Court, Dublin 2, D02 TW84, Ireland
- **Opening Hours:** Monday–Thursday 10:30 AM – 11:30 PM, Friday–Saturday 10:30 AM – 12:30 AM, Sunday 12:30 PM – 11:00 PM
- **Insider Tip:** Visit midweek around 5:00 PM to experience it bustling with after-work Dubliners without the overwhelming weekend crowds.

An Spailpín Fánach – Cork

In a city known for its strong sense of identity, An Spailpín Fánach stands proudly as one of Cork's most beloved traditional pubs. Its name, meaning "the wandering laborer," hints at its deep folk roots. Inside, low ceilings, roaring fires, and faded posters of folk legends set the mood for nights of raucous music and storytelling. While it attracts plenty of tourists, locals fiercely guard it as an authentic slice of old Cork.

- **Location:** 28 South Main Street, Cork, T12 AE81, Ireland
- **Opening Hours:** Monday–Thursday 4:00 PM – 11:30 PM, Friday 4:00 PM – 12:30 AM, Saturday 2:00 PM – 12:30 AM, Sunday 2:00 PM – 11:00 PM
- **Insider Tip:** Head there late on Saturday night when the best traditional sessions unfold spontaneously by the fireplace.

The Temple Bar – Dublin

An institution in the heart of Dublin's historic quarter, The Temple Bar is perhaps the city's most famous pub. Its bright red facade, bustling atmosphere, and impressive whiskey collection draw visitors from all over the world. Despite its popularity among tourists, the pub retains a lively, traditional Irish spirit with nightly live music sessions featuring folk, ballads, and lively jigs. It's a great place to immerse yourself in Dublin's vibrant pub culture, though it can get very busy during peak times.

- **Location:** 47-48 Temple Bar, Dublin, D02 N725, Ireland
- **Opening Hours:** Daily, 10:30 AM – 2:30 AM
- **Insider Tip:** Visit earlier in the day to enjoy a quieter atmosphere and to snap a photo without the crowds.

The Crane Bar – Galway

For travelers searching for authentic Irish music, The Crane Bar in Galway stands out as a temple of traditional sounds. It is located slightly off the main tourist trail and maintains a loyal local following. The ground floor has a welcoming, lively pub vibe, but it is the upstairs "listening room" that sets it apart, hosting nightly performances where audiences gather around close to the musicians, hanging onto every note of the fiddles, flutes, and bodhráns.

- **Location:** 2 Sea Road, Galway, H91 YP97, Ireland
- **Opening Hours:** Monday–Thursday 5:00 PM – 11:30 PM, Friday 5:00 PM – 12:30 AM, Saturday 4:00 PM – 12:30 AM, Sunday 4:00 PM – 11:00 PM
- **Insider Tip:** Attend an early evening session if you prefer sitting up close — latecomers often stand along the back walls during busier performances.

The Long Hall – Dublin

Steeped in Victorian elegance, The Long Hall is one of Dublin's oldest and most beautiful pubs, operating since 1766. With mahogany woodwork, ornate mirrors, and antique lighting, the pub has a timeless charm. It's favored by locals who appreciate its authentic atmosphere and excellent pint of Guinness. Though it doesn't serve food, its focus on traditional pub vibes and perfectly poured pints makes it a standout among Dublin's historic watering holes.

- **Location:** 51 South Great George's Street, Dublin 2, D02 HP86, Ireland
- **Opening Hours:** Monday–Thursday, 12:00 PM – 11:30 PM; Friday–Saturday, 12:00 PM – 12:30 AM; Sunday, 12:30 PM – 11:00 PM
- **Insider Tip:** If you love history, ask the barman about the pub's role during the Irish War of Independence.

O'Connor's Famous Pub – Salthill, Galway

Stepping into O'Connor's Famous Pub is like stepping back in time. Located in the seaside village of Salthill, this atmospheric pub is decorated with vintage memorabilia hanging from every inch of the ceiling and walls. Known for its cozy fires, friendly locals, and legendary live music sessions, O'Connor's even appeared in Ed Sheeran's "Galway Girl" music video. It's a must-visit for anyone wanting an authentic, music-filled Irish night out.

- **Location:** Upper Salthill Road, Galway, H91 N9TD, Ireland
- **Opening Hours:** Monday–Saturday, 12:00 PM – 12:30 AM; Sunday, 12:30 PM – 11:00 PM
- **Insider Tip:** Arrive early for live music nights as seating fills up fast, especially on weekends.

Dick Mack's Pub – Dingle, County Kerry

Dick Mack's Pub is a Dingle institution, once a combination pub and leather shop — and traces of its artisan past still line the walls. This iconic spot offers cozy snugs, a courtyard beer garden, and an impressive whiskey bar featuring hundreds of Irish varieties. It regularly hosts music sessions and attracts visitors and locals alike with its relaxed, welcoming vibe.

- **Location:** 47 Green Street, Dingle, County Kerry, V92 FF97, Ireland
- **Opening Hours:** Monday–Sunday, 12:00 PM – 11:30 PM
- **Insider Tip:** Head to the back courtyard, where you might catch a spontaneous folk session under the stars.

John Kavanagh's "The Gravediggers" – Dublin

Tucked away beside Glasnevin Cemetery, The Gravediggers is one of Dublin's most cherished hidden gems. It's a no-frills pub that has barely changed since the 19th century, famous for serving one of the best pints of Guinness in the city. There's no music or TVs — conversation and atmosphere reign supreme. It's called "The Gravediggers" because cemetery workers used to slip in for a pint after digging graves.

- **Location:** 1 Prospect Square, Glasnevin, Dublin 9, D09 CF72, Ireland
- **Opening Hours:** Monday–Saturday, 10:30 AM – 11:30 PM; Sunday, 12:30 PM – 11:00 PM

- **Insider Tip:** Try their tapas-style traditional Irish food — it's surprisingly excellent for a pub that looks so old-school.

Best Restaurants in Ireland

Ireland's culinary scene has blossomed into a world-class affair, blending traditional flavors with daring innovation. From Michelin-starred dining rooms to cozy, passion-driven kitchens, each restaurant offers a deep sense of place and a taste of Ireland's finest ingredients.

Chapter One – Dublin

Chapter One is a beacon of fine dining in Dublin, renowned for its artful balance of elegance and warmth. Under the guidance of chef Mickael Viljanen, the restaurant crafts dishes that are as visually stunning as they are flavorful. Think Irish lobster with bergamot or salt-aged duck with wild Irish berries. The tasting menus highlight locally sourced ingredients with a refined, modern twist, yet the atmosphere remains unpretentious. It is a place where both serious gourmets and relaxed celebrators feel entirely at home.

- **Cuisine Highlight:** Modern Irish with French techniques
- **Location:** 18–19 Parnell Square North, Dublin 1, D01 T3V8, Ireland
- **Opening Hours:** Tuesday–Saturday 5:00 PM – 9:00 PM
- **Contact Information:** +353 1 873 2266 | www.chapteronerestaurant.com

- **Insider Tip:** Book the Chef's Table experience for a unique behind-the-scenes glimpse into the kitchen action — spaces fill quickly, often months ahead.

Aniar – Galway

Aniar, meaning "from the west" in Irish, is a Michelin-starred restaurant that pays homage to the wild terroir of Ireland's west coast. Chef JP McMahon's menu is an ever-changing symphony built around hyperlocal, foraged, and seasonal ingredients. Dishes often include Atlantic seaweed, native lamb, and heirloom vegetables, crafted with minimal interference to preserve their natural integrity. Dining at Aniar is not just a meal; it is a narrative of the land, told plate by plate, with quiet reverence.

- **Cuisine Highlight:** Contemporary Irish tasting menus focused on terroir
- **Location:** 53 Lower Dominick Street, Galway, H91 XVP2, Ireland
- **Opening Hours:** Wednesday–Saturday 6:00 PM – 9:00 PM
- **Contact Information:** +353 91 535 947 | www.aniarrestaurant.ie
- **Insider Tip:** Take advantage of their "Aniar At Home" classes if you're staying longer — a fantastic way to learn Irish culinary techniques directly from the team.

Ichigo Ichie – Cork

Ichigo Ichie brings an extraordinary kaiseki dining experience to the heart of Cork. Japanese chef Takashi Miyazaki seamlessly merges the precision of Japanese haute cuisine with Irish ingredients, creating an exquisite seasonal menu that defies easy categorization. Dishes are tiny works of art, like miso-cured Clare Island salmon or Connemara crab paired with yuzu kosho. Each plate flows into the next with meditative grace, offering an unforgettable journey of flavor and craftsmanship that lingers long after the final bite.

- **Cuisine Highlight:** Japanese Kaiseki with Irish ingredients
- **Location:** 5 Fenn's Quay, Sheares Street, Cork City, T12 W5TD, Ireland
- **Opening Hours:** Thursday–Saturday 6:00 PM – 9:00 PM
- **Contact Information:** +353 21 427 9997 | www.ichigoichie.ie
- **Insider Tip:** Seats are extremely limited — book 2–3 months in advance for weekends, and ask for counter seating for a closer view of Chef Miyazaki's artistry.

House Restaurant at Cliff House Hotel – Ardmore

Suspended dramatically on a cliff edge overlooking Ardmore Bay, the House Restaurant at the Cliff House Hotel delivers one of Ireland's most romantic and sensory dining experiences. Chef Ian Doyle's cooking is elegant yet deeply rooted in the coastal environment, featuring treasures like Helvick cod, organic vegetables, and foraged herbs. Every dish is elevated by a stunning ocean view.

The multi-course tasting menus are complemented by a carefully curated wine list, making every meal an occasion.

- **Cuisine Highlight:** Modern Irish coastal cuisine
- **Location:** Middle Road, Ardmore, Co. Waterford, P36 DK38, Ireland
- **Opening Hours:** Thursday–Sunday 6:00 PM – 9:00 PM
- **Contact Information:** +353 24 87800 | www.thecliffhousehotel.com
- **Insider Tip:** Book a table around sunset to enjoy breathtaking views as the light shifts across the sea.

The Oak Room at Adare Manor – Limerick

The Oak Room exudes grandeur fitting of its setting in the stately Adare Manor. With a Michelin star under chef Michael Tweedie, the menu showcases the best of Irish produce, treated with classic French precision and contemporary flair. Dishes like roasted pigeon with beetroot or wild Irish turbot with brown butter bear the mark of craftsmanship, creating an immersive dining experience framed by oak-paneled walls and centuries-old history. Service is polished but warmly welcoming.

- **Cuisine Highlight:** Contemporary Irish fine dining
- **Location:** Adare Manor, Adare, Co. Limerick, V94 W8WR, Ireland
- **Opening Hours:** Wednesday–Sunday 6:00 PM – 9:00 PM

- **Contact Information:** +353 61 605 200 | www.adaremanor.com
- **Insider Tip:** Ask for a pre-dinner stroll through the manor's grounds; the gardens and architecture set the perfect mood for an unforgettable meal.

Wild Honey Inn – Lisdoonvarna

Wild Honey Inn is Ireland's only Michelin-starred pub and a shining example of refined, rustic dining. Chef Aidan McGrath's dedication to showcasing local Clare produce shines through in dishes like Burren lamb, wild Atlantic fish, and fresh garden vegetables. The food is elegant yet unfussy, designed to highlight natural flavors rather than overwhelm them. Set in a charming Victorian building on the edge of the Burren, the inn is as much about slow, soulful eating as it is about convivial country hospitality.

- **Cuisine Highlight:** Seasonal Irish country fare
- **Location:** Kincora Road, Lisdoonvarna, Co. Clare, V95 KP86, Ireland
- **Opening Hours:** Wednesday–Sunday 6:00 PM – 9:00 PM (April to October seasonally)
- **Contact Information:** +353 65 707 4300 | www.wildhoneyinn.com
- **Insider Tip:** Book one of their cozy guest rooms and stay overnight to fully savor the peaceful rural surroundings after dinner.

Campagne – Kilkenny

Campagne stands proudly as one of Ireland's best examples of modern French-inspired cuisine with an Irish soul. Located just outside Kilkenny's medieval center, it boasts a Michelin star and a menu brimming with vibrant, seasonal ingredients. Chef Garrett Byrne's dishes — such as Kilkenny venison with smoked beetroot or rich foie gras terrine — reflect flawless technique without pretension. The cozy, contemporary décor, highlighted by bold local artwork, creates an inviting atmosphere that perfectly balances elegance and warmth.

- **Cuisine Highlight:** Modern French-Irish fine dining
- **Location:** Gashouse Lane, Kilkenny, R95 XKR9, Ireland
- **Opening Hours:** Wednesday–Saturday 6:00 PM – 9:30 PM; Sunday 12:30 PM – 3:00 PM
- **Contact Information:** +353 56 777 2858 | www.campagne.ie
- **Insider Tip:** Try the early evening prix fixe menu for excellent value — same exceptional cooking at a friendlier price.

Dede at Customs House – Baltimore, West Cork

Turkish chef Ahmet Dede has created something truly unique at Dede, where Michelin-starred precision meets the rich bounty of West Cork. His deeply personal menu weaves together local seafood, artisanal lamb, and foraged greens with Ottoman flavors and contemporary techniques. Dishes like lobster with Anatolian spices or Gubbeen lamb with yogurt and mint are both comforting and surprising. Set in the pretty seaside village of Baltimore, dining here feels like a serene, sensorial journey by the sea.

- **Cuisine Highlight:** Turkish-influenced modern Irish
- **Location:** Customs House, The Square, Baltimore, West Cork, P81 YE14, Ireland
- **Opening Hours:** Thursday–Sunday 6:00 PM – 9:00 PM
- **Contact Information:** +353 28 20600 | www.customshousebaltimore.com
- **Insider Tip:** Spend the day exploring the rugged coast before your dinner — the fresh sea air seems to make the flavors even more vivid.

Kai – Galway

Kai ("food" in Maori) has become a culinary institution in Galway, famous for its fearless devotion to seasonal, local produce. Chef Jess Murphy crafts ever-evolving menus that embrace whatever is freshest from land and sea.

Expect hearty, vibrant dishes such as crab and seaweed risotto or spiced lamb shoulder with flatbreads. The setting — a bright, rustic room with salvaged wood and wildflowers — matches the earthy, generous spirit of the food perfectly. It's lively, casual, and distinctly West of Ireland in character.

- **Cuisine Highlight:** Seasonal, rustic modern Irish
- **Location:** 22 Sea Road, Galway, H91 DX47, Ireland
- **Opening Hours:** Tuesday–Saturday 9:00 AM – 3:00 PM (Lunch), 6:00 PM – 9:30 PM (Dinner)
- **Contact Information:** +353 91 526 003 | www.kaigalway.com
- **Insider Tip:** Their brunch is legendary — arrive early or prepare for a relaxed queue; the lemon ricotta hotcakes alone are worth it.

The Tannery – Dungarvan

Located in the charming coastal town of Dungarvan, The Tannery is where chef Paul Flynn serves up heartfelt, flavor-packed modern Irish cuisine. Known for championing rich, bold flavors without fuss, Flynn's menus are built around whatever is freshest from the sea and nearby farms. Dishes like pan-roasted hake with shellfish bisque or slow-cooked pork belly with cider reduction are favorites. The atmosphere is stylish yet deeply welcoming, making it a popular destination for both special occasions and relaxed feasting.

- **Cuisine Highlight:** Flavorsome modern Irish
- **Location:** Quay Street, Dungarvan, Co. Waterford, X35 EE93, Ireland
- **Opening Hours:** Wednesday–Saturday 6:00 PM – 9:00 PM; Sunday Lunch 12:30 PM – 3:00 PM
- **Contact Information:** +353 58 45420 | www.tannery.ie
- **Insider Tip:** Combine your visit with a stroll or cycle along the nearby Waterford Greenway — a perfect pairing of coastal scenery and culinary reward.

Whiskey Trails & Distillery Tours

Ireland's love affair with whiskey spans centuries, entwined with the country's cultural identity and legendary hospitality. Traversing Ireland's whiskey trails feels like embarking on a journey through its heart — each distillery offering not only spirits but the rich stories, craftsmanship, and landscapes that shaped them. From ancient pot still traditions to contemporary craft innovators, visiting these distilleries uncovers an essential flavor of Ireland.

Old Jameson Distillery – Midleton, County Cork

The Jameson Distillery in Midleton is a pilgrimage site for whiskey lovers, offering an enthralling dive into the craftsmanship behind Ireland's most iconic whiskey. Guided tours unfold in the sprawling grounds of the historic distillery complex, where ancient copper pot stills, fragrant maturation warehouses, and interactive exhibits bring the distilling process vividly to life. Tasting sessions let visitors compare Jameson with American and Scotch whiskeys, while the premium whiskey tastings and cask draws elevate the experience to something truly unforgettable.

- **Location:** Distillery Walk, Midleton, Co. Cork, P25 Y394
- **Opening Hours:** Daily 10:00 AM – 6:00 PM
- **Contact Information:** +353 21 461 3594 | www.jamesonwhiskey.com
- **Insider Tip:** Book the "Behind the Scenes" Distillery Experience for a rare chance to visit working production areas not open to standard tours.

Teeling Whiskey Distillery – Dublin

In the heart of Dublin's historic Liberties district, Teeling Whiskey Distillery brought whiskey-making back to the city after nearly half a century. This vibrant, working distillery blends old-world tradition with new-world innovation. Tours walk visitors through the sights, sounds, and aromas of fermentation and distillation before culminating in lively guided tastings. With its dynamic atmosphere, urban energy, and award-winning small-batch whiskeys, Teeling reflects the contemporary spirit of Irish distilling.

- **Location:** 13-17 Newmarket, Dublin 8, D08 KD91
- **Opening Hours:** Daily 10:00 AM – 5:30 PM
- **Contact Information:** +353 1 531 0888 | www.teelingwhiskey.com
- **Insider Tip:** Try the distillery-exclusive releases available only on-site — perfect souvenirs for serious collectors.

Bushmills Distillery – County Antrim, Northern Ireland

Standing proudly since 1608, Bushmills holds the title of Ireland's oldest licensed whiskey distillery. Nestled near the rugged beauty of the Giant's Causeway, Bushmills offers an evocative glimpse into centuries of whiskey-making tradition. Tours wind through atmospheric stone buildings, copper still rooms, and cask warehouses infused with the scent of maturing whiskey.

Tasting sessions feature the signature smoothness of Bushmills whiskeys, including rare single malts aged up to 21 years.

- **Location:** 2 Distillery Road, Bushmills, Co. Antrim, BT57 8XH
- **Opening Hours:** Monday–Saturday 10:00 AM – 5:00 PM; Sunday 12:00 PM – 4:30 PM
- **Contact Information:** +44 28 2073 3218 | www.bushmills.com
- **Insider Tip:** Combine your distillery visit with a scenic drive along the Causeway Coastal Route — among the most breathtaking landscapes in Ireland.

Dingle Distillery – Dingle, County Kerry

Small, fiercely independent, and fiercely proud, Dingle Distillery has earned a devoted following for its artisan approach to craft whiskey. Set against the backdrop of the dramatic Kerry coast, the distillery produces limited batches of whiskey, gin, and vodka, with every step meticulously managed in-house. Tours are intimate and educational, offering an up-close look at the distillation process along with generous tastings. The Dingle Single Malt, matured in bourbon, sherry, and port casks, has already reached cult status among aficionados.

- **Location:** Farranredmond, Dingle, Co. Kerry, V92 E7YD
- **Opening Hours:** Monday–Saturday 10:00 AM – 5:00 PM (Tours by booking)
- **Contact Information:** +353 66 402 9011 | www.dingledistillery.ie
- **Insider Tip:** Arrive a little early and stroll along Dingle's harbor before your tour — the perfect way to soak up the local charm.

Slane Distillery – County Meath

On the historic grounds of Slane Castle, where rock legends have performed and history echoes through ancient stone walls, Slane Distillery offers a whiskey experience infused with both heritage and bold innovation. Using triple-casked maturation (virgin oak, seasoned oak, and sherry casks), Slane Irish Whiskey achieves a smooth, rich flavor profile that nods to both tradition and contemporary tastes. Tours explore the historic stables, working distillery, and conclude with tastings in a beautifully restored lounge.

- **Location:** Slane Castle Estate, Slane, Co. Meath, C15 XP83
- **Opening Hours:** Friday–Sunday 11:00 AM – 5:00 PM (Tours by appointment)
- **Contact Information:** +353 41 988 4477 | www.slaneirishwhiskey.com

- **Insider Tip:** Pair your distillery tour with a visit to nearby Slane Castle itself — music and history enthusiasts will find it a real highlight.

Craft Beer Scene & Irish Breweries

Ireland's brewing tradition stretches back over a thousand years, but the modern craft beer movement has sparked a thrilling renaissance. Today, microbreweries, independent brewpubs, and innovative beer festivals breathe fresh life into an ancient craft, delighting both locals and travelers with their creativity. From Dublin's urban taprooms to wild coastal breweries in remote corners of the island, Ireland's craft beer scene offers a world of flavor, storytelling, and discovery.

Galway Bay Brewery – Galway

Galway Bay Brewery stands as one of Ireland's most celebrated craft brewing pioneers. Founded in 2009 by two friends with a passion for American-style craft beer, the brewery quickly made waves across the country. Their flagship "Of Foam and Fury," a bold Double IPA, along with seasonal experimental releases, reflect the brewery's fearless approach to brewing. Guided tours lead visitors through the brewing process, while tastings offer a dynamic experience across their wide-ranging styles — from crisp pilsners to rich barrel-aged stouts.

- **Location:** Galway Bay Brewery, Oranmore, Galway, H91 V04C
- **Opening Hours:** Monday–Saturday 12:00 PM – 6:00 PM (Tours by appointment)
- **Contact Information:** +353 91 792 999 | www.galwaybaybrewery.com
- **Insider Tip:** Visit their Oslo Bar in Salthill for an unforgettable pint by the seaside paired with superb local seafood.

The White Hag Brewery – Ballymote, County Sligo

The White Hag embraces Irish mythology and tradition while pushing brewing boundaries. Specializing in bold IPAs, sour beers, and traditional Irish ales, the brewery has built a reputation for both innovation and reverence for history. Their annual Hagstravaganza Festival draws brewers and beer lovers from around the world. Visitors to the brewery can expect a vibrant, hands-on tasting experience, featuring flights that range from their sessionable "Little Fawn" IPA to richly complex barrel-aged beers.

- **Location:** Unit 1, Industrial Estate, Ballymote, Co. Sligo, F56 KR24

- **Opening Hours:** Monday–Friday 9:00 AM – 5:00 PM (Tours on request)
- **Contact Information:** +353 71 930 8570 | www.thewhitehag.com
- **Insider Tip:** Plan your visit around Hagstravaganza in August — a festival celebrating the global craft beer community right in Sligo.

Eight Degrees Brewing – Mitchelstown, County Cork

Eight Degrees Brewing, founded by a New Zealander and an Australian who fell in love with Ireland, embodies adventurous brewing with an international flair. Their award-winning beers include seasonal lagers, barrel-aged special releases, and their wildly popular "Full Irish" Single Malt IPA. Rooted at the foot of the Galtee Mountains, the brewery balances innovation with an artisan approach, favoring locally sourced ingredients whenever possible.

- **Location:** Unit 3, Coolnanave Business Park, Mitchelstown, Co. Cork, P67 VW42
- **Opening Hours:** Monday–Friday 9:00 AM – 5:00 PM (Tours by arrangement)
- **Contact Information:** +353 25 84 122 | www.eightdegrees.ie
- **Insider Tip:** Their limited-edition barrel-aged stouts, released every winter, are collectors' treasures — ask in advance if any are still available.

Porterhouse Brewing Company – Dublin

Porterhouse Brewing Company carved out its place in history as Dublin's first craft brewpub back in 1996, long before craft beer was a trend. Renowned for creating Ireland's first microbrewed stout to rival Guinness, Porterhouse offers a lively introduction to the Dublin craft scene. Their beers, ranging from hop-forward IPAs to rich porters, reflect a commitment to both quality and character. The flagship Temple Bar venue is an essential stop for beer enthusiasts seeking a vibrant atmosphere paired with exceptional brews.

- **Location:** 16-18 Parliament Street, Temple Bar, Dublin 2, D02 VR94
- **Opening Hours:** Daily 12:00 PM – 12:00 AM
- **Contact Information:** +353 1 679 8847 | www.porterhousebrewco.com
- **Insider Tip:** Try their Oyster Stout, uniquely brewed with fresh oysters, for a distinctive and unforgettable taste of the sea.

Kinnegar Brewing – Letterkenny, County Donegal

Located in a beautifully rustic farm setting near the stunning Donegal coastline, Kinnegar Brewing champions farmhouse-style brewing with a modern twist.

Their range focuses on balanced, flavorful beers that respect traditional brewing methods while embracing contemporary creativity. From crisp pale ales like "Scraggy Bay" to earthy saisons and aromatic IPAs, Kinnegar's beers evoke the landscapes and weather of Ireland's Wild Atlantic Way.

- **Location:** Ballyraine, Letterkenny, Co. Donegal, F92 XYV4
- **Opening Hours:** Monday–Friday 10:00 AM – 5:00 PM (Tours by booking)
- **Contact Information:** +353 74 912 2733 | www.kinnegarbrewing.ie
- **Insider Tip:** Enjoy a guided tasting experience and pick up limited-batch brews not available outside of Donegal.

Afternoon Tea & Café Scene

Ireland's café culture has blossomed into one of the most delightful experiences for visitors, blending traditional hospitality with contemporary creativity. Whether you're looking for a refined afternoon tea in an elegant setting or a cozy café offering artisanal pastries and specialty coffee, the atmosphere is invariably warm, inviting, and brimming with character. From Dublin's grand hotels to Galway's indie coffee houses, Ireland serves every mood — from luxurious to laid-back — always with an authentic sense of place.

The Shelbourne Hotel – Dublin

One of the most iconic destinations for a traditional afternoon tea, The Shelbourne delivers a truly opulent experience steeped in Irish history.

Guests enjoy tiers of meticulously prepared finger sandwiches, freshly baked scones with clotted cream, and a selection of delicate pastries. The tea menu offers a thoughtful mix of classic blends and rare selections sourced from across the globe, complemented by the elegant setting of The Lord Mayor's Lounge.

- **Location:** 27 St Stephen's Green, Dublin 2, D02 K224
- **Opening Hours:** Daily 12:00 PM – 6:00 PM
- **Contact Information:** +353 1 663 4500 | www.theshelbourne.com
- **Insider Tip:** Reserve well in advance for weekends and request a window seat overlooking St. Stephen's Green for an unforgettable view.

The Westbury Hotel – Dublin

The Westbury's afternoon tea exudes sophistication and creativity, offering a contemporary twist on the beloved tradition. Served in the art-filled Gallery, it features exquisitely crafted pastries, imaginative savory bites, and luxurious scones. Signature teas curated by experts, as well as champagne pairings, enhance the experience. The setting, lined with plush armchairs and rich textiles, perfectly complements the sensory delight of the food and drink.

- **Location:** Balfe Street, Dublin 2, D02 CH66
- **Opening Hours:** Daily 1:00 PM – 5:00 PM
- **Contact Information:** +353 1 679 1122 | www.doylecollection.com

- **Insider Tip:** Opt for the champagne afternoon tea package for a more celebratory experience, especially if marking a special occasion.

Cupán Tae – Galway

Cupán Tae, meaning "cup of tea" in Irish, offers a whimsical, vintage-style afternoon tea experience in the heart of Galway's Latin Quarter. The charming setting, complete with floral china, antique décor, and pastel hues, sets the tone for a truly nostalgic afternoon. Guests can choose from an extensive menu of loose-leaf teas, complemented by an array of homemade treats, from traditional scones to delightfully inventive pastries.

- **Location:** 8 Quay Lane, Galway City, H91 W212
- **Opening Hours:** Monday–Sunday 10:00 AM – 6:00 PM
- **Contact Information:** +353 91 561 404 | www.cupantae.ie
- **Insider Tip:** Try their signature "Galway Cream Tea" featuring locally sourced jam and Irish cream for a true taste of the region.

The Merchant Hotel – Belfast

The Merchant Hotel's afternoon tea experience stands as a beacon of luxury in Northern Ireland. Served in the elegant Great Room, complete with a gilded dome ceiling and grand chandeliers, the service matches the setting with flawless precision.

Guests savor an artful selection of delicate sandwiches, scones with homemade preserves, and sumptuous desserts, accompanied by an expansive tea selection or fine champagne.

- **Location:** 16 Skipper Street, Belfast, BT1 2DZ
- **Opening Hours:** Daily 12:00 PM – 4:30 PM
- **Contact Information:** +44 28 9023 4888 | www.themerchanthotel.com
- **Insider Tip:** Dress smartly; the Merchant's setting and tradition maintain a refined dress code, adding to the experience.

Bewley's Grafton Street – Dublin

A beloved Dublin institution since 1840, Bewley's offers a more casual but richly atmospheric afternoon tea option. With its stained glass windows by Harry Clarke and intricate mosaic floors, the café feels timeless. Afternoon tea includes freshly baked scones, sandwiches, and a selection of mini desserts, all made in-house. Bewley's also offers a fine range of house-blend coffees for those preferring caffeine in a different form.

- **Location:** 78-79 Grafton Street, Dublin 2, D02 K033
- **Opening Hours:** Daily 8:00 AM – 8:00 PM
- **Contact Information:** +353 1 564 0900 | www.bewleys.com
- **Insider Tip:** Arrive early for a seat in the grand main hall and enjoy people-watching along busy Grafton Street.

Top Coffee and Brunch Spots

Brother Hubbard (North & South) – Dublin

Brother Hubbard has become synonymous with inventive, Middle Eastern-inspired brunch and excellent coffee in Dublin. Both the Northside and Southside locations feature vibrant, wholesome menus that balance indulgence with health-conscious options. Think pulled lamb sandwiches with harissa yogurt, Moroccan eggs with feta, and fluffy buttermilk pancakes. Their in-house roasted coffee is equally superb, brewed with passion and precision.

Location:

- North: 153 Capel Street, Dublin 1, D01 V9V0
- South: 46 Harrington Street, Dublin 8, D08 NP9Y

Opening Hours: Monday–Sunday 8:00 AM – 4:00 PM

Insider Tip: Go early on weekends; the queue can build quickly, but the staff move it efficiently, and it's worth the wait.

3fe Coffee – Dublin

Regarded as the pioneer of Ireland's third-wave coffee movement, 3fe Coffee roasts its beans and serves what many argue is the best coffee in Dublin. Their Grand Canal Street café offers a simple yet exceptional brunch menu focusing on quality ingredients, from decadent eggs Benedict to avocado toast on their signature house-made sourdough. Coffee lovers will appreciate the carefully calibrated espresso drinks and tasting flights.

- **Location:** 32 Grand Canal Street Lower, Dublin 2, D02 Y970
- **Opening Hours:** Monday–Sunday 8:00 AM – 3:00 PM
- **Insider Tip:** Visit during weekdays if possible for a quieter, more relaxed experience and a chance to chat with the knowledgeable baristas.

Urban Grind – Galway

Urban Grind redefines brunch in Galway with an edgy, industrial-chic vibe and a menu that is inventive without being overcomplicated. Dishes like duck confit hash with poached eggs, spicy vegan shakshuka, and French toast with whiskey mascarpone set the tone. Their specialty coffee program rivals Dublin's best, featuring Irish roasters like Calendar Coffee alongside guest beans from Europe.

- **Location:** 8 William Street West, Galway, H91 YR5P
- **Opening Hours:** Tuesday–Sunday 9:00 AM – 4:00 PM
- **Insider Tip:** Keep an eye on their rotating specials board; dishes change with the seasons and often spotlight local seafood or foraged ingredients.

Café du Parc – Killarney

Located at the edge of Killarney National Park, Café du Parc offers a brunch setting that feels both sophisticated and serene. Think sourdough crumpets with smoked salmon, free-range egg omelets, and cold-pressed juices, all enjoyed in a chic, glass-walled dining room. The coffee program is outstanding, using organic beans and precision brewing methods to highlight delicate flavors.

- **Location:** Kenmare Place, Killarney, Co. Kerry, V93 X3VW
- **Opening Hours:** Daily 8:00 AM – 5:00 PM
- **Insider Tip:** Plan a walk through Killarney Park before or after brunch — it's only a minute's stroll away and incredibly beautiful in the morning light.

Alchemy Coffee and Books – Cork

Alchemy fuses the love of specialty coffee with a passion for books, creating an artistic, relaxed brunch venue in Cork. The menu features a small but impeccably curated selection of dishes, from sweet potato hash to Turkish-style eggs with sumac yogurt. Their V60 pour-overs and creamy flat whites are crafted from micro-roasted beans, often sourced from small Irish roasters.

- **Location:** 123 Barrack Street, Cork City, T12 R6YE
- **Opening Hours:** Monday–Saturday 8:30 AM – 4:30 PM
- **Insider Tip:** Spend some time browsing the indie bookshelves — they often stock rare or locally published titles you won't find elsewhere.

Established Coffee – Belfast

One of Northern Ireland's top destinations for serious coffee lovers, Established Coffee serves world-class espresso and filter brews in a minimalist, Scandinavian-inspired space. The brunch menu matches the quality, offering house-made granola, sourdough with whipped ricotta and honey, and rotating specials that often highlight Northern Irish produce.

- **Location:** 54 Hill Street, Belfast, BT1 2LB
- **Opening Hours:** Monday–Sunday 8:00 AM – 5:00 PM

- **Insider Tip:** Order a batch brew alongside a brunch dish for an ideal pairing — their baristas are masters at matching flavor notes with food.

Vegan & Vegetarian Friendly Options

Ireland's culinary landscape has evolved tremendously, and today, it offers exceptional options for vegans and vegetarians across cities and towns. Fresh local produce, plant-based innovation, and globally inspired flavors come together to create a dining scene that rivals any major foodie destination. Whether in Dublin, Cork, Galway, or beyond, plant-based diners will find a thriving range of dedicated vegan eateries, stylish vegetarian cafés, and restaurants with outstanding vegan menus.

Cornucopia – Dublin

One of Ireland's pioneering vegetarian restaurants, Cornucopia has been a cornerstone of plant-based dining since 1986. Located in a beautiful Georgian building, it offers a vibrant menu of vegetarian, vegan, and gluten-free dishes. From hearty stews and vegan lasagna to colorful salads and rich desserts, every item is crafted with wholesome, organic ingredients.

- **Cuisine Highlights:** Vegan Shepherd's Pie, Aubergine Casserole, Vegan Chocolate Cake
- **Location:** 19–20 Wicklow Street, Dublin 2, D02 FK27
- **Opening Hours:** Monday–Sunday 12:00 PM – 9:00 PM
- **Contact Information:** +353 1 677 7583 | www.cornucopia.ie
- **Insider Tip:** Arrive slightly before peak lunch or dinner times for the best selection of freshly made dishes before they sell out.

The Lighthouse Café – Galway

The Lighthouse Café has become a beloved spot in Galway for vegetarian and vegan cuisine. Offering a menu of warming curries, homemade soups, decadent vegan cakes, and excellent coffee, it is perfect for casual dining in a cozy atmosphere. The café also hosts yoga workshops and sustainability events, reflecting its holistic ethos.

- **Cuisine Highlights:** Vegan Thai Green Curry, Lentil Shepherd's Pie, Raw Vegan Cheesecake
- **Location:** 8 Abbeygate Street Upper, Galway, H91 AY72

- **Opening Hours:** Tuesday–Saturday 10:00 AM – 5:00 PM
- **Contact Information:** +353 91 567 279 | Facebook Page
- **Insider Tip:** Try their homemade vegan caramel slice — it's a local secret treat that sells out fast.

My Goodness – Cork

My Goodness started as a market stall and has grown into a cult favorite among Cork locals. Specializing in probiotic-rich vegan foods like kimchi, kombucha, and raw cakes, the eatery also serves hearty mains such as vegan burrito bowls and tempeh salads. Everything is made with organic and locally sourced ingredients, embracing a deeply sustainable philosophy.

- **Cuisine Highlights:** Vegan Buddha Bowls, Raw Cacao Treats, Fermented Drinks
- **Location:** English Market, Grand Parade, Cork City, T12 DH02
- **Opening Hours:** Monday–Saturday 9:00 AM – 5:30 PM
- **Contact Information:** +353 87 779 8428 | www.mygoodnessfood.com
- **Insider Tip:** Pick up a bottle of their house-made kombucha — it is one of the finest, small-batch brewed options in Ireland.

Blazing Salads – Dublin

Blazing Salads is a staple for health-focused vegans and vegetarians in the heart of Dublin. Operating as a deli-style eatery, it allows diners to build their plates from an array of colorful salads, vegan quiches, hearty stews, and baked goods. Everything is made fresh daily using organic and whole foods.

- **Cuisine Highlights:** Vegan Thai Noodle Salad, Organic Lentil Soup, Vegan Carrot Cake
- **Location:** 42 Drury Street, Dublin 2, D02 T210
- **Opening Hours:** Monday–Saturday 11:00 AM – 5:00 PM
- **Contact Information:** +353 1 671 9552 | www.blazingsalads.com
- **Insider Tip:** Their vegan samosas and desserts are particularly popular — buy a few extra to enjoy later.

Umi Falafel – Dublin, Cork, Belfast

Offering some of the best Middle Eastern vegan fare in Ireland, Umi Falafel has locations across Dublin, Cork, and Belfast.

Their menu centers around freshly made falafel wraps, mezze platters, and traditional Palestinian and Lebanese specialties. The ingredients are simple, authentic, and full of flavor.

Cuisine Highlights: Palestinian Falafel Wrap, Baba Ghanoush, Vine Leaves

Location:

- Dublin: 13 Dame Street, Dublin 2
- Cork: 37 Oliver Plunkett Street, Cork City .
- Belfast: 96 Botanic Avenue, Belfast

Opening Hours: Monday–Sunday 12:00 PM – 9:00 PM

Contact Information: +353 1 670 6866 (Dublin) | www.umifalafel.ie

Insider Tip: Order the mezze selection for a full taste experience — it is perfect for sharing or a varied solo meal.

Veginity – Dublin

Veginity brings a fine-dining sensibility to vegan cuisine, offering globally inspired tasting menus and a brunch service that has won countless awards. Dishes are inventive and beautifully plated, ranging from jackfruit tacos to tofu Benedict. Everything is crafted from scratch with local and sustainable ingredients.

- **Cuisine Highlights:** Vegan Bao Buns, Tofu Benedict, Korean Fried Cauliflower
- **Location:** 101 Dorset Street Upper, Dublin 1, D01 P9Y9
- **Opening Hours:** Thursday–Sunday 10:00 AM – 3:00 PM (Brunch), 5:00 PM – 10:00 PM (Dinner)
- **Contact Information:** +353 85 721 2120 | www.veginitydublin.com
- **Insider Tip:** Book a table for their themed tasting nights — each menu draws inspiration from a different country's culinary traditions.

Sweet Beat Café – Sligo

Sweet Beat Café showcases vibrant plant-based cuisine using organic and local produce from Sligo and the surrounding region. Their menu includes smoothie bowls, vegan breakfasts, colorful salads, and mouthwatering desserts. They also make their nut milks and ferments, ensuring a clean-eating experience rooted in community values.

- **Cuisine Highlights:** Vegan Breakfast Bowl, Avocado Toast, Raw Snickers Bars
- **Location:** 4 Bridge Street, Abbeyquarter North, Sligo, F91 DW58
- **Opening Hours:** Monday–Saturday 9:00 AM – 4:00 PM
- **Contact Information:** +353 87 972 0131 | www.sweetbeat.ie
- **Insider Tip:** Try their raw desserts — especially the Raw Snickers Bar, which has a loyal following.

Cooking Classes & Culinary Experiences

Ireland's culinary culture goes beyond dining — it's about heritage, storytelling, and the deep connection between land and plate. Whether you're learning to bake traditional soda bread or foraging along the wild Atlantic coast, these cooking classes and culinary experiences invite you to immerse yourself in Irish flavors hands-on.

1. Ballymaloe Cookery School – Shanagarry, County Cork

Set on a 100-acre organic farm, Ballymaloe Cookery School is world-renowned for its commitment to farm-to-fork education. Founded by culinary legend Darina Allen, the school offers everything from half-day workshops to full 12-week professional programs. Expect rustic Irish baking classes, seafood masterclasses, and full immersion into sustainable cooking.

- **Experience Highlight:** Traditional Irish Cooking, Baking, and Organic Farming
- **Location:** Shanagarry, Midleton, County Cork
- **Opening Hours:** Classes vary; generally Monday–Saturday
- **Contact Information:** +353 21 464 6785
- **Insider Tip:** Book a garden tour along with your class — it offers fascinating insights into the organic philosophy behind their food.

2. Dublin Cookery School – Blackrock, Dublin

Just a short drive from Dublin city center, Dublin Cookery School offers practical, inspiring courses suitable for all skill levels. From classic Irish dishes like lamb stew and boxty to international cuisines, it's a modern, lively learning environment. The school also hosts specialized wine-pairing evenings and artisan baking classes.

- **Experience Highlight:** Hands-On Irish and Global Cuisine Workshops
- **Location:** Brookfield Terrace, Blackrock, Dublin

- **Opening Hours:** Classes typically run Monday–Saturday
- **Contact Information:** +353 1 210 0555
- **Insider Tip:** Their full-day Irish Baking course is a must for lovers of breads, cakes, and scones.

3. Aniar Boutique Cookery School – Galway

Located behind the Michelin-starred Aniar Restaurant, the Aniar Boutique Cookery School offers an exceptional opportunity to cook at the level of a Michelin kitchen. Classes focus on traditional Irish techniques, fermentation, pickling, and the use of local, seasonal ingredients — all hallmarks of west coast Irish cuisine.

- **Experience Highlight:** Michelin-Star Kitchen Skills and Traditional Preservation Techniques
- **Location:** 53 Lower Dominick Street, Galway
- **Opening Hours:** Scheduled classes mainly on Saturdays
- **Contact Information:** +353 91 535 947
- **Insider Tip:** Sign up early for the "Wild Atlantic Way" class — spots fill quickly due to limited group sizes.

4. Cookery Cottage – Douglas, Cork

A cozy, family-run culinary school, Cookery Cottage is perfect for travelers seeking friendly, relaxed classes in traditional Irish cooking. The hands-on workshops range from Irish country kitchen classics to artisan breadmaking and home-preserving. It's particularly good for families and beginners.

- **Experience Highlight:** Irish Comfort Food and Baking for Beginners
- **Location:** South Douglas Road, Douglas, Cork
- **Opening Hours:** Tuesday–Saturday (schedule varies)
- **Contact Information:** +353 21 489 2973
- **Insider Tip:** They offer fun "Cook & Dine" evenings — a great alternative to a standard restaurant night out.

5. Foraging Experiences with Wild Food Mary – County Clare

If you want to get truly close to nature, Wild Food Mary offers unforgettable guided foraging walks along Ireland's wild landscapes. Learn to identify edible plants, mushrooms, and seaweeds — then cook a meal with your gathered ingredients. It's a unique way to understand Ireland's ancient relationship with the land.

- **Experience Highlight:** Foraging, Wild Cooking, and Plant Identification
- **Location:** Various coastal and woodland locations around County Clare
- **Opening Hours:** Seasonal, usually Spring to Autumn
- **Contact Information:** +353 87 741 8536
- **Insider Tip:** Wear sturdy shoes and bring a small basket for collecting your finds — you'll be amazed at how much you can gather.

6. The Tannery Cookery School – Dungarvan, County Waterford

Owned by celebrated chef Paul Flynn, The Tannery Cookery School is attached to the famous Tannery Restaurant and Townhouse. The school offers accessible, hands-on courses emphasizing bold flavors and modern Irish cooking. Choose from half-day sessions, full-day courses, or weekend retreats combining cooking, dining, and relaxing stays.

- **Experience Highlight:** Vibrant, Modern Irish Cuisine Workshops
- **Location:** Quay Street, Dungarvan, County Waterford
- **Opening Hours:** Scheduled courses, mainly Friday–Sunday
- **Contact Information:** +353 58 45420
- **Insider Tip:** Their weekend packages are perfect for couples or friends looking for a full gourmet getaway.

7. An Grianán Cookery School, County Louth

Part of the Irish Countrywomen's Association, An Grianán offers a unique culinary experience rooted deeply in Irish traditions. Courses focus on hearty country cooking, Irish baking, and festive holiday foods. It's a wonderful opportunity to explore traditional methods and recipes, often taught by local Irish "mammies" who pass down generations of culinary wisdom in a friendly and communal environment.

- **Cuisine Highlight:** Traditional Irish Cooking and Baking
- **Location:** Termonfeckin, Co. Louth, Ireland
- **Opening Hours:** Monday–Friday, 9:00 AM – 5:00 PM (residential stays often included)
- **Contact Information:** +353 41 982 2119 | icaw.ie

- **Insider Tip:** Don't miss their scone and brown bread baking workshops — the recipes are treasured heirlooms.

8. Clonakilty Food Tours & Cookery Experiences, County Cork

While Clonakilty is famous for its black pudding, it's also home to fantastic local produce and innovative culinary experiences. Some tours include market visits followed by cooking classes where participants prepare a menu with ingredients gathered earlier. It's a very "market-to-table" experience, led by local food experts and chefs who offer insider insights into Cork's food scene.

- **Cuisine Highlight:** Local Irish Cuisine with a Focus on Artisan Produce
- **Location:** Clonakilty, Co. Cork, Ireland
- **Opening Hours:** Tour and class times vary; most run late morning into afternoon
- **Contact Information:** +353 86 172 8656 | clonakiltyfoodtours.com
- **Insider Tip:** Ask about seasonal foraging walks combined with cooking sessions for a true taste of wild Ireland.

Chapter 15: Shopping in Ireland

What to Buy in Ireland

Ireland's craftsmanship is as rich as its storytelling tradition. Across the island, artisans have honed their skills over centuries, weaving heritage into every fabric, carving history into every piece of crystal, and shaping identity into each handmade item. Here's what to look for when shopping for authentic Irish treasures:

1. Irish Woolens and Knitwear

Ireland's windswept landscapes birthed a deep tradition of wool craftsmanship. Aran sweaters (jumper or geansaí in Irish) from the Aran Islands are world-famous for their intricate patterns, each design symbolizing luck, clan identity, and daily life. You'll also find cozy scarves, capes, and socks made from pure new Irish wool — ideal for layering during chilly days.

- **Where to Buy:** Aran Sweater Market (Galway, Dublin, Killarney), Blarney Woollen Mills (Cork)
- **Insider Tip:** Look for hand-knit pieces rather than machine-made — they're heavier, softer, and last for generations.

2. Irish Tweed

Ireland's tweed, especially from County Donegal, is celebrated for its colorful flecks and rugged warmth. Traditionally woven by hand, Donegal tweed jackets, caps, and coats offer a classic, timeless Irish style. Many modern designers blend tradition with sleek tailoring, making Irish tweed both heritage-rich and fashionable.

- **Where to Buy:** Magee 1866 (Donegal Town), Kevin & Howlin (Dublin)
- **Insider Tip:** Invest in a Donegal tweed flat cap — it's a lightweight, packable souvenir that you'll use.

3. Irish Crystal

Irish crystal is world-renowned for its clarity, craftsmanship, and brilliance. The most iconic name, Waterford Crystal, has been producing luxury glassware since the late 18th century. From delicate goblets and vases to intricate chandeliers, each piece is cut by hand using centuries-old techniques.

- **Where to Buy:** House of Waterford Crystal (Waterford City), Kilkenny Shop (nationwide)
- **Insider Tip:** Visit the Waterford factory to see master blowers and cutters at work — and access exclusive designs.

4. Irish Pottery and Ceramics

The raw, earthy beauty of Ireland's landscapes inspires its ceramicists. Studios like Nicholas Mosse (Kilkenny) and Belleek Pottery (Fermanagh) produce handcrafted pottery ranging from rustic tableware to ornate figurines, often decorated with Irish florals and Celtic motifs.

- **Where to Buy:** Nicholas Mosse Pottery (Bennettsbridge), Belleek Pottery Visitor Centre (County Fermanagh)
- **Insider Tip:** Choose hand-painted pieces — each has slight variations, making it uniquely yours.

5. Handmade Jewelry

Ireland's jewelry reflects its mythology and symbolism. Look for Claddagh rings (symbolizing love, loyalty, and friendship), Celtic knotwork designs, and locally mined Connemara marble jewelry. Many pieces are still crafted by small family workshops.

- **Where to Buy:** Celtic & Heraldic Jewelry (Dublin), Brian de Staic Jewelry (Dingle)
- **Insider Tip:** Authentic Claddagh rings should be hallmarked by the Assay Office at Dublin Castle — check for the stamp!

6. Irish Linen

Irish linen has been treasured for centuries for its crisp quality and cool touch. Fine tablecloths, napkins, and handkerchiefs made from flax-grown linen make elegant, long-lasting souvenirs.

- **Where to Buy:** Thomas Ferguson Irish Linen (County Down), Avoca Stores (nationwide)
- **Insider Tip:** Pure Irish linen will feel stiffer at first, but softens beautifully with washing.

7. Traditional Irish Music Instruments

If you're a music lover, a bodhrán (Irish frame drum), a tin whistle, or a handcrafted fiddle make for a special keepsake. Many shops also sell beginner sets with tutorials.

- **Where to Buy:** McNeela Instruments (Dublin), Custy's Traditional Music Shop (Ennis)
- **Insider Tip:** Attend a trad session in a pub first to appreciate the magic before picking your instrument!

Final Shopping Tips:

- **Tax-Free Shopping:** Visitors from outside the EU can claim VAT refunds — keep your receipts!
- **Shop Local:** Artisan cooperatives and small boutiques often offer better quality and authenticity than mass-produced souvenir shops.
- **Shipping Services:** Many Irish stores offer international shipping if you're buying delicate crystal or bulky woolens.

Markets & Artisan Boutiques

Ireland's creative spirit shines in its bustling markets and artisan boutiques, where you can find handmade treasures, local foods, original art, and traditional crafts. Markets are lively hubs where heritage meets contemporary creativity, while boutique shops often feel like stepping into the workshop of a master artisan.

1. English Market, Cork

Operating since 1788, the English Market is one of Europe's oldest and best-covered markets. Step inside to find a wonderland of Irish artisan foods: farmhouse cheeses, handmade chocolates, fresh seafood, and specialty meats. Several stalls also showcase crafts like hand-carved wooden wares and local preserves. The market atmosphere is buzzing but warmly welcoming, with generations of vendors sharing recipes and stories.

- **Location:** Grand Parade, Cork City
- **Opening Hours:** Monday–Saturday, 8:00 AM–6:00 PM
- **Insider Tip:** Grab a gourmet sandwich at the Farmgate Café upstairs, made with market ingredients.

2. Galway Market

Nestled beside St. Nicholas' Collegiate Church, this vibrant open-air market has been a fixture for centuries. On weekends, you'll find local artists selling watercolors, photographers displaying stunning Connemara landscapes, and jewelers offering handmade pieces. Farmers and food producers sell artisan bread, cheeses, and fresh produce, making it a feast for the senses.

- **Location:** Church Lane, Galway City
- **Opening Hours:** Saturday and Sunday, 8:00 AM–6:00 PM
- **Insider Tip:** Look for handmade Connemara marble goods and original Galway hooker boat models.

3. George's Street Arcade, Dublin

Ireland's oldest shopping arcade (opened in 1881) is a Victorian red-brick gem packed with quirky independent shops. Inside, discover artisan boutiques specializing in Irish-made jewelry, vintage clothing, handmade candles, art prints, and rare vinyl. It's the perfect place to browse for unusual and creative souvenirs.

- **Location:** South Great George's Street, Dublin 2
- **Opening Hours:** Monday–Saturday, 9:30 AM–6:30 PM; Sunday, 12:00 PM–6:00 PM
- **Insider Tip:** Visit the tiny record shops and indie bookstores tucked away in the corners.

4. Kilkenny Design Centre

Situated across from Kilkenny Castle, the Design Centre champions Irish design in fashion, ceramics, jewelry, textiles, and art. Featuring over 200 designers and artisans, it's a treasure trove of quality craftsmanship. Workshops and galleries showcase evolving contemporary styles alongside traditional techniques.

- **Location:** The Parade, Kilkenny City
- **Opening Hours:** Daily, 10:00 AM–6:00 PM
- **Insider Tip:** Check out the craft gallery upstairs, often overlooked by casual visitors.

5. Limerick Milk Market

This historic covered market is one of Ireland's best for artisan foods and crafts. Saturday mornings are a sensory delight: aromas of freshly baked breads, the clink of handmade jewelry displays, and colorful stands of artwork and ceramics. Many vendors sell direct-from-maker, making it easy to meet the artisans.

- **Location:** Cornmarket Row, Limerick City
- **Opening Hours:** Friday–Sunday, 8:00 AM–3:00 PM
- **Insider Tip:** Arrive early on Saturdays for the best handmade pastries and hot food stalls.

6. Crafted Design, Wexford

A boutique that feels like an artist's studio, Crafted Design specializes in high-quality Irish-made products: handmade lamps, scarves, wall art, and designer ceramics. Every piece tells a story, supporting local makers from all over Ireland.

- **Location:** South Main Street, Wexford Town
- **Opening Hours:** Monday–Saturday, 10:00 AM–5:30 PM
- **Insider Tip:** Ask about limited-edition pieces from emerging Irish designers — perfect for collectors.

7. St. George's Market, Belfast

Though technically in Northern Ireland, St. George's Market deserves mention. Built in the 1890s, this iconic Victorian market is bursting with artisan crafts, antiques, designer clothes, and delicious local foods. Live music performances create a lively and uniquely Belfast atmosphere.

- **Location:** East Bridge Street, Belfast
- **Opening Hours:** Friday–Sunday, 8:00 AM–4:00 PM
- **Insider Tip:** Look out for local artists offering prints of Northern Ireland's landscapes and historic sites.

8. Avoca Stores

Founded in 1723 as a weaving mill, Avoca has grown into Ireland's most beloved lifestyle brand, combining fashion, homewares, artisan foods, and gifts. Their boutiques across Ireland carry cozy throws, stylish Irish fashion, handmade soaps, and gourmet treats.

- **Locations:** Avoca Kilmacanogue (Co. Wicklow), Avoca Suffolk Street (Dublin), and others
- **Opening Hours:** Typically Monday–Saturday, 9:30 AM–6:00 PM; Sunday hours vary
- **Insider Tip:** Visit a flagship location like Kilmacanogue, which includes a café and garden center.

Final Market Shopping Tips:

- **Go Early:** Morning visits often mean the best stock and more time to chat with makers.
- **Cash Helps:** Some small vendors still prefer cash, especially in rural markets.
- **Ask for Stories:** Irish artisans love to share the inspiration behind their work, and you'll bring home a souvenir rich in meaning, not just material.

Irish Design: Fashion & Home Goods

Ireland's design scene blends centuries of craft tradition with fresh, contemporary innovation. Whether it's a soft tweed jacket, a minimalist ceramic vase, or a handwoven throw, Irish design emphasizes quality, authenticity, and a deep connection to nature and heritage. Across fashion and home goods, you'll find pieces that are timeless yet modern, rooted in Ireland's landscapes, myths, and craftsmanship.

1. Irish Fashion Design

Irish fashion stands out for its love of natural materials like wool, linen, and leather, often designed with subtle nods to Celtic traditions or wild Irish landscapes.

Tweed & Wool: Brands like Magee 1866 and Triona Design transform Donegal tweed into stylish contemporary coats, suits, and accessories. Look for pieces in earthy tones inspired by the Irish countryside.

Knitwear: Irish Aran sweaters (Geansaí Árann) from Inis Meáin and Fisherman Out of Ireland are luxurious updates of the traditional fisherman's sweater, using ultra-soft merino and cashmere blends.

Contemporary Labels: Designers like Simone Rocha, JW Anderson, and Richard Malone are internationally celebrated, pushing Irish fashion into bold, artistic territory.

Jewelry: Makers like Chupi (Dublin) and Enibas (West Cork) blend Irish mythology and nature into delicate, modern jewelry crafted in gold and silver.

2. Irish Home Goods and Interiors

Irish home design is all about warmth, simplicity, and soul. Many artisans craft pieces that reflect a sustainable and thoughtful way of living.

Textiles: Avoca's colorful throws, McNutt of Donegal's woven blankets, and Foxford Woollen Mills' elegant bedding collections are luxurious yet timeless investments.

Ceramics: Makers like Nicholas Mosse (Kilkenny) and Arran Street East (Dublin) create handcrafted pottery that's both functional and beautiful. Expect rustic glazes, organic shapes, and rich textures.

Furniture & Lighting: Orior Furniture (Newry) designs bold, sculptural furniture pieces, while Mullan Lighting (County Monaghan) handcrafts industrial-inspired lights that have found homes around the world.

Handcrafted Decor: Look for handblown glassware from Jerpoint Glass Studio and intricate, nature-inspired prints from Jam Art Factory in Dublin.

3. Where to Shop for Irish Design

Brown Thomas (Dublin, Cork, Galway, Limerick): For luxury Irish fashion labels and cutting-edge designers.

Irish Design Shop (Dublin): A curated boutique filled with jewelry, homewares, and art from leading Irish artisans.

Kilkenny Shop (various locations): A great place to discover Irish-made fashion, ceramics, linens, and gifts.

Design House (Dublin): Supports independent designers with a special focus on sustainable fashion and crafts.

Insider Tips for Buying Irish Design:

- **Look for "Made in Ireland" labels:** Many brands are inspired by Ireland but made elsewhere. True Irish-made pieces will clearly state it.
- **Visit Studios:** Many artisans open their studios to visitors — it's a fantastic way to see craft in action and find one-of-a-kind pieces.

- **Invest in Quality:** Irish woollens, tweeds, and ceramics are built to last — these aren't just souvenirs; they're heirlooms in the making.

Souvenirs with Authentic Irish Flair

Ireland's rich culture, stunning landscapes, and artistic spirit inspire some of the world's most memorable souvenirs. Rather than settling for mass-produced trinkets, true Irish souvenirs carry a deep sense of place, crafted with tradition, skill, and a connection to the land. Whether you're looking for gifts or personal keepsakes, these authentic treasures embody the heart of Ireland.

1. Aran Knitwear

A genuine Aran sweater from the Aran Islands or Irish brands like Inis Meáin or Carraig Donn répresents both heritage and craftsmanship. Traditionally knitted with intricate patterns symbolizing fishermen's hopes for luck and safety, today's sweaters offer a stylish and practical reminder of Ireland's maritime culture.

Tip: Choose hand-knit pieces for the finest quality, usually heavier and softer to the touch.

2. Irish Tweed Products

Donegal tweed, known for its vibrant flecks and rugged charm, has been woven in County Donegal for centuries. Scarves, caps, jackets, and even bags crafted from authentic tweed bring a piece of Ireland's wild landscapes back home.

Tip: Visit family-run mills like Magee 1866 in Donegal Town for truly authentic finds.

3. Celtic Jewelry

Jewelry featuring Celtic knots, Claddagh designs, or ogham script (ancient Irish writing) makes for meaningful gifts. Crafted in gold, silver, or even Connemara marble, these pieces symbolize love, loyalty, and eternity.

Tip: Shop at established Irish jewelers like Blarney Woollen Mills or independent studios like Chupi in Dublin for unique craftsmanship.

4. Irish Whiskey & Gin

Bringing home a bottle of Irish whiskey or craft gin is a classic — and delicious — souvenir. Distilleries like Jameson, Teeling, Redbreast, and boutique producers such as Dingle and Drumshanbo offer beautifully bottled spirits that tell the story of Ireland's distilling heritage.

Tip: Some distilleries offer exclusive, distillery-only editions that you won't find elsewhere.

5. Handcrafted Pottery

Ireland's pottery scene offers rustic and beautiful creations perfect for home decor. Studios such as Nicholas Mosse in Kilkenny and Stephen Pearce Pottery in Cork create plates, mugs, and serving pieces decorated with traditional Irish motifs and natural glazes.

Tip: Many potteries offer personalized items, making a one-of-a-kind souvenir even more special.

6. Traditional Irish Music

A handpicked album of traditional Irish music — whether it's sean-nós singing, lively reels, or atmospheric harp music — makes a sentimental and easy-to-carry memento. Many local shops, especially in towns like Galway and Dingle, feature indie musicians you won't find abroad.

Tip: Buy from local record shops to support independent Irish artists.

7. Irish Linen and Lace

Irish linen, known for its durability and elegance, has been produced for centuries, particularly in Northern Ireland. Linen tablecloths, handkerchiefs, and lace-trimmed accessories are lightweight, practical souvenirs with timeless charm.

Tip: Visit towns like Banbridge or Belfast's Linen Quarter for authentic selections.

8. Connemara Marble

Often called "Ireland's gemstone," Connemara marble boasts stunning shades of green and has been quarried for over 600 million years. Jewelry, coasters, and keepsakes made from this marble are deeply tied to Ireland's geological and cultural heritage.

Tip: Authentic Connemara marble has natural variations; no two pieces are exactly alike.

9. Art Prints and Local Photography

Irish landscapes are endlessly inspiring. High-quality art prints and photographs of the Cliffs of Moher, the Dingle Peninsula, or ancient castles allow you to bring a piece of that magic home. Many local galleries in cities and small towns carry works by Irish artists.

Tip: Choose signed or limited-edition prints for greater value and authenticity.

10. Handmade Candles & Soaps

Scented with Irish flora like wild gorse, heather, and sea salt, artisan candles and soaps make a sensory souvenir. Brands like FieldDay Ireland and The Handmade Soap Company use local ingredients and sustainable practices.

Tip: Natural Irish products often avoid synthetic additives, making them ideal for sensitive skin and eco-conscious travelers.

Insider Tips for Buying Authentic Irish Souvenirs:

- **Seek out local artisans:** Craft fairs, village shops, and farm markets often hide the best finds.
- **Look for official seals:** Some goods, like Irish linen or Connemara marble, have authenticity stamps.
- **Avoid airport-only gifts:** While convenient, these often lack the craftsmanship and story behind truly memorable Irish souvenirs.

Chapter 16: Ireland Suggested Itinerary

Classic Ireland: 7-Day Itinerary Tour

Experience the timeless charm of Ireland on this carefully designed 7-day journey. From vibrant cities and ancient castles to breathtaking cliffs and cozy villages, this itinerary blends cultural highlights, natural wonders, and authentic Irish experiences for an unforgettable week.

Day 1: Arrival in Dublin – City Exploration

Welcome to Dublin, Ireland's energetic capital, steeped in history, creativity, and lively culture. Your first day balances iconic sights with immersive local experiences, ensuring a perfect start to your Irish journey.

Morning: Arrival and Trinity College Visit

Begin your Dublin adventure at **Trinity College**, Ireland's oldest university, founded in 1592. Step through the grand wooden doors and walk the cobbled paths to the Long Room Library, one of the most stunning libraries in the world. Inside, discover the Book of Kells, a 9th-century manuscript famous for its intricate illustrations and profound cultural significance.

- **Location:** Trinity College, College Green, Dublin 2
- **Opening Hours:** Monday–Saturday: 8:30 AM–5:00 PM; Sunday: 9:30 AM–5:00 PM
- **Pro Tip:** Pre-book your timed entry tickets online to skip long queues, especially during peak seasons.

Afterward, enjoy a gentle stroll through the nearby **Grafton Street**, Dublin's premier shopping avenue filled with buskers, charming cafes, and vibrant flower stalls.

Afternoon: Temple Bar and Historic Core

Head into the cultural heart of Dublin – **Temple Bar**. While known for its nightlife, during the afternoon, this area reveals its more authentic side: colorful galleries, indie boutiques, and cozy cafés tucked along cobbled lanes. Visit the **Temple Bar Food Market** (open Saturdays) for a taste of artisanal Irish produce or pop into the **Irish Photography Centre** for a creative fix.

- **Location:** Temple Bar District, Dublin 2
- **Opening Hours:** The district is open at all times; shops typically 10:00 AM–6:00 PM
- **Pro Tip:** Explore Temple Bar's side streets like Crow Street and Cow's Lane for quieter, more authentic experiences away from the main tourist crowd.

Continue to **Dublin Castle**, once the seat of British rule in Ireland. Wander through the State Apartments, medieval undercroft, and the Chapel Royal to get a sense of Ireland's layered political history.

- **Location:** Dame Street, Dublin 2
- **Opening Hours:** Daily: 9:45 AM–5:45 PM (last admission at 5:15 PM)
- **Pro Tip:** Join a guided tour to access the full State Apartments and Viking Excavation areas, not available on self-guided visits.

Evening: Dinner, Pubs & Traditional Music

As the sun sets, head toward **Dame Lane** and **George's Street** for dinner at one of Dublin's celebrated gastropubs like **The Bank on College Green** or **The Hairy Lemon** — both serve hearty Irish classics in atmospheric historic settings. After dinner, enjoy an evening of traditional Irish music at one of Dublin's iconic pubs. **The Cobblestone** in Smithfield offers genuine, uncommercialized Irish sessions led by skilled musicians, perfect for a cultural first night.

- **Location:** The Cobblestone, 77 King Street North, Dublin 7
- **Opening Hours:** Monday–Thursday: 5:00 PM–11:30 PM; Friday–Sunday: 2:00 PM–12:30 AM
- **Pro Tip:** Arrive early for a good seat near the musicians, as it fills up quickly, especially on weekends.

For a final nightcap or stroll, the **Ha'penny Bridge** offers a magical nighttime view of the River Liffey, reflecting the city's sparkling lights.

Day 2: Dublin – Museums, Parks & Nightlife

Today you'll uncover Dublin's artistic treasures, enjoy its green lungs, and immerse yourself in its vibrant evening culture. A perfectly balanced day of history, nature, and city buzz.

Morning: National Museum of Ireland – Archaeology & National Gallery

Start your morning at the **National Museum of Ireland – Archaeology**, a treasure trove of Ireland's ancient past. Marvel at the dazzling gold artifacts of the Bronze Age, Viking relics, and the eerily preserved "bog bodies" from prehistoric times.

- **Location:** Kildare Street, Dublin 2

- **Opening Hours:** Tuesday–Saturday: 10:00 AM–5:00 PM; Sunday–Monday: 1:00 PM–5:00 PM
- **Pro Tip:** Admission is free, but arriving early means you can explore the popular exhibitions like the Tara Brooch without crowds.

Next, walk to the **National Gallery of Ireland**, home to an impressive collection of European and Irish art. Highlights include works by Caravaggio, Vermeer, and Jack B. Yeats. The gallery's new wings and peaceful courtyard café make it a lovely place to spend a leisurely morning.

- **Location:** Merrion Square West, Dublin 2
- **Opening Hours:** Monday: 11:00 AM–5:30 PM; Tuesday–Saturday: 9:15 AM–5:30 PM; Sunday: 11:00 AM–5:30 PM
- **Pro Tip:** Pick up a free highlights map at the entrance to easily navigate to the must-see paintings if you're short on time.

Afternoon: St. Stephen's Green & Iveagh Gardens

Recharge by heading to St. Stephen's Green, a beautiful Victorian park right in the heart of Dublin. Wander its landscaped gardens, cross ornate bridges over duck ponds, and find monuments to Irish history hidden among the greenery. Ideal for a casual picnic or coffee break.

- **Location:** St. Stephen's Green, Dublin 2
- **Opening Hours:** Daily: Dawn to Dusk
- **Pro Tip:** Bring a takeaway coffee or snack from a Grafton Street café to enjoy on one of the park's many benches for a peaceful break.

Afterwards, step into the **Iveagh Gardens**, Dublin's "Secret Garden." Quieter and lesser-known than St. Stephen's Green, these gardens feature a beautiful rose garden, cascading fountains, and a maze. It's a perfect hidden gem if you're seeking a serene escape from the city's bustle.

- **Location:** Clonmel Street (off Harcourt Street), Dublin 2
- **Opening Hours:** Daily: 8:00 AM–Dusk
- **Pro Tip:** Visit in late spring or summer when the roses are in full bloom, making it one of the most photogenic spots in the city.

Evening: Dublin's Nightlife – From Traditional to Trendy

Start your evening with dinner in **Dublin's Creative Quarter**, centered around South William Street and Drury Street. Restaurants like **Fade Street Social** and **Pitt Bros BBQ** offer a wide range of stylish dining options with Irish twists.

Later, dive into Dublin's famous nightlife. You have two standout experiences to choose from, depending on your mood:

Traditional Irish Night at O'Donoghue's Pub

The birthplace of The Dubliners, this historic pub offers nightly live folk music where locals and visitors gather to sing, clap, and share pints.

- **Location:** 15 Merrion Row, Dublin 2
- **Opening Hours:** Monday–Thursday: 10:30 AM–11:30 PM; Friday–Saturday: 10:30 AM–12:30 AM; Sunday: 12:30 PM–11:00 PM
- **Pro Tip:** Grab a table early, especially on weekends, as space fills up quickly for music sessions.

Trendy Night Out at The Dean's Sophisticated Rooftop Bar, Sophie's

If you prefer a modern night out, head to Sophie's Rooftop Bar for panoramic views of the city skyline, craft cocktails, and a lively ambiance.

- **Location:** 33 Harcourt Street, Dublin 2
- **Opening Hours:** Daily: 7:00 AM–Late (Bar from 12:00 PM)

- **Pro Tip:** Reserve a spot at sunset for incredible photo opportunities over Dublin's rooftops.

End your night with a stroll through buzzing **Harcourt Street**, packed with stylish bars and late-night venues, if you still have energy left!

Day 3: Kilkenny – Medieval Magic

Today, you step back into Ireland's medieval heartland. Kilkenny, with its majestic castle, charming cobbled streets, and thriving arts scene, feels like walking through living history — but with all the vibrancy of a modern Irish town.

Morning: Kilkenny Castle & Parklands

Begin your day at the magnificent **Kilkenny Castle**, a symbol of Norman power dating back to the 12th century. Tour the restored Victorian rooms, the grand picture gallery, and the beautiful gardens. The lush parklands surrounding the castle are perfect for a relaxing morning stroll.

- **Location:** The Parade, Kilkenny, Ireland
- **Opening Hours:** Daily: 9:30 AM–5:30 PM (last admission 5:00 PM)
- **Pro Tip:** Book your ticket online to avoid queues, especially in summer. Don't miss the Rose Garden and the stunning view from the terrace over the River Nore.

Afternoon: Medieval Mile Exploration

Spend your afternoon walking the "**Medieval Mile**," a historic trail that connects Kilkenny Castle with St. Canice's Cathedral. Along the way, explore quaint alleys, historic pubs, and artisan shops.

Stop at the **Medieval Mile Museum**, located in a converted 13th-century church, to dive deeper into the city's medieval history through interactive exhibits and tomb carvings.

- **Location:** St. Mary's Church, High Street, Kilkenny
- **Opening Hours:** Monday–Saturday: 9:30 AM–5:00 PM; Sunday: 11:00 AM–5:00 PM
- **Pro Tip:** Take the guided walking tour offered by the museum — the stories behind the buildings and the colorful characters of medieval Kilkenny bring the stones to life.

Afterward, visit **St. Canice's Cathedral & Round Tower**, one of Ireland's best-preserved medieval cathedrals. Climb the 9th-century round tower for panoramic views of the city — a true highlight!

- **Location:** Coach Road, Kilkenny
- **Opening Hours:** Monday–Saturday: 10:00 AM–5:00 PM; Sunday: 2:00 PM–5:00 PM

- **Pro Tip:** Wear sturdy shoes for the tower climb — the steps are steep, but the 360-degree view is worth it!

Evening: Dining & Traditional Pubs

In the evening, settle in for a delicious Irish dinner. Try Zuni Restaurant, a local favorite offering modern Irish cuisine with an elegant atmosphere. Dishes like Kilkenny venison and seafood chowder pair beautifully with Irish craft beer or wine.

- **Location:** 26 Patrick Street, Kilkenny
- **Opening Hours:** Dinner from 5:30 PM–9:30 PM
- **Pro Tip:** Reserve in advance, especially on weekends, as this spot is popular among both visitors and locals.

After dinner, explore Kilkenny's lively pub scene. **Kyteler's Inn**, founded in 1324, is one of Ireland's oldest inns, brimming with atmosphere, live traditional music, and legends of witches and magic.

- **Location:** St. Kieran's Street, Kilkenny
- **Opening Hours:** Monday–Thursday: 11:30 AM–11:30 PM; Friday–Saturday: 11:30 AM–12:30 AM; Sunday: 12:00 PM–11:00 PM
- **Pro Tip:** Catch a live music session and ask the bartenders about Dame Alice Kyteler's ghostly tales — the storytelling here is as memorable as the Guinness!

Day 4: Killarney & The Ring of Kerry

Today brings you into some of Ireland's most breathtaking landscapes. Killarney acts as the gateway to the legendary Ring of Kerry, a scenic drive wrapped in wild coastal beauty, ancient history, and charming villages.

Morning: Killarney National Park & Muckross House

Start your morning exploring Killarney National Park, Ireland's first national park and a true paradise of lakes, woodlands, and rugged mountains.

Visit **Muckross House and Gardens**, a 19th-century Victorian mansion perfectly set against the mountains of Killarney. Tour the beautifully preserved rooms and learn about life in grand Irish estates.

- **Location:** Muckross, Killarney, County Kerry

- **Opening Hours:** Muckross House: Daily 9:00 AM–5:30 PM; Park open year-round
- **Pro Tip:** Rent a bike near the entrance to the park and cycle the scenic trails around the lakes for an unforgettable way to experience the landscape.

Afternoon: The Ring of Kerry Drive

Dedicate your afternoon to the iconic Ring of Kerry, a 179-kilometer loop showcasing Ireland's raw coastal beauty.

Depart from Killarney and follow the route clockwise, stopping at highlights such as:

- **Ladies View** (a stunning panoramic lookout named after Queen Victoria's ladies-in-waiting)
- **Torc Waterfall**, a dramatic cascade surrounded by lush forest
- **Sneem Village**, a colorful and charming riverside spot ideal for a lunch break
- **Cahergall Stone Fort**, one of the best-preserved ring forts in Ireland

Each stop blends natural beauty with history and storytelling.

- **Location:** Ring of Kerry, County Kerry
- **Opening Hours:** Always open (road access); some individual attractions have opening times

- **Pro Tip:** Start early and take your time — this is a journey meant for leisurely discovery. Bring layers for changing weather and a fully charged camera!

Evening: Relax in Killarney Town

After your drive, return to Killarney for a well-deserved evening of good food and traditional Irish hospitality.

Dine at **The Laurels Pub & Restaurant**, a beloved spot serving hearty Irish dishes like beef and Guinness stew and fresh Atlantic salmon.

- **Location:** 29 Main Street, Killarney, County Kerry
- **Opening Hours:** Daily 12:00 PM–10:00 PM
- **Pro Tip:** Book a table if you're arriving after 7:00 PM — this place fills up quickly with both visitors and locals.

Later, step into a pub like **O'Connor's Traditional Pub** for live music and lively craic (Irish fun and banter). Killarney's pub scene is legendary for its authenticity, with nightly music sessions featuring fiddles, bodhráns, and storytelling.

- **Location:** 7 High Street, Killarney
- **Opening Hours:** Monday–Saturday: 10:30 AM–11:30 PM; Sunday: 12:00 PM–11:00 PM
- **Pro Tip:** Order a pint of local craft beer and join in the singing — locals love it when visitors participate!

Day 5: Ring of Kerry – Scenic Drive

Today is dedicated to fully immersing yourself in the extraordinary beauty of the Ring of Kerry, one of the most iconic and majestic driving routes in the world. With rugged coastlines, ancient ruins, seaside villages, and wild landscapes, every twist and turn offers a new scene worth savoring.

Morning: Depart Killarney – Head for Killorglin and Glenbeigh

Begin your morning journey heading west from Killarney, first reaching Killorglin, known for its famous Puck Fair festival. Continue toward Glenbeigh, a village offering spectacular views over Rossbeigh Strand, a long sandy beach perfect for a refreshing stroll. If the tide allows, take a short beach walk to admire the endless Atlantic views.

- **Location:** Killorglin and Glenbeigh, County Kerry
- **Opening Hours:** Scenic drives are accessible all day
- **Pro Tip:** Start early, ideally by 8:30 AM, to beat the tour buses and have the roads mostly to yourself for relaxed stops and photographs.

Mid-Morning Stop: Cahersiveen & Stone Forts

Continue to **Cahersiveen**, a historic town near the birthplace of Daniel O'Connell, the "Liberator" of Ireland.

Just outside town, visit **Leacanabuaile** and **Cahergall Stone Forts**, circular stone structures from the 9th century that whisper of ancient clan life. These ruins offer a peaceful, uncrowded window into early Irish history.

- **Location:** Cahergall Stone Fort, Ballycarbery, Cahersiveen, County Kerry
- **Opening Hours:** Open-air sites, accessible all day
- **Pro Tip:** Wear sturdy shoes — while easy to reach, the ground around the forts can be uneven, especially after rain.

Afternoon: Skellig Ring, Portmagee & Valentia Island

Break away from the main Ring of Kerry for the **Skellig Ring**, a smaller loop that's even more dramatic and less crowded.

Stop in **Portmagee**, a colorful fishing village with a lively harbor — ideal for lunch with seafood fresh from the Atlantic.

Then cross the bridge to **Valentia Island** to visit the **Bray Head Walk** or the **Valentia Island Lighthouse**, offering sweeping ocean views and a glimpse of Skellig Michael in the distance, a UNESCO World Heritage Site.

- **Location:** Portmagee and Valentia Island, County Kerry
- **Opening Hours:** Valentia Island sites generally open daylight hours (lighthouse 10:00 AM–6:00 PM)

- **Pro Tip:** Bring binoculars to get a closer look at the rugged Skellig Islands from Valentia's viewpoints.

Mid-Afternoon: Sneem & Moll's Gap

Return to the Ring route and drive toward **Sneem**, a postcard-perfect village with bright houses and a relaxed atmosphere. Stop for a coffee and explore the riverbanks before heading toward Moll's Gap.

At **Moll's Gap**, the road winds through rocky mountains, offering panoramic views over lakes and valleys — one of the most stunning parts of the drive.

- **Location:** Sneem and Moll's Gap, County Kerry
- **Opening Hours:** Accessible all day
- **Pro Tip:** Pause at the Avoca Café at Moll's Gap — it's one of the best places for a scenic tea break with sweeping views of the MacGillycuddy's Reeks.

Evening: Return to Killarney via Ladies View

Conclude your day with a magical stop at **Ladies View**, named after Queen Victoria's ladies-in-waiting who fell in love with the panorama in 1861. As the sun lowers, the golden light bathes the lakes and hills, making this one of the most memorable moments of the trip.

Continue down to **Killarney** for dinner at one of its cozy pubs or restaurants, soaking in the relaxed, friendly atmosphere after a full day of natural wonders.

- **Location:** Ladies View, Killarney National Park
- **Opening Hours:** Always open; café usually open 9:00 AM–5:00 PM
- **Pro Tip:** Arrive about an hour before sunset to see the landscape at its most beautiful — it's a photographer's dream.

Day 6: Cliffs of Moher & Galway

Today brings together the breathtaking grandeur of Ireland's most iconic cliffs with the lively spirit of the west's cultural capital. Prepare for awe-inspiring landscapes followed by a warm, vibrant city vibe in Galway.

Morning: Depart for the Cliffs of Moher

Start your day early from Killarney or wherever you're staying nearby, heading toward the **Cliffs of Moher** in County Clare.

These cliffs soar up to 214 meters (702 feet) above the Atlantic, stretching for about 8 kilometers (5 miles).

Walk along the cliff-top trails, soak in panoramic views, and, if clear, you can even glimpse the Aran Islands. Visit the **Cliffs of Moher Visitor Experience** to learn about the geology, history, and wildlife of this natural wonder.

- **Location:** Cliffs of Moher, Liscannor, County Clare
- **Opening Hours:** 8:00 AM – 7:00 PM (seasonal; last entry usually 1 hour before closing)
- **Entrance Fee:** €12 per adult (includes parking and visitor center access); book online for discounts
- **Pro Tip:** Arrive before 10:00 AM to avoid the tour bus crowds and catch the soft morning light for perfect photos.

Midday: Explore the Burren National Park

After visiting the Cliffs, take a scenic drive through the nearby Burren National Park, a unique karst limestone landscape home to rare plants and ancient monuments.

Stop at **Poulnabrone Dolmen**, a 5,800-year-old portal tomb, and marvel at the surreal, otherworldly terrain around you.

- **Location:** Burren National Park, County Clare
- **Opening Hours:** Open access year-round; Burren Visitor Centre typically 10:00 AM – 5:00 PM
- **Entrance Fee:** Free entry to the park; some guided tours may have a fee
- **Pro Tip:** Wear sturdy walking shoes — the limestone terrain is uneven and can be slippery when wet.

Drive to Galway, often called the "City of the Tribes."

Start with a casual walking tour through **Eyre Square**, the **Latin Quarter**, and along Shop Street. The city bursts with energy — buskers playing music, colorful shopfronts, and lively crowds.

Pop into **St. Nicholas' Collegiate Church** and maybe sneak a peek at the famous Galway Market if open.

- **Location:** Galway City Centre, County Galway
- **Opening Hours:** Public spaces open all day; shops generally 9:00 AM – 6:00 PM
- **Pro Tip:** Park outside the center and walk in; Galway's medieval streets are beautiful but tight and challenging for driving.

Evening: Dinner and Live Music in Galway

Settle into the evening with a hearty meal at a local pub or seafood restaurant. Galway is famous for its oysters, seafood chowder, and artisan cheeses. Afterward, enjoy live traditional music at one of Galway's famous pubs like Tigh Neachtain, **The Crane Bar**, or Taaffes.

Let the lively music and friendly atmosphere round off your day perfectly.

- **Location:** Latin Quarter and West End, Galway City
- **Opening Hours:** Pubs and restaurants generally 5:00 PM – late (music usually starts around 9:00 PM)
- **Pro Tip:** Arrive early for a seat at popular pubs — Galway's music sessions fill up quickly, especially on weekends!

Day 7: Galway – Relaxed Farewell

After an exhilarating journey through Ireland's iconic landscapes and historic towns, today is about unwinding and soaking up the last moments of Irish charm at a gentler pace in Galway.

Morning: Leisurely Breakfast and Stroll Along the Promenade

Start your morning with a relaxed breakfast at a cozy café like **Dela** or **The Kitchen Café**. Then, head to Salthill Promenade, a scenic seaside walkway stretching along Galway Bay.

Breathe in the salty air, watch locals jogging or walking their dogs, and maybe even partake in the tradition of kicking the wall at the end of the promenade for good luck.

- **Location:** Salthill Promenade, Galway
- **Opening Hours:** Public promenade, open 24 hours
- **Pro Tip:** Pick up a coffee to-go and enjoy it during your walk — it's a favorite morning ritual for Galwegians.

Afternoon: Explore the Galway City Museum and Shop for Last-Minute Gifts

After your seaside stroll, wander back into the city and visit the Galway City Museum to dive into the city's rich history, from medieval times to modern life. Afterward, spend some time shopping for authentic souvenirs — wool sweaters, Claddagh rings, artisanal pottery, and more — in the Latin Quarter's boutiques and local craft shops.

- **Location:** Galway City Museum, Spanish Parade, Galway
- **Opening Hours:** Tuesday–Saturday, 10:00 AM – 5:00 PM
- **Entrance Fee:** Free
- **Pro Tip:** Visit the museum terrace for beautiful views over the Claddagh and the River Corrib.

Treat yourself to a memorable final meal at a restaurant overlooking the bay, such as **O'Grady's on the Pier** in Barna or **Ard Bia** at Nimmos by the Spanish Arch. Enjoy fresh seafood, toast with a glass of Irish whiskey or a pint of Guinness, and savor the last tastes of Ireland.

After dinner, if time allows, take a final gentle walk along the **River Corrib** or catch an early trad session in one of the local pubs before your departure.

- **Location:** Ard Bia at Nimmos, Spanish Arch, Galway, or O'Grady's on the Pier, Barna, Galway
- **Opening Hours:** Generally 5:00 PM – 9:30 PM (confirm in advance)
- **Contact:** Ard Bia: +353 91 561 114 | O'Grady's: +353 91 592 223
- **Pro Tip:** Reserve a table with a view — Galway Bay at sunset offers a peaceful, unforgettable farewell to your Irish journey.

Family-Friendly Ireland

Ireland is a fantastic destination for families, offering a blend of captivating landscapes, historical charm, and activities that appeal to every member of the family. From outdoor adventures to engaging cultural experiences, Ireland provides a welcoming atmosphere for parents and children alike. With its friendly locals, safety, and wealth of fun things to see and do, Ireland promises unforgettable family memories.

Explore Majestic Castles & Ancient Ruins

Ireland is home to numerous stunning castles and ancient ruins that will spark the imagination of young adventurers.

- **Blarney Castle (County Cork):** Home to the famous Blarney Stone, children will love climbing to the top of the castle tower and exploring the beautiful surrounding gardens.
- **Kilkenny Castle (Kilkenny):** This castle features a fascinating history, beautiful parklands for picnics, and an interactive visitor center.
- **Dublin Castle (Dublin):** Offering tours suitable for families, Dublin Castle's history and impressive architecture make it a fun place for kids to learn about Irish history.

These castles often host interactive exhibits, medieval reenactments, and kid-friendly activities, making them ideal spots for families.

Visit Zoos & Wildlife Parks

Ireland's zoos and wildlife parks allow children to connect with nature and learn about native and exotic species in fun, engaging environments.

- **Dublin Zoo (Phoenix Park, Dublin):** One of the oldest zoos in the world, Dublin Zoo is a great family outing. It has a variety of animal habitats and interactive exhibits that are educational and entertaining.
- **Fota Wildlife Park (County Cork):** This expansive wildlife park allows families to get up close to rare animals, including giraffes, zebras, and cheetahs, in a natural, open environment.
- **The Galway Atlantaquaria (Galway):** Perfect for marine life lovers, this aquarium offers fascinating exhibits on the local aquatic life of the Atlantic coast.

Adventure in Nature: Parks, Trails & Outdoor Fun

Ireland's dramatic natural landscapes provide a wide variety of outdoor activities for families, from hikes to bike rides to beach days.

- **Killarney National Park (County Kerry):** A stunning location with family-friendly walking and cycling paths, as well as boat tours of the lakes. Children can spot wildlife, visit Muckross House, and explore the cascading Torc Waterfall.
- **The Burren (County Clare):** Known for its unique limestone landscape, The Burren offers easy, family-friendly walks where kids can learn about the unique flora and fauna of the area.
- **Wicklow Mountains National Park (County Wicklow):** Perfect for families who enjoy outdoor activities, this park offers scenic trails, stunning views, and the chance to explore ancient monastic sites like Glendalough.

Ride the Rails: Fun Train Journeys

Take a leisurely train ride through some of Ireland's most scenic areas, ideal for families looking to relax while soaking in the views.

- **The DART (Dublin Area Rapid Transit)** offers an easy and affordable way to explore the coastal beauty of Dublin and its surroundings, with stops at places like Howth and Dun Laoghaire.
- **The West Cork Railway:** Although not operational as a full train service, families can experience a nostalgic steam train ride through the beautiful countryside in season.
- **The Beltany Stone Circle (County Donegal):** For a blend of history and adventure, families can travel through scenic landscapes while discovering Ireland's ancient sites.

Beach Days & Coastal Adventures

Ireland's coastline boasts some of the most stunning beaches, perfect for family fun.

- **Inch Beach (County Kerry):** Ideal for a family day out, this long sandy beach offers shallow waters, safe swimming, and plenty of space for picnics and games.
- **Curracloe Strand (County Wexford):** Famously featured in Saving Private Ryan, this beach is perfect for sandcastle building, kite flying, and simply soaking in the natural beauty.
- **Tramore Beach (County Waterford):** A family favorite with a lively boardwalk, amusements, and safe swimming areas.

In addition to beach activities, Ireland's coastline offers family-friendly coastal walking trails, rock-pooling, and sea kayaking for more adventurous families.

Fun Activities for Children

Ireland boasts a variety of theme parks, adventure centers, and kid-friendly attractions.

- **Tayto Park (County Meath):** A fun-filled park with rides, roller coasters, and an animal park. This is a must-visit for families with younger children.
- **Ireland's Ancient East (Across multiple counties):** Families can explore over 5,000 years of history with interactive storytelling, exhibits, and archaeological sites that engage children with Ireland's rich heritage.
- **Epic Ireland (Dublin):** A unique interactive experience that brings Ireland's emigration history to life in a fun and informative way, especially for older kids.

- **Aquazone (Dublin):** An exciting water park with wave pools, lazy rivers, and water slides, ideal for a day of fun and excitement.

Family-Friendly Dining

Irish dining is relaxed and welcoming, with many restaurants offering kid-friendly menus and early dining hours.

- **The Woollen Mills (Dublin):** A casual spot where families can enjoy classic Irish dishes like fish and chips, with plenty of space for children to sit comfortably.
- **Bunsen Burger (Dublin):** This no-frills burger joint is perfect for kids who love a good burger, served quickly in a casual, relaxed atmosphere.
- **The Kingfisher (Galway):** A family-run, cozy restaurant serving fresh, local ingredients in a friendly setting. The children's menu includes favorites like pasta, fish, and chips.

Many local pubs in rural areas also offer a friendly atmosphere for families, with hearty meals and the chance to enjoy a relaxed evening out.

Cultural Experiences for Young Minds

Encourage kids to explore Ireland's cultural richness through interactive and hands-on exhibits.

- **The National Museum of Ireland (Dublin):** With multiple locations, including Archaeology, Decorative Arts & History, and Natural History, the museum offers a wealth of exhibits that are both educational and fun for children of all ages.
- **The Ark (Dublin):** A dedicated children's cultural center, featuring a wide array of events, workshops, and performances designed specifically for young audiences.
- **The Galway City Museum:** This museum offers family-friendly exhibits that explore the heritage of the area, along with interactive displays for children to enjoy.

City Explorations: Dublin, Cork & Beyond

- **Dublin:** Ireland's capital city is a treasure trove of family activities, from visiting the Dublin Zoo to touring the interactive Dublinia Viking Museum.

Families can also enjoy the National Aquatic Centre or take a river cruise along the Liffey for a different perspective of the city.

- **Cork:** Beyond its beautiful streets and rich history, Cork offers kid-friendly attractions such as Fota Wildlife Park and the Cork City Gaol.
- **Belfast:** In Northern Ireland, the Titanic Belfast museum provides an engaging experience for all ages, allowing families to learn about the ill-fated ship through interactive displays and multimedia.

Tips for Families Traveling in Ireland

- **Plan Ahead:** Many attractions offer family discounts or free entry for younger children. Booking tickets in advance for popular attractions can save time.
- **Weather Preparedness:** Ireland's weather can be unpredictable. Pack waterproofs, layers, and sturdy shoes for both adults and children to keep everyone comfortable during outdoor excursions.
- **Public Transport:** Ireland's public transport system is generally family-friendly, with buses and trains offering discounts for children. Many car rental companies offer booster seats and other child-specific accommodations.
- **Stay in Family-Friendly Accommodation:** Many hotels, guesthouses, and even self-catering cottages cater to families, offering amenities like family rooms, play areas, and kid-friendly activities.

Romantic & Honeymoon Ireland

Ireland's timeless landscapes, intimate hideaways, and warm hospitality create the perfect backdrop for a romantic getaway or unforgettable honeymoon. Across its rolling green hills, dramatic coasts, and ancient towns, couples will find endless opportunities to celebrate love, adventure, and shared memories.

Stay in a Castle

Nothing says "fairy tale romance" like staying in a centuries-old Irish castle.

- **Ashford Castle, County Mayo:** Luxurious rooms, award-winning dining, and a lakeside setting combine to create an unforgettable experience. Couples can enjoy private boat rides, falconry lessons, and spa treatments.

- **Dromoland Castle, County Clare:** A masterpiece of historic elegance, Dromoland offers candlelit dinners, horse-drawn carriage rides, and manicured gardens perfect for strolling hand-in-hand.
- **Lough Eske Castle, County Donegal:** Nestled at the foot of the Blue Stack Mountains, this castle retreat blends five-star luxury with dramatic natural beauty, ideal for a secluded, romantic stay.

Romantic Landscapes and Drives

The wild beauty of Ireland's countryside offers dreamlike settings for couples who love exploration and scenic views.

- **Ring of Kerry, County Kerry:** Panoramic drives past mountains, lakes, and Atlantic beaches invite frequent stops for photos, picnics, and shared moments.
- **The Cliffs of Moher, County Clare:** Standing together at the edge of these towering cliffs, gazing out over the Atlantic, feels almost cinematic.
- **Causeway Coastal Route, Northern Ireland:** A drive along this rugged coastline, with stops at castles, beaches, and the Giant's Causeway, makes for an adventurous and romantic journey.

Secluded Villages and Quiet Escapes

Small towns offer a slower pace, charming accommodations, and plenty of intimate moments.

- **Kenmare, County Kerry:** A colorful town filled with artisan shops, cozy restaurants, and stunning nearby landscapes.
- **Kinsale, County Cork:** Famous for its seafood and harbor views, Kinsale's cobbled streets are perfect for evening strolls.
- **Doolin, County Clare:** A tiny village near the Cliffs of Moher, Doolin is a gateway to the Aran Islands and a center for traditional Irish music.

Water Adventures for Two

Ireland's coasts, lakes, and rivers set the stage for unforgettable water-based experiences.

- **Kayaking under the stars on Lough Hyne, County Cork:** A rare chance to experience bioluminescence as the waters glow with natural light during night paddles.

- **Boat trips on Lough Corrib, County Galway:** Private cruises take couples through serene waters surrounded by rolling hills and ancient ruins.
- **Sailing along the Wild Atlantic Way:** Charter a private boat for a day, exploring hidden coves and remote beaches.

Spa Retreats and Wellness Escapes

Pampering and relaxation are an essential part of any romantic trip.

- **Monart Destination Spa, County Wexford:** Often rated among Europe's best, this adult-only spa focuses entirely on wellness and tranquility.
- **The Spa at Powerscourt Hotel, County Wicklow:** A luxurious spa experience combined with views of Wicklow's "Garden of Ireland" countryside.
- **The Europe Hotel & Resort, Killarney:** Offering panoramic lakeside spa pools and private couples' massages with mountain views.

Intimate Dining Experiences

Ireland's dining scene sets the table for romance, from cozy traditional pubs to world-class fine dining.

- **The Cliff House Hotel, County Waterford:** Michelin-starred dining overlooking the wild Atlantic—perfect for a special celebration.
- **Chapter One, Dublin:** Elegant, innovative cuisine in a sophisticated setting.
- **Moran's Oyster Cottage, County Galway:** Share freshly shucked oysters and seafood by the fireside in a charming 250-year-old thatched cottage.

Unique Couple Experiences

- **Horseback riding on the beach in County Sligo:** Gallop side-by-side along a deserted strand at sunset.
- **Hot air balloon rides over County Kildare:** Drift over lush fields and ancient castles for an unforgettable bird's-eye view.
- **Private whiskey tasting tours:** Visit distilleries together and enjoy behind-the-scenes tastings of Ireland's famous spirits.

Best Time for a Romantic Trip

- **Spring (April to June):** Gardens in bloom, mild weather, and longer daylight hours.

- **Autumn (September to October):** Fewer tourists, golden landscapes, and cozy evenings by the fire.
- **Winter (November to February):** Ideal for castle stays, spa retreats, and intimate indoor experiences, with festive Christmas lights adding a magical glow.

Hidden Gems & Off-the-Beaten-Path Ireland

Ireland's best-kept secrets lie far from the crowded tourist trails — in wild peninsulas, quiet villages, and ancient landscapes where tradition and raw beauty reign. These hidden gems invite travelers to slow down, savor authentic experiences, and witness a side of Ireland few visitors ever truly see.

1. Beara Peninsula, County Cork

Tucked away between the better-known Ring of Kerry and West Cork, the Beara Peninsula feels like a step back in time. Narrow, winding roads curve past craggy mountains, stone walls, and tiny fishing villages untouched by mass tourism. Colorful towns like Allihies and Eyeries offer glimpses into traditional Irish life, and the Healy Pass — a winding mountain drive — delivers some of the most jaw-dropping views in Ireland. Outdoor lovers will relish the Beara Way walking trail that loops the entire peninsula.

- **Location:** Southwest County Cork and County Kerry
- **Must Experience:** Drive the Healy Pass at sunset for unforgettable golden light over the mountains.

- **Insider Tip:** Visit Dzogchen Beara, a cliffside Buddhist retreat open to visitors — the meditation garden has one of the most peaceful views in Ireland.

2. Slieve League Cliffs, County Donegal

While the Cliffs of Moher draw massive crowds, the Slieve League Cliffs tower almost three times higher and remain blissfully uncrowded. Rising nearly 2,000 feet from the Atlantic Ocean, these cliffs are among Europe's highest sea cliffs. Their sheer drop and rugged beauty feel overwhelmingly wild and untouched. Hike the Pilgrim's Path or Bunglas View Walk for panoramic vistas stretching to Sligo and even Scotland on clear days.

- **Location:** Southwest County Donegal
- **Must Experience:** Hike to the "One Man's Pass," a thrilling narrow ridge offering dramatic photo opportunities.
- **Insider Tip:** Go early in the morning for soft lighting and near solitude; bring sturdy shoes as paths can be slippery after rain.

3. Loop Head Peninsula, County Clare

Loop Head remains one of Ireland's most breathtaking yet under-visited corners. Jutting into the Atlantic, its raw cliffs, powerful waves, and lighthouses evoke an ancient and elemental Ireland. At the tip, Loop Head Lighthouse offers tours, and if you're lucky, you might spot dolphins frolicking below.

Unlike other popular coastal routes, Loop Head's driving loop rarely sees traffic, allowing for a true "edge of the world" experience.

- **Location:** County Clare, west coast of Ireland
- **Must Experience:** Walk the Loop Head Heritage Trail and stand at the edge where the Atlantic roars against the cliffs.
- **Insider Tip:** Stop at Keating's Pub in Kilbaha, which claims to be the "nearest pub to New York," for a drink with stunning sea views.

4. Inishbofin Island, County Galway

Off the coast of Connemara, Inishbofin Island is a haven of untouched beauty, traditional culture, and wild Atlantic landscapes. With no large hotels and minimal traffic, the island feels preserved in time. Crystal-clear waters lap at deserted beaches, and craggy walking trails offer views of dramatic cliffs and historic ruins like Cromwell's Barracks. Life on Inishbofin moves slowly, inviting visitors to simply be present.

- **Location:** Off the coast of County Galway (ferry from Cleggan)
- **Must Experience:** Swim in the turquoise waters of the East End beaches, some of the clearest in Ireland.
- **Insider Tip:** Rent a bike from a local shop on arrival — it's the best way to explore the island's hidden coves and headlands at your own pace.

5. Gougane Barra, County Cork

In the shadow of the Shehy Mountains, Gougane Barra is one of Ireland's most serene and spiritual spots. A small, picture-perfect chapel stands on an island in a glacial lake, surrounded by thick forests and misty hills. The scene feels almost mythical. The nearby national forest park offers gentle hiking trails, streams, and countless quiet spots for picnics or contemplation, making it a favorite among locals for day trips and small weddings.

- **Location:** County Cork, near Macroom
- **Must Experience:** Visit St. Finbarr's Oratory early in the morning when mist often rises off the lake.
- **Insider Tip:** Book a stay at the Gougane Barra Hotel to wake up with the lake and chapel right outside your window.

6. The Arigna Mining Experience, County Roscommon

Hidden in the hills of Roscommon, the Arigna Mining Experience offers a fascinating dive into Ireland's coal mining history. Guided by former miners, tours lead visitors deep into the original narrow tunnels. Their personal stories bring to life the hardships and camaraderie that shaped this tight-knit community. It's a moving, authentic experience that connects visitors to a lesser-known chapter of Irish life.

- **Location:** County Roscommon, near Lough Allen
- **Must Experience:** Take the underground tour led by a retired miner who worked in the tunnels for decades.
- **Insider Tip:** Combine your visit with a drive along the nearby Lough Allen Scenic Drive for peaceful lake views and pretty picnic spots.

7. The Black Valley, County Kerry

Nestled deep within the MacGillycuddy's Reeks mountains, the Black Valley is an untouched pocket of Ireland where nature reigns supreme. Known for being one of the last places in Ireland to receive electricity, it remains one of the country's most isolated areas. Expect dramatic mountain vistas, lonely stone cottages, sheep-dotted roads, and absolute silence. Hiking or cycling through the Black Valley offers a profoundly peaceful experience far removed from crowds.

- **Location:** County Kerry, near the Gap of Dunloe
- **Must Experience:** Cycle the route from Moll's Gap through the Black Valley to the Gap of Dunloe for an unforgettable day.
- **Insider Tip:** Pack snacks and water — there are no shops or services in the valley, reinforcing the sense of pure remoteness.

8. Valentia Island, County Kerry

Connected to the mainland by a small bridge, Valentia Island is one of Ireland's most enchanting and little-visited islands.

It offers spectacular scenery ranging from dramatic cliffs and subtropical gardens to ancient fossils embedded in its rocks. The island's modest size makes it easy to explore in a day, but the tranquil atmosphere often tempts travelers to linger longer. The Skellig Experience Visitor Centre, just off the bridge, brings the story of the nearby Skellig Islands to life.

- **Location:** County Kerry, off the Iveragh Peninsula
- **Must Experience:** Visit the Valentia Island Lighthouse and the Bray Head Walk for sweeping Atlantic views.
- **Insider Tip:** Drive the full Skellig Ring, a lesser-known but stunning extension of the famous Ring of Kerry, especially magical at sunset.

9. Dunmore East, County Waterford

This charming fishing village hugs a dramatic coastline, featuring secluded coves, pastel-colored cottages, and a relaxed, timeless atmosphere. Dunmore East is a perfect blend of seaside escape and traditional Irish village life. In summer, the beaches come alive with swimmers and kayakers, while seafood lovers savor some of the freshest catch in the country. Its sleepy vibe, beautiful harbor, and cliff walks offer a restful break from more tourist-heavy coastal spots.

- **Location:** County Waterford, southeast coast of Ireland
- **Must Experience:** Walk the Dunmore East Cliff Path for breathtaking views of hidden beaches and rugged coastline.
- **Insider Tip:** Visit during the Dunmore East Festival of Food, Fish & Fun in early summer — locals serve up unbeatable seafood platters.

10. Belmullet Peninsula, County Mayo

Raw, remote, and windswept, the Belmullet Peninsula feels like the edge of the earth. Surrounded by the Atlantic on both sides, its landscape is a tapestry of bogland, white-sand beaches, and traditional peat fields. Gaelic is still spoken in parts of this rugged region, offering a glimpse into authentic Irish culture. Belmullet's beaches are perfect for those who crave isolation, wild beauty, and some of the best surfing waves in Ireland.

- **Location:** County Mayo, northwest coast
- **Must Experience:** Explore Elly Bay and Cross Beach, endless stretches of sand framed by shifting Atlantic skies.

Understanding Irish Etiquette

Navigating social customs in Ireland comes naturally once you understand the warmth and wit that shape everyday interactions. Irish etiquette values friendliness, humility, and good humor, often blending old traditions with a relaxed modern spirit.

Warm Greetings Matter

A firm handshake paired with a friendly smile is the typical way to greet in Ireland, whether meeting for business or pleasure. It's polite to address people with their titles (Mr., Mrs., or Dr.) until invited to use first names, which usually happens quickly, given the informal Irish character. Eye contact is important and signals sincerity.

Conversation and Humor

The Irish are famed storytellers, and engaging in light conversation is an important social skill. Topics like family, travel, local culture, and sports (especially Gaelic games and rugby) are safe and welcome. Politics and religion can be sensitive and are best avoided unless you're familiar with the audience. Humor, often self-deprecating and clever, is appreciated — being able to laugh at yourself is seen as a sign of good character.

Hospitality and Invitations

If invited into someone's home, it is courteous to bring a small gift such as wine, chocolates, or flowers. Complimenting the home and accepting food or drink when offered shows respect. Offering to help clear the table is appreciated but not expected; however, a heartfelt thank-you is essential before leaving.

Pub Culture

Ordering at the bar is the norm rather than waiting for table service. Taking your turn to buy a round of drinks for your group — called "buying your round" — is an important social ritual. Skipping your turn can be considered impolite. It's common to exchange light conversation with strangers at pubs, but pushing serious topics onto new acquaintances is discouraged.

Respect for Traditions

Ireland's deep respect for its history, folklore, and national pride is woven into everyday life. Standing respectfully for national anthems, honoring traditions during cultural events, and acknowledging Irish efforts in literature, music, and sports earns genuine goodwill.

Queuing and Public Manners

Respecting queues (lines) is taken seriously. Cutting in line is considered very rude. Saying "please," "thank you," and offering apologies even for small inconveniences keeps social exchanges smooth and pleasant.

Tipping Customs

While not as obligatory as in the United States, tipping is appreciated. In restaurants, a tip of around 10–15% is customary if service is good and not already included. Tipping small amounts to taxi drivers, hotel porters, and hairdressers is also common.

Personal Space and Physical Contact

The Irish tend to be warm but maintain moderate personal space, particularly with strangers. Physical affection, like hugging, is common among friends but usually reserved until a stronger relationship is built. A light touch on the arm during conversation is a natural part of animated Irish storytelling, but should not be misunderstood.

Religion and Traditions

Ireland's strong Catholic heritage still shapes social customs, especially in rural areas. While society is increasingly secular, religious holidays like Christmas and Easter retain significant cultural importance. Respecting religious customs and sites, even if you are not a believer, is important for visitors.

Language Tips & Useful Gaelic Phrases

English is spoken everywhere in Ireland, but you will also encounter the beautiful, ancient Irish language — known locally as Gaeilge. Seeing road signs, public notices, and even hearing conversations in Gaelic, especially in western regions and Gaeltacht areas, adds a deeper layer to your journey.

Knowing a few phrases opens doors, sparks smiles, and shows a heartfelt appreciation for Irish culture.

Understanding the Role of Gaelic

Irish is a living language with deep national significance. While most conversations take place in English, Gaelic is taught in schools and cherished as a symbol of identity. In Gaeltacht areas such as Connemara, the Dingle Peninsula, and parts of Donegal, Irish is spoken daily and proudly maintained. Even if you use only a few words, your efforts are warmly appreciated.

Pronunciation Tips

- Irish vowels have a softer sound compared to English.
- The letter combination "bh" often sounds like "v."
- "Mh" can sound like "w" or "v" depending on the word.
- Stress usually falls on the first syllable of words.

Listening carefully and not worrying about getting it perfect is the key. Irish people are encouraging when visitors attempt to speak Gaelic.

Useful Gaelic Phrases for Travelers

- **Hello** — Dia duit (Jee-ah gwitch)
- **Reply to Hello** — Dia is Muire duit (Jee-ah iss Mwir-ah gwitch)
- **Goodbye** — Slán (Slawn)
- **Thank you** — Go raibh maith agat (Guh rev mah agat)
- **Please** — Le do thoil (Leh duh hull)
- **Yes** — Tá (Taw)
- **No** — Níl (Neel)
- **How are you?** — Conas atá tú? (Kun-us a-taw too?)
- **I'm well, thank you** — Tá mé go maith, go raibh maith agat (Taw may guh mah, guh rev mah agat)
- **Excuse me / Sorry** — Gabh mo leithscéal (Gow muh leh-shkale)
- **Cheers!** — Sláinte! (Slawn-cha)

Signs and Everyday Gaelic

- **An Ghaeltacht** — Areas where Irish is the first language
- **Garda** — Police
- **Tóg go bog é** — Take it easy

- **Céad míle fáilte** — A hundred thousand welcomes (a common phrase symbolizing Irish hospitality)

Cultural Tip

Using simple greetings like "Dia duit" when entering a shop in the Gaeltacht or saying "Sláinte!" during a toast shows not just courtesy but real cultural respect. Locals often reward these small efforts with great warmth, sometimes even teaching you a few more phrases on the spot.

Accessibility Travel Tips

Ireland is becoming increasingly welcoming to travelers with mobility, hearing, vision, or cognitive needs. While older infrastructure and historic sites sometimes present challenges, many modern facilities, hotels, public transport services, and attractions are committed to accessibility. Planning ahead and knowing what to expect ensures a smoother, more enjoyable trip.

Transportation Access

Most airports, including Dublin, Shannon, and Cork, provide excellent accessibility services such as wheelchair assistance, priority security screening, and accessible shuttle transport. Booking assistance in advance — ideally 48 hours before travel — guarantees the smoothest experience. In cities, many public buses are low-floor with ramps and designated wheelchair spaces. The DART (Dublin Area Rapid Transit) offers step-free access at many stations, but some rural train stations may require advance notice for assistance. Irish Rail's Travel Assistance Scheme helps passengers who may need extra support navigating stations or boarding. Accessible taxis can be booked through apps and dedicated services, especially in major cities. Renting an adapted vehicle is possible through specialized providers but should be reserved well in advance, particularly in peak season.

Accommodation for All

Large hotel chains and many boutique hotels offer accessible rooms fitted with roll-in showers, wider doorways, and support rails. When booking a hotel or guesthouse, it's important to confirm specific needs directly with the property, as standards vary.

Self-catering cottages and B&Bs sometimes provide fully accessible units, particularly in the countryside where newer developments consider accessibility from the design phase.

Tourist Attractions and Tours

Many of Ireland's top attractions are improving their accessibility offerings. Dublin Castle, Kilmainham Gaol, and the Guinness Storehouse, for instance, provide ramps, lifts, and accessible restrooms. Some castles and historic ruins, given their medieval design, may have partial access only. Specialized accessible tours are available, offering adapted vehicles and customized itineraries to accommodate mobility devices or sensory needs. Companies like Accessible Ireland and Mobility Mojo offer trusted resources to help plan barrier-free experiences. Outdoor sites like the Cliffs of Moher now feature wheelchair-accessible visitor centers and paths, though weather conditions can affect ease of movement. Many national parks provide accessible trails and viewing platforms.

Mobility Equipment & Assistance

Hiring mobility aids such as scooters or wheelchairs is possible through national services and medical supply companies based in Dublin, Cork, and Galway. Delivery to hotels or private accommodations can usually be arranged. Assistance dogs are legally recognized throughout Ireland. Travelers bringing an assistance dog must meet Ireland's entry requirements under the Pet Travel Scheme and should ensure documentation is complete before traveling.

Accessible Dining and Nightlife

Major cities offer restaurants, pubs, and cafés with step-free access, though older buildings can sometimes have narrow entrances or tight spaces. Calling ahead to check about ramps, restrooms, or assistance is advisable, especially for smaller, independent venues. Many traditional music nights, theaters, and festivals incorporate accessibility seating and facilities, though early booking may be necessary to secure spots.

Practical Tips for Smooth Travel

- Plan transportation early and inform airlines, trains, and hotels of any specific needs.

- Carry a basic phrase card explaining any critical medical information, mobility needs, or allergies.
- Download accessibility apps such as Access Earth or Wheelmap to check reviews of public spaces and venues.
- Build in extra time when moving between sites, particularly in rural areas where ramps and lifts might be less common.

Cultural Note

The Irish are known for their helpfulness. If assistance is needed — whether for directions, boarding transport, or navigating a site — locals are typically more than happy to lend a hand.

LGBTQ+ Travel in Ireland

Ireland stands as one of Europe's most welcoming destinations for LGBTQ+ travelers. Since the historic legalization of same-sex marriage by popular vote in 2015 — the first country in the world to do so — the Emerald Isle has embraced LGBTQ+ rights with genuine warmth and pride. Today, the country offers a thriving LGBTQ+ scene, inclusive events, and a cultural atmosphere where travelers can feel both safe and celebrated.

LGBTQ+ Rights in Ireland

Same-sex marriage, adoption rights, and anti-discrimination laws have been fully implemented, making Ireland a leader in LGBTQ+ legal protections. Public attitudes toward LGBTQ+ individuals are overwhelmingly positive, particularly in cities and larger towns. Displays of affection between same-sex couples are widely accepted, although, like anywhere, smaller rural areas may feel more conservative at times.

Best Cities for LGBTQ+ Travelers

Dublin

Ireland's capital boasts a lively and visible LGBTQ+ community. The Panti Bar, run by renowned drag queen and activist Panti Bliss, is a Dublin institution. The George, Dublin's oldest LGBTQ+ bar, remains a vibrant cornerstone for locals and visitors alike. Annual events like Dublin Pride transform the city into a joyful celebration of diversity.

Cork

The second-largest city offers a welcoming LGBTQ+ atmosphere with smaller, close-knit venues like Loafers, a beloved gay bar that has long served as a safe social space. Cork Pride in August draws thousands, blending political activism with vibrant festivities along the River Lee.

Galway

Known for its bohemian vibe, Galway provides a friendly and artistic setting. LGBTQ+ travelers will find inclusive spaces scattered throughout the city's pubs, art galleries, and music venues. The Galway Community Pride Festival, each August, captures the spirit of the West Coast's progressive heartbeat.

Belfast

Though located in Northern Ireland, Belfast deserves mention for its evolving LGBTQ+ landscape. While same-sex marriage became legal here more recently (2020), the city's community events and nightlife have blossomed. Union Street Bar and Maverick are favorite gathering spots.

LGBTQ+ Events and Festivals

Dublin Pride (June)

One of Europe's most dynamic Pride festivals, featuring a colorful parade, street parties, political marches, and cultural events that span a full week.

Outburst Queer Arts Festival (November, Belfast)

A cutting-edge celebration of queer arts, showcasing theater, film, literature, and visual art.

Cork Pride (August)

A week-long series of events culminating in a parade that is both family-friendly and high-energy, emphasizing community solidarity.

Pink Training (November)

Europe's largest LGBTQ+ student training event, held annually by the Union of Students in Ireland, fosters activism and leadership among young people.

Safety and Practical Tips

Ireland ranks among the safest countries for LGBTQ+ travel. Violent crime targeting LGBTQ+ individuals is extremely rare. That said, rural villages may have a more reserved atmosphere; discretion is advisable in very small or isolated communities if unsure of local attitudes.

Public transport, hotels, and major tourist attractions are LGBTQ+ inclusive. Most accommodations, from luxury hotels to charming guesthouses, warmly welcome LGBTQ+ guests without issue. Booking platforms often indicate LGBTQ+ friendly properties. When attending major events or festivals, it's wise to arrange accommodations well in advance, as hotels fill quickly, especially around Dublin Pride and Galway Arts Festival.

Insider Tips for LGBTQ+ Travelers

- **Stay in Dublin's "Creative Quarter"** around South William Street for the best mix of LGBTQ+-friendly bars, cafés, and boutique shopping.
- **Explore Ireland's queer literary tradition** — from Oscar Wilde to Emma Donoghue — through literary walking tours in Dublin.
- **Join local community meetups** and LGBTQ+ walking tours offered seasonally in Dublin and Galway, ideal for solo travelers seeking new connections.

WiFi, SIM Cards & Connectivity

Ireland is well-equipped for travelers who need to stay online, whether you're posting scenic shots of the Cliffs of Moher or navigating the Wild Atlantic Way. Here's everything you need to know about staying connected:

WiFi in Ireland

Public WiFi is widely available throughout Ireland. Many hotels, cafés, restaurants, pubs, shopping centers, and even public buses and trains offer free WiFi. Larger cities like Dublin, Cork, Galway, and Limerick have good coverage, while rural areas can be a little spottier, especially along the west coast and in remote countryside spots.

- **Hotels and Accommodation:** Almost all hotels, B&Bs, and guesthouses offer complimentary WiFi. Always check when booking to ensure it's included.
- **Public Spaces:** Dublin offers free WiFi in select zones like Temple Bar, St. Stephen's Green, and O'Connell Street.

- **Pubs and Cafés:** Chains like Costa Coffee and Starbucks always have WiFi, but you'll also find it in most local pubs and independent cafés.
- **Transportation:** Irish Rail offers WiFi on most InterCity trains; Dublin Bus and Aircoach buses often provide free WiFi too.

Pro Tip: Always use a VPN when accessing public WiFi to keep your data secure.

SIM Cards in Ireland

If you need constant access to mobile data, buying a local SIM card is a smart and affordable choice. Ireland's three main mobile operators offer tourist-friendly prepaid SIMs:

1. Vodafone Ireland

- **Best for:** Wide coverage and good speed nationwide.
- **Tourist SIM:** "Vodafone X" plans for visitors, including unlimited social media and generous data allowances.
- **Cost:** Around €20–€30 for 20GB to unlimited data packages.
- **Where to buy:** Vodafone shops (found in airports, city centers), some supermarkets, and online.

2. Three Ireland

- **Best for:** Heavy data users.
- **Tourist SIM:** "Prepay SIM" offering all-you-can-eat data.
- **Cost:** About €20 for unlimited data for 28 days.
- **Where to buy:** Three stores, airport kiosks, and convenience shops like Tesco and Spar.

3. Eir Mobile

- **Best for:** Good value in urban areas.
- **Tourist SIM:** Prepay plans with solid data allowances, international calling credit included.
- **Cost:** Around €20 for 20–30GB plans.
- **Where to buy:** Eir stores and major retailers.

Pro Tip: Some providers offer free SIM cards at airports — look for kiosks in Dublin Airport (T1 and T2 arrivals).

How to Get a SIM Card at the Airport

- **Dublin Airport (T1 & T2):** Vodafone and Three kiosks at Arrivals offer ready-to-go SIM cards for tourists.
- **Cork, Shannon, Knock Airports:** Tourist SIMs available at newsagents like WHSmith or vending machines near arrivals.

Just bring an unlocked phone — otherwise, you'll need to have it unlocked before traveling.

eSIMs in Ireland

If your phone supports eSIM (like recent iPhones, Google Pixels, and some Samsung Galaxy models), you can purchase an eSIM online before you even land. Providers like Airalo, Nomad, and GigSky offer affordable Irish eSIMs.

- **Cost:** Around €5–€30 depending on the data package (1GB to 20GB).
- **Activation:** Instant — you simply scan a QR code.

Pro Tip: Using an eSIM allows you to keep your home SIM active for calls/texts if needed.

Coverage Overview

- **Cities:** Excellent 4G/LTE coverage in Dublin, Cork, Galway, Limerick, and Waterford.
- **Countryside:** Coverage is good but can be patchy on mountain roads, in the Burren, or rural Kerry.
- **5G:** Available in Dublin and some parts of Cork, Limerick, and Galway for Vodafone and Eir users (device must support 5G).

Emergency Contacts & Assistance

Traveling with peace of mind means knowing exactly where to turn in the event of an emergency. Ireland offers well-organized and accessible support services for visitors, ensuring that help is never far away when needed.

Emergency Services (Police, Fire, Ambulance)

Ireland uses a single emergency number: 112 or 999.

Both numbers connect callers to the same emergency services — police (Gardaí), fire department, ambulance services, and coast guard. Calls are free from any phone, including mobile phones without an active SIM card. When calling, stay calm, state the type of emergency, your exact location (or nearest landmark), and follow the operator's instructions carefully. English-speaking operators are always available, and translation services for other languages can be accessed if required.

Garda Síochána (Irish Police)

The Garda Síochána, often simply called "Gardaí," is Ireland's national police service. Garda stations are found in every town and city, with larger stations open 24 hours a day. Gardaí are known for their approachability and helpfulness, making them a reassuring resource for travelers seeking assistance or advice.

Contact for Non-Emergencies: +353 1 666 0000

Website: www.garda.ie

If in doubt, travelers can always approach Garda officers directly on the street for assistance with directions, safety concerns, or reporting lost property.

Medical Assistance

For non-emergency medical situations, such as minor illnesses or injuries, General Practitioners (GPs) are widely available. Many GPs offer same-day or next-day appointments. Private clinics often accept walk-ins.

Hospitals with Accident & Emergency (A&E) departments are located in all major cities and larger towns. University Hospital Galway, St. Vincent's University Hospital Dublin, Cork University Hospital, and Limerick's University Hospital are among the largest facilities.

HSE Health Service Executive Info Line: 1800 700 700 (from within Ireland)

Private Doctor Service (Nationwide): Doctor on Duty – 0818 22 44 76

Pharmacies (Chemists) can provide advice and over-the-counter medication for minor health concerns. Pharmacists are highly trained and an excellent first step for non-urgent issues.

Roadside Assistance

Roadside support is widely available for travelers renting cars or using their vehicles. Insurance policies for car rentals in Ireland usually include an emergency breakdown service. It's essential to double-check this before driving off.

Top services include:

- **AA Ireland Roadside Assistance:** 0818 66 77 88
- **RAC Europe (for British travelers):** 00 800 82 82 82 82

In case of accidents, contacting local Gardaí is mandatory if there is injury or significant damage.

Lost or Stolen Passports

Losing a passport can be stressful, but swift steps help resolve the situation efficiently. The first step is contacting the local Gardaí to report the loss. An official report is necessary for reissuing a travel document.

Travelers should then reach out to their national embassy or consulate:

- **U.S. Embassy Dublin:** +353 1 668 8777
- **UK Embassy Dublin:** +353 1 205 3700
- **Canadian Embassy Dublin:** +353 1 234 4000
- **Australian Embassy Dublin:** +353 1 664 5300

Many embassies offer online appointment bookings to streamline the process of obtaining emergency travel documents.

Tourist Assistance

Fáilte Ireland operates tourist information centers across the country where staff can assist with emergencies related to travel plans, accommodation changes, or general advice.

Tourist Information Center Dublin (Suffolk Street): +353 1 884 7700

These centers are valuable hubs for troubleshooting non-life-threatening travel issues quickly.

Embassy Contacts

Keeping embassy details handy is essential for any international traveler. Embassies can assist with lost documents, legal matters, emergencies involving citizens abroad, and general travel advice. A full list of embassies and consulates in Ireland can be found on the Department of Foreign Affairs website: www.dfa.ie

Sustainable & Responsible Travel

Exploring Ireland's landscapes, heritage sites, and vibrant cities comes with the opportunity — and responsibility — to protect and preserve them. Practicing sustainable and responsible travel ensures that the beauty of the Emerald Isle remains intact for future generations.

Respecting Natural Environments

Ireland's coastlines, national parks, forests, and wild spaces are delicate ecosystems. Staying on designated trails, avoiding the removal of plants or rocks, and minimizing impact during hikes are simple but vital actions. Always take litter home or use proper recycling and waste facilities.

- **Leave No Trace Principles:** Adopt the Leave No Trace ethos — pack out what you pack in, respect wildlife, and leave natural objects undisturbed.
- **Support Protected Areas:** Visiting Ireland's national parks and nature reserves often involves a small fee or donation, which directly supports conservation efforts.

Supporting Local Communities

Choosing accommodations, dining, tours, and products that are locally owned contributes significantly to community well-being. When travelers invest in local economies, they help small businesses thrive and maintain cultural authenticity.

- **Stay Local:** Opt for family-run guesthouses, farm stays, and eco-lodges.
- **Buy Local:** Purchase crafts, food, and souvenirs made in Ireland rather than mass-produced imports.
- **Dine Local:** Eat at locally-owned restaurants and enjoy menus that highlight regional produce and traditional Irish recipes.

Ethical Wildlife Experiences

Ireland's wild inhabitants, from puffins to red deer, are part of its charm. Responsible wildlife watching means maintaining respectful distances, avoiding feeding animals, and choosing ethical tour operators who follow conservation guidelines.

- **Seal Watching in Dingle:** Observe seals and dolphins from boats that maintain proper distance regulations.
- **Birdwatching in the Cliffs of Moher:** Follow the cliff path guidelines to avoid disturbing nesting seabirds.

Low-Impact Transportation Choices

Reducing your carbon footprint while traveling across Ireland makes a meaningful difference. Buses, trains, and cycling are highly effective and scenic ways to explore the country.

- **Use Public Transport:** Irish Rail and Bus Éireann services offer efficient routes between major cities and towns.
- **Rent a Bike:** Cities like Dublin, Galway, and Cork have excellent bike rental programs and dedicated lanes.
- **Car Share:** If renting a car is necessary, consider car-sharing platforms or renting electric vehicles when available.

Eco-Friendly Accommodation

An increasing number of accommodations in Ireland have adopted green policies, from solar energy and water conservation to farm-to-table dining experiences.

- **Green Hospitality Certified Properties:** Look for stays certified by Green Hospitality Ireland, a recognized eco-standard.
- **Sustainable Stays:** Choose lodgings that promote energy efficiency, recycling programs, and local sourcing.

Cultural Sensitivity

Respect for Irish customs, traditions, and languages strengthens the connection between visitors and local communities.

Recognizing Gaelic language signage, participating respectfully in cultural events, and dressing appropriately for sacred sites demonstrate thoughtfulness and appreciation.

- **Participate Thoughtfully:** Attend céilí dances, festivals, and storytelling events with an open mind and respect for local customs.
- **Sacred Sites:** Be mindful when visiting ancient sites like Newgrange, Clonmacnoise, and Celtic ruins — these locations often have spiritual significance.

Reducing Waste

Simple habits go a long way toward reducing waste while traveling:

- Carry a reusable water bottle and coffee cup.
- Say no to single-use plastics whenever possible.
- Use digital tickets and maps instead of printed versions.

Volunteering and Giving Back

Some travelers seek deeper connections through volunteering. Opportunities range from helping with conservation projects to participating in cultural preservation efforts.

- **Conservation Projects:** Join initiatives focused on coastal cleanups, bog restoration, or reforestation.
- **Community Programs:** Participate in local events that support rural development or historical preservation.

Apps & Tools for Ireland Travel

Technology can greatly enhance a journey through Ireland, making everything from navigation to dining reservations seamless. Downloading a few essential apps ensures smoother experiences, better planning, and more authentic exploration.

Navigation and Transportation

Google Maps: Essential for driving, walking, or public transit directions throughout Ireland. Offline maps are highly recommended, especially when traveling through rural areas with limited reception.

Transport for Ireland (TFI) App: Offers real-time public transportation information for buses, trains, trams, and ferries across the country. Perfect for planning journeys between cities and navigating urban transport networks.

Leap Top-Up App: For travelers using Dublin's public transportation, this app allows quick top-ups for Leap Cards, used on buses, trains, and the Luas tram system.

Free Now: Ireland's leading taxi app allows for fast and safe taxi bookings in cities like Dublin, Cork, Galway, and Limerick. It often offers fare estimates before confirming rides.

Accommodation

Booking.com: A reliable platform for finding a wide range of accommodations, from cozy B&Bs to luxury hotels. Reviews, flexible booking options, and price comparisons simplify the process.

Airbnb: Ideal for travelers seeking local stays, private rentals, or countryside retreats. It often provides more character-rich options compared to traditional hotels.

Hostelworld: For budget-conscious travelers, Hostelworld specializes in hostels across Ireland, offering user reviews, ratings, and detailed amenities lists.

Food and Dining

OpenTable: Essential for making restaurant reservations, especially in popular dining cities like Dublin and Galway. It allows browsing by cuisine type, price range, and ratings.

Deliveroo: Food delivery from top restaurants is possible through this app in major cities — perfect after a long day exploring.

Activities and Tours

GetYourGuide: A comprehensive app for booking tours, activities, and attractions across Ireland. From Cliffs of Moher tours to whiskey tastings, GetYourGuide often includes user reviews and flexible cancellation policies.

Viator: Similar to GetYourGuide, Viator offers thousands of travel experiences, including day trips, skip-the-line tickets, and private tours.

Eventbrite: Useful for finding concerts, festivals, workshops, and local events happening across Ireland during your stay.

Language and Communication

Duolingo: For travelers eager to learn a few words of Irish Gaelic or refresh basic English phrases before and during their trip. Short, engaging lessons fit easily into any travel day.

Google Translate: Helpful for translating signs, menus, or simple conversations. Although English is dominant across Ireland, occasional Gaelic signage, especially in the Gaeltacht regions, can appear.

Connectivity

WiFi Map: A handy tool for locating free or paid WiFi hotspots across Ireland, reducing mobile data costs.

WhatsApp: Essential for keeping in touch with accommodation hosts, tour operators, or new friends made along the way. It remains one of the most used messaging apps throughout Ireland.

Weather

Met Éireann App: Developed by Ireland's national meteorological service, this app offers highly accurate, localized weather forecasts — vital when planning hikes, coastal drives, or outdoor excursions.

YR.no: Another excellent weather app, developed by the Norwegian Meteorological Institute, offering reliable and detailed forecasts even for rural and coastal areas.

Money and Budgeting

Revolut: Widely popular in Ireland, Revolut is great for currency exchanges, online payments, and managing travel budgets. Many locals use it for fast, contactless payments.

XE Currency: Real-time currency conversion tool — helpful for managing expenses and understanding euro costs when budgeting.

Conclusion and Farewell

Traveling through Ireland is not just a journey across a beautiful land; it's an encounter with deep-rooted traditions, sweeping landscapes, timeless hospitality, and a spirit that lingers long after you return home. From the rugged cliffs of the Wild Atlantic Way to the story-soaked streets of Dublin and the quiet magic of village life in the Gaeltacht, Ireland reveals its heart in countless ways — often in the simplest of moments.

Whether sipping a creamy pint in a cozy pub, listening to the haunting strains of a traditional fiddle, or standing in awe before a medieval fortress battered by time, each experience layers into a story uniquely your own. The Emerald Isle invites exploration not just with the eyes, but with the soul, urging every traveler to slow down, savor, and truly connect.

Ireland in 2025 offers even more: modern comforts intertwined with old-world charm, renewed festivals, sustainable travel options, and a deepening embrace of diverse cultures and communities. Every corner holds discovery for those willing to wander.

As you set out on your Irish adventure, travel with curiosity, respect, and an open heart. The more you give to Ireland — in attention, in conversation, in appreciation — the more it will reward you with moments of wonder that no guidebook can script.

Thank you for trusting this guide to light your way. May your journey be filled with vivid sunsets, lively music, warm welcomes, and stories that become cherished memories.

Slán agus beannacht — goodbye and blessings — on your unforgettable journey across Ireland.

— Logan Matthews

Printed in Dunstable, United Kingdom